D0948753

CAPITALISM, PATRIARCHY, AND CRIME

CAPITALISM, PATRIARCHY, AND CRIME

Toward a
Socialist Feminist Criminology

JAMES W. MESSERSCHMIDT
UNIVERSITY OF SOUTHERN MAINE

ROWMAN & LITTLEFIELD
PUBLISHERS

FOR ULLA

ROWMAN & LITTLEFIELD
Published in the United States of America in 1986
by Rowman & Littlefield, Publishers
(a division of Littlefield, Adams & Company)
81 Adams Drive, Totowa, New Jersey 07512

Copyright © 1986 by Rowman & Littlefield

Library of Congress Cataloging-in-Publication Data

Messerschmidt, James W.
  Capitalism, patriarchy, and crime.

  Bibliography: p. 193
  Includes index.
  1. Crime and criminals.   2. Women and socialism.
3. Feminism.   I. Title.
HV6030.M47   1986   364.2'5   86-15608
ISBN 0-8476-7496-7
ISBN 0-8476-7497-5 (pbk.)

88 87 86
5 4 3 2 1

Printed in the United States of America

Contents

Acknowledgments

A number of people devoted much time and energy to help make this book possible. I am particularly indebted to four individuals: Ray Michalowski, Varda Burstyn, Peg Strobel and Steven Box. Ray provided detailed comments on each chapter and valuable insights throughout. I feel very lucky to have had his input. Varda, through her encouragement, criticism, advice, and keen sense of theory, helped immeasurably to strengthen many of the arguments presented here. Peg, who took time away from a very demanding and busy schedule, read the entire manuscript, contributing important suggestions on each chapter. And finally, Steve provided valuable comments on the whole manuscript, and his book *Power, Crime and Mystification* (see References), which I believe is one of the most important contributions to criminology in recent years, helped guide some of my ideas. I thank all of them for everything.

I also want to thank Mark Hansel, Marjorie Shostak, Eleanor Miller, Sandra Bartky, and Bill Chambliss for reading certain parts of the manuscript and furnishing critical comments that helped me clarify what I wanted to say.

Several socialist feminists and criminologists, many of whom I have never met, have had a major influence on my work. This book would have never been written if it were not for the work of these individuals: Varda Burstyn, Bill Chambliss, Zillah Eisenstein, Heidi Hartmann, Alison Jaggar, Tony Platt, Janet Schmidt, and Julia and Herman Schwendinger.

Special thanks goes to Tami Feland, Twyla Ereth, and Tammie Grisner for their typing and to John Sherman and Sarah Held for editing.

Finally, I am especially grateful to Ulla Eurenius-Messerschmidt for her warmth, comfort, support, and criticism, and to Erik and Jan Messerschmidt, whose interruptions reminded me that the personal is political.

Introduction

Within criminology, whether Marxist, liberal, or conservative, there is an almost total neglect of the sexual division of labor and its impact on crime. Similarly, the feminist community has not examined the way the sexual division of labor affects crime overall, although there has been considerable interest in crimes against women. Finally, neither criminologists nor feminists have attempted theoretically to account for the way gender, in conjunction with class, relates to crime. This is the project I have begun.

In the recent flowering of feminist theory, a body of work has emerged, commonly known as *socialist feminism* which, while "tentative, impressionistic and clearly unfinished" (Bartky 1982, 127), fundamentally challenges not only traditional and Marxist thought, but also traditional and Marxist frameworks for comprehending crime and social control. Most important in this challenge is the insight that reproduction—the production of human life through procreation, socialization, and daily maintenance—does not simply "reflect" or derive from what has until recently been known as the mode of production, but rather that production and reproduction codetermine the base of society. While Marxism recognizes the labor in the production sphere, socialist feminism recognizes the labor performed in both production and reproduction.

Although socialist feminists differ on how to structure socialist feminism, they are now in the process of developing a vocabulary to describe accurately phenomena that have been until now largely invisible. Thus, it is important to discuss briefly some of the specific terminology in this book.

In all societies, people have the material needs of food, clothing, and shelter. Consequently, members of a given society organize themselves into *relations of production* to satisfy these needs. In contemporary U.S. society, relations of production take the form of *capitalist class relations,* in which the capitalist class appropriates the labor power of the working class. Additionally, in all societies, people need to reproduce, socialize, and maintain the species. Consequently, people organize themselves into *relations of reproduction* to satisfy these needs. In contemporary U.S. society, relations of reproduction take the form

ix

of *patriarchal gender relations,* in which the male gender appropriates the labor power and controls the sexuality of the female gender. From this perspective, then, the "base" of society entails production *and* reproduction, interacting and interpenetrating, for relations of class and gender exist in both the productive and reproductive spheres. Moreover, the dialectical interaction between production and reproduction sets limits to the "superstructure"—the legal, political, religious, aesthetic, and philosophic forms of society.

Defining patriarchy has caused considerable debate in the feminist literature. Others have defined patriarchy as an ideology that arose out of the exchange of women, as simply being the power of the father, and as the sexual hierarchical ordering of society for political control. Following Heidi Hartmann (1981a), I define patriarchy as a set of social relations of power in which the male gender appropriates the labor power of women and controls their sexuality. This appropriation and control—in both the home and market—provide the material base of patriarchy. Patriarchy is a hierarchical system of power relations, providing control among men and of men over women. Thus, patriarchy entails a relation of domination, with the male gender dominating. "Patriarchy," as used here, conceptualizes a system of gender hierarchy, that while appearing in different forms at different times, has crossed what has traditionally been referred to as the mode of production. Patriarchal gender relations, then, are similar to class relations in that they entail appropriation, control, domination, and conflict.

Patriarchal gender relations are a form of relations of reproduction. However, "reproduction," as understood here, differs from the traditional Marxist usage. For Marxists, the term covers two major areas: the replacement of the means of production, including human labor power (procreation and consumption), and the reproduction of the social relations of production. Within Marxist theory, reproduction is essentially functional for capital, so, while reproductive labor is socially necessary, Marxism pays no theoretical attention to who it is that primarily performs that labor and equally, who it is that appropriates it. However, as Alison Jaggar (1983, 74–75) has pointed out, producing a meal, for example,

> is the result of an enormously long and complex labor process that includes growing, picking, transporting, packaging, shopping and cooking. In Marxist theory, however, the last two processes count as consumption rather than production, at least if they are done in a household rather than in a restaurant.

The socialist feminist understanding of reproduction points to the fact that labor is performed through procreation, socialization, and daily maintenance, and under certain relations of reproduction—

patriarchy—men-as-a-group appropriate the labor power of women-as-a-group.

However, and this is important, socialist feminism does not see simply two parallel systems of labor. Class domination and gender domination cut across and interpenetrate each other. For instance, women labor in both the market and the home, and suffer masculine* dominance in each. But in addition, their experience in both realms is determined by their class. While the two "spheres" are separated in this work *for analytical purposes,* we should see them as interdependent and intertwined social relations.

Still in its infancy as theory, socialist feminism has not dealt adequately with the question of race and racism. While I believe that racial oppression is as important as class and gender oppression, socialist feminism has not linked it systematically with patriarchy and capitalism. However, a complete theory on crime and social control requires this conceptualization. This is a limitation not only of socialist feminism, but this work as well. While I have considered racial oppression, the analysis, I feel, is still inadequate.

I have not attempted to analyze all forms of criminality—an endeavor clearly beyond the scope of this work. Consequently, this book should be read as an analysis of crime and social control from a new and as yet incomplete theoretical orientation—hence its subtitle, "Toward a Socialist Feminist Criminology." I offer it in the hope of stimulating the kind of comment and critical controversy that will advance social theory and help us to break "the chains of outmoded ideology" in order to construct a "criminology committed to human liberation" (Krisberg 1975, 170).

---

*I use the terms "masculine" and "male gender" rather than "male" throughout the book since "male" behavior is learned rather than biologically determined.

1
The Patriarchal Nature of Marxist Criminology

While a number of scholars have pointed out the patriarchal bias within Marxism generally (Rubin 1975; Flax 1976; Kuhn and Wolpe 1978; Eisenstein 1979; Ferguson 1979; Harding 1981; Hartmann 1981a; Burstyn 1983a, 1983b), Marxist criminology has been practically ignored, with only minor references to its masculine bias (Leonard 1982). This chapter demonstrates that Marxist criminology ignores the equal importance of gender stratification and reproduction (the production of human life through procreation, socialization, and daily maintenance), as against class stratification and production, to an understanding of crime. I first examine Marx and Engels' views on gender stratification and reproduction and then analyze the work of some contemporary Marxist criminologists. Marx and Engels set the stage for a patriarchal dogmatism in Marxist criminology by arguing that reproduction is "superstructural"—that is, derived from production. Marx and Engels ignored the fundamental fact that in all societies humans must reproduce as well as produce to sustain their society. Consequently, Marxist social theory is flawed, since production *and* reproduction—distinct yet interdependent structural social systems—constitute the material base of society. Continuing to overlook the codeterminative nature of the base, the writings of later Marxists on crime reflect the same error.

The Legacy of Marx and Engels

"Every child knows," Marx (1868) wrote, "that a country that ceased to work would die." In other words, every society must produce food, shelter, and clothing simply to survive. Moreover, according to Marx and Engels, for a society to maintain itself, it must organize its own form of reproduction (see the discussion in the Introduction). It is these two systems, according to Marx and Engels, that create the conditions for everyday existence. As Engels (1972, 5–6) states,

1

production and reproduction are central to understanding any society according to "the materialistic conception."

> According to the materialistic conception, the determining factor in history is, in the final instance, the production and reproduction of immediate life. This, again, is of a two-fold character: on the one side, the production of the means of existence, of food, clothing and shelter and the tools necessary for that production; on the other side, the production of human beings themselves, the propagation of the species. The social organization under which the people of a particular historical epoch and a particular country live is determined by both kinds of production; by the stage of development of labour on the one hand and of the family on the other.

Marx and Engels, however, never developed a materialist perspective accounting for both production and reproduction "as the determining factor in history" (Eisenstein 1979; Flax 1976). Their work concentrates on production and class relations, abstracting away from reproduction and gender relations. Although recognizing the importance of both production and reproduction as *codetermining* the "social organization under which the people of a particular historical epoch and a particular country live," their analysis subsumes reproduction and the family to the economy and production. In this way, gender relations are made subordinate to class relations and the oppression of women becomes for Marx and Engels simply a reflection of the more important and fundamental class oppression (Eisenstein 1979).

The materialist conception eventually developed by Marx and Engels focuses on the particular society's social arrangement of production. This *mode of production* contains two important elements: the forces and social relations of production. The *forces of production* include the human labor power that transforms raw materials into other objects by using means of production such as tools, factories, machinery, and so on. The level of development of these productive forces determines a society's capacity to produce. According to Marx and Engels, in all but "primitive societies," the productive forces have developed to the point of producing a social surplus—more goods than the society requires for subsistence. The *social relations of production* is the process by which this social surplus is produced and appropriated. In all societies beyond the "primitive" stage, one class produces the surplus while another appropriates it through some form of coercion. Thus, for Marx and Engels, social classes develop through peoples' common relation to the production and appropriation of the surplus. Since these two classes—the producing and appropriating classes—have antagonistic interests, class struggle becomes inherent in any class society. According to Marx and Engels (1970, 16), "the history of all hitherto existing society is the history of class struggle." By reason of surplus production, a division of labor emerges, and with it exploitative relations and class conflict.

However, for Marx and Engels, the first division of labor is biologically based in the family. The act of procreation gives rise to a "natural" division of labor in the family that "develops spontaneously or 'naturally' by virtue of natural predisposition (e.g., physical strength), needs, accidents, etc.," (Marx and Engels 1947, 51). Discussing the peasant family in *Capital*, Marx (1967, 77–78) notes that this type of family system possesses a "spontaneously developed system of division of labor." The distribution of work and the regulation of labor time of family members "depends upon the differences of age and sex as upon natural conditions varying with the seasons" (ibid.). The division of labor in the home, arising from differences in sex and age, is "a division that is consequently on a purely physiological foundation" (ibid., 351).

For Marx and Engels then, the division of labor within the family is "natural," since it is biologically based. From the earliest times, this "natural" division of labor results in men producing the means of subsistence while women work in the household. Discussing "primitive societies," Engels (1972, 145) writes in *The Origin of the Family, Private Property, and the State,*

> The division of labour is purely primitive, between the sexes only. The man fights in wars, goes hunting and fishing, procures the raw materials of food and the tools necessary for doing so. The woman looks after the house and the preparation of the food and clothing, cooks, weaves, sews. They are each master in their own sphere: the man in the forest, the woman in the house. Each is the owner of the instruments which he or she uses: the man of weapons, the hunting and fishing implements, the woman of the household gear.

Thus, Engels does not view this sexual division of labor as placing women in a subordinate position. Men and women had their own spheres, each vital to the survival of the community. In fact, Engels (1972, 113) states that in primitive societies women were *dominant,* and this female supremacy has a material foundation. "The communistic household, in which most or all of the women belong to one and the same gens, while men come from various gentes, is the material foundation of that supremacy of the women which was general in primitive times."

This alleged supremacy is destroyed, according to Engels, by developments in the productive sphere. The invention of agriculture and the domestication of animals greatly expand the forces of production and create a surplus. These developments make engaging in slavery profitable and lead to the emergence of a class society. Engels argues that since these developments occurred in the "male sphere"—production—men came to dominate women. Moreover, because men accumulated wealth, they wanted to pass it on to their children, so men changed a matrilineal communal system to a patrilineal private property system. This overthrowing of "mother right" was for Engels (1972, 120), "the world historic defeat of the female sex."

Engels' account suffers from severe anthropological inaccuracies, which is not surprising given the infancy of anthropological research in his time. While it is true in hunting and gathering societies (what Engels calls "primitive" societies) that men hunt, fight wars, and make weaponry, they do not procure all or even most of the raw materials for food, nor the tools that are necessary to carry out this labor. Varda Burstyn (1983a), in analyzing a large body of anthropological evidence on the genesis of women's oppression, concludes that female involvement in "gathering" provides the major and consistent source of food, even in those societies where hunting is accorded greater prestige. Moreover, in horticultural (small scale cultivation) societies, women are primarily involved in cultivation, and therefore provide not only the major and consistent source of food, but also any surplus (ibid.; Reiter 1975; Blumberg 1978; Fisher 1979). However, to Engels, female labor, for the most part, was unknown, unrecognized, and therefore invisible. In those horticultural societies that produced a surplus, it was women primarily who produced it, but Engels inaccurately portrays this sphere as male. Women's labor was therefore both productive and reproductive in hunting and gathering societies.

Engels uses the Iroquois as an example of how the surplus produced by women was appropriated by the community as a whole. However, the Iroquois were atypical and represented only one type of surplus appropriation. In other horticultural societies, the surplus produced by women is appropriated by *men* and used to increase their social standing. As Rae Lesser Blumberg (1978, 36) argues in her analysis of the rise of class and gender stratification, this latter type of appropriation

> emerges when men use women's labor in cultivation in order to deliberately produce surplus—and prestige—for their own benefit. Typically, the chief beneficiary is the man for whom the woman labors, in most cases, her husband. . . . In this way, the surplus of one group is appropriated for the benefit of another—the hallmark of class stratification.

While in most hunting and gathering societies women maintained control over their productive and reproductive labor power (see below), with the development of certain kinds of horticultural societies, masculine control of the labor power of women emerges. In addition, female labor comes to be manipulated as a scarce good, therefore polygyny (males having more than one wife at a time) becomes prevalent as a family form and restrictions "on sexual activity develop differentially for women and for men, and differentially among women on the basis of their affiliation to (families of) leading men once surplus accumulation and private appropriation begins." As Burstyn (1983a, 27) goes on to argue, the woman loses control of her sexuality and becomes an "affiliated and controlled wife" in many horticultural societies. Thus, with the development of masculine appropriation of the productive labor power of women in horticultural societies, masculine control over women's reproductive labor and thus sexuality emerges. Economic classes, in the Marxist sense, eventually arise once the greater surplus produced by agriculture and the domestication of animals becomes prevalent. Therefore, the growth of surplus accumulation and the rise of social classes is grounded in women's labor and its appropriation by men, as well as in the control of women's sexuality (Burstyn 1983a; Blumberg 1978). Women were the first "producing class" and men the first "appropriating class." With the development of certain types of horticultural societies, incipient patriarchal gender relations emerge, entailing appropriation and domination in both the productive and reproductive spheres. Engels was evidently unaware that the sexual division of labor was the first "great social division of labor" where an exploiter-exploited relationship existed.

Engels ignored the internal dynamics of the reproductive sphere, and its codeterminative aspect with production. As a result, Engels account of "the world historic defeat of the female sex" fails to answer a number of important questions. If his analysis is accurate, why did women not come to dominate since they produced the surplus in horticulture societies? If female supremacy was dominant, as Engels seems to argue, why did women not remain in control? And why do men, who did not bequeath property to their biological children under matrilineality, suddenly desire to do so? The empirical fact is that in certain horticultural societies, men appropriate the surplus produced by women. Engels explanation for women's oppression is therefore based "not only on an incorrect assessment of the nature and role of women's labor, but on changes he incorrectly believes took place completely exterior to the sexual division of labor" (Burstyn 1983a, 24). Consequently, he fails to account for that oppression, for as Varda Burstyn (1983a, 25) concludes,

> In locating women's oppression "out there" in the abstract social relations of a class society rather than in the real relations of masculine control and appropriation of women's labor, Engels renders the sexual division of labor itself as a non-issue and, in strategic terms, essentially unimportant.

Engels' failure to analyze accurately the sexual division of labor, and therefore masculine appropriation of female labor, led him to concentrate on what he understood—in a limited way—to constitute the sphere of production. While he acknowledged the equal importance of production and reproduction in "primitive societies," his incomplete understanding of production comes to dominate upon the emergence of class society, and reproduction becomes "superstructural."

> Within this structure of society based on kinship groups the productivity of labor increasingly develops, and with it private property and exchange, differences of wealth, the possibility of utilizing the labor power of others, and hence the basis of class antagonisms: new social elements, which in the course of generations strive to adapt the old social order to the new conditions, until at last their incompatibility brings about a complete upheaval. In the collision of the newly developed social classes, the old society founded on kinship groups is broken up. In its place appears a new society, with its control centered in the state, the subordinate units of which are no longer kinship associations; a society in which the system of the family is completely dominated by the system of property, and in which there now freely develop those class antagonisms and class struggles that have hitherto formed the content of all written history. [Engels 1972, 72]

In short, Marx and Engels, having failed to analyze the relations between men and women in society, view the relations of reproduction in societies beyond the "primitive" stage as secondary to relations of production and determined ultimately by production. The Marxist materialist conception of history simply excludes the dynamics and effects of gender relations and hierarchy, thereby concealing, rather than illuminating, masculine dominance.

According to Engels (1972, 137), women's opppression results from her exclusion from social production as the husband maintains his position of supremacy in the household by reason of his economically privileged position. As a result, the "emancipation of women will only be possible when women can take part in production on a large scale and domestic work no longer claims anything but an insignificant amount of her time" (Engels 1972, 158). Engels (1958, 162–66) argued that as women and children became wage laborers, the authority of the male (husband/father) would be undermined and patriarchal relations eventually destroyed. Both Marx and Engels believed that capitalism itself would set the stage for the destruction of sex differences; women would become economically independent and therefore "true" proletarians to struggle alongside men for emancipation of the working class. After the revolution, women would be liberated from both masculine and capital exploitation. While today women are increasingly entering the wage labor force, they are far from liberated. Patriarchal sex segregation in the labor market is as prevalent today as it has ever been, and men continue to appropriate the labor power of women in the home (see chapters 2 and 4). Patriarchy, while always changing, has persisted through over two hundred years of capitalist development.

In sum, Marx and Engels acknowledge that the sexual division of labor is the first division of labor. However, they see it as "natural" and unproblematic in and of itself; consequently, they develop the thesis that women's oppression derives from the mode of production, not the codetermination of reproduction and production. For them, gender relations do not need theoretical analysis. Even though they state that production and reproduction structure society simultaneously, they ignore this perception and subordinate reproduction and the family to the category of completely determined parts of the superstructure. This superstructure is made up of legal, political, and ideological institutions resting upon and helping to maintain the social relations of production. As part of this superstructure, the state articulates and enforces laws to bolster productive relations. The family then, is only one of many ideological institutions of the superstructure, socializing its members to support and accept the social relations of production. Thus, the family is derivative and subordinate to the economy. Although the family has a dynamic of its own, economic factors ultimately dominate, and gender relations are subsumed under class relations. The preconditions for the elimination of patriarchy are found within the framework of the capitalist mode of production. Clearly, the evidence does not support these arguments of Marx and Engels.

Both Marx and Engels lived and wrote during the mid-nineteenth-century Victorian period, which emphasized monogamy and the subordination of women. Moreover, both were influenced by liberal philosophers such as Kant and Hegel who articulated very degrading views of women (Jaggar 1983, 36). Hegel, for instance, believed women to be so deficient in the "universal faculty" (reason) that they were as different from men as plants are from animals (ibid.). It is within this intellectual and cultural context that the work of Marx and Engels, and as a result, Marxist social theory, developed.

A New Criminology?

In the early 1970s what has become known as "The New Criminology" emerged in the United States and England. While initially this new school in the United States may have been a "theoretically incoherent amalgam—a pastiche of Marxism and other political philosphies and sociological perspectives" (Greenberg 1983, 12), it has now outgrown this stage and greatly enhances our understanding of crime and social control. The "new" Marxist sociologists have put forth a devastating critique of the state definition of crime (Schwendinger and Schwendinger 1970), the relation between class power and the law (Chambliss and Seidman 1982), and the overall ideological hegemony that crime and the legal system provide for the powerful (Quinney 1973; Reiman 1984). Moreover, today's Marxist criminologists have produced, in various forms, a more sophpisticated understanding of crime. Using Marxist social theory to develop a methodology that gives priority to historical analysis and focuses on production, economic relations, class struggle, capital accumulation, the role of the reserve army of labor, and other central concepts, they offer a coherent theoretical comprehension of crime, the state, and ideology (Balkan et al. 1980; Michalowski 1985; Eitzen and Timmer 1985).

Nevertheless, while this "new" criminology has yielded many valuable insights, its exclusive preoccupation with a class-based analysis of crime limits its usefulness. Although class analysis is very important, it only partially explains crime and society. Ignoring gender relations and reproduction, it leaves untouched such issues as the differences between male and female crime, and how relations of reproduction affect human behavior and therefore crime generally. Gender relations are either ignored or subsumed under the class issue. A mode of analysis that eschews such an important social relation as that of gender is clearly not rich enough to explain criminality satisfactorily. A workable theory leads us to identify certain questions as important. When a theory overlooks important questions, the theory itself becomes dubious.

Dissatisfied with the predominant "radical" sociological approaches to crime of the time (labeling and conflict perspectives) and influenced by certain aspects of the social and political climate of the 1960s (new left, civil rights, and antiwar movements), a number of criminologists turned to the work of Marx and Engels, where they found a more adequate structural understanding of power, conflict, the state, and therefore of crime. However, while these aspects of the cultural and intellectual climate influenced the new criminology, the concurrent emerging feminism had relatively little impact. The new wave of feminism, going well beyond the Suffragist movement of the "Progressive Era", questions the sexual division of labor as a whole and examines the concomitant subordination of women in all aspects of contemporary capitalism. The new criminology of the 1970s largely ignored this important contribution, or in some cases acknowledged it, yet subsumed it under an orthodox Marxist analysis of crime.

While differing specifically in the way they analyze crime, the new Marxist criminologists have in common their commitment to understanding crime solely in terms of relations of production and class. Gender relations are scarcely considered. For example, Michalowski (1985, 303) spends one page (of a 422-page textbook), discussing "gender and common crime," while Eitzen and Timmer (1985, 142–49) devote seven out of 640 pages to "sex and street crime." The best-known theoretical works of the new criminology *completely* ignore gender, sexuality, and women (Gordon 1971a; Quinney 1973, 1980; Chambliss 1975; Spitzer 1975; Greenberg 1983). Consequently, from a feminist point of view, what is striking about the new criminology is that it is simply not that *new*, being merely a sophisticated application of the analytical legacy of Marx and Engels.

Marxist criminologists have failed to analyze crime in terms of the social relations of reproduction, not because of hidden sexism, but because Marxist theory is almost exclusively a theory of class society, and in particular, capitalist society. As a theory of capitalism, it explains how this particular mode of production develops through capital accumulation and the exploitation of wage labor. Throughout this process a political and social structure develops in which the majority of people are "proletarianized," and therefore live at or below a subsistence level, while a few (the economic elite) dominate society and enjoy affluent lifestyles. Concomitantly, a "capitalist ideology" arises characterized by individualism, competitiveness, domination, and commodity fetishism. Within this (very simplified) framework the new criminology examines crime. However, Marx's theory of the development of capitalism is, as Heidi Hartmann (1981a, 10–11) has pointed out, essentially a theory of the development of "empty places."

> Marx predicted, for example, the growth of the proletariat and the demise of the petit bourgeoisie. More precise and in more detail, Braverman among others has explained the creation of the "places" clerical worker and service worker in advanced capitalist societies. Just as capital creates these places indifferent to the individuals who fill them, the categories of Marxist analysis, class, reserve army of labor, wage-laborer, do not explain why particular people fill particular places. They give no clues about why women are subordinate to men inside and outside the family and why it is not the other way round. Marxist categories, like capital itself, are sex-blind.

To explain who fills these empty places, Marxists today have appealed to Engels, but as we have seen, his account is clearly unsatisfactory. It is for the same reason—sex-blindness—that the new Marxist criminology has failed to analyze relations of reproduction as related to crime.

While a growing number of articles and books by feminists have analyzed crimes against women, crimes by women, and the sexist nature of the legal system, neither feminists nor criminologists have attempted to understand how reproduction and gender, in connection with production and class, have influenced the entire spectrum of criminality. Only two major works in the criminological literature have thought it important to attempt to understand gender in relation to class (Balkan et al. 1980; Schwendinger and Schwendinger 1983). Yet even these two works are marked with masculine bias; in the sense that, when discussing gender, they subordinate it to economic relations. Moreover, they discuss gender only in ideological terms and ignore the material dynamics of gender relations. This theoretical direction not only distorts our understanding of the position of men and women and the role masculine dominance plays in society, it also fails to provide an adequate understanding of all forms of criminality and their social control.

The Emerging Marxist Feminist Criminology

The two books cited above are prototypes of an emerging "Marxist feminist criminology" and an outgrowth of Marxist feminist theory (classical Marxist feminist works are Benston 1969; Smith 1975; Rowbotham 1973). In the late 1960s and early 1970s, a number of leftist women, questioning the masculine bias in Marxist social theory, created a Marxist feminist thought. However, much Marxist feminism is not markedly different from earlier Marxist work, since this "new" perspective still understands the "woman question" as an epiphenomenon of relations of production, and considers gender stratification and reproduction relatively unimportant. For most Marxist feminists, the class and sexual divisions of labor are both responsible for the position of women in any society, but the sexual division of labor is considered to be *derived* from the class division of labor. The family and reproduction are thus "superstructural," molded by the more primary relations of production. Reproduction is viewed as being only reactive, never an active force in history. For instance, Marxist feminists view the capitalist mode of production as the basic organization of U.S. society, which determines the social relations of production *and* reproduction. Sex and class inequality in this society result from property relations and the capitalist mode of production. Masculine dominance then is ideological—not material—and women are primarily dominated by capital and only secondarily by men, and even that domination results from the mode of production. While some Marxist feminists advocate analyzing masculine dominance and sexism in society, they understand the roles of men and women in relation to capital, not in relation to a system of masculine power. Women's labor in the home is analyzed not in terms of the way it serves the interests of men, but rather, as it benefits profit-making by the capitalist class.

It is in this light that the two works considered below can be understood, as they represent an emergent "Marxist feminist criminology." While these works have advanced Marxist criminology, they still suffer from severe masculine bias, in subordinating reproduction, women, and gender to production, men, and class, and provide an inadequate basis for understanding crime.

Balkan, Berger, and Schmidt

In 1980, Shiela Balkan, Ron Berger, and Janet Schmidt published a very comprehensive Marxist textbook on crime and deviance. Unfortunately, this work, following the Marxist feminist paradigm, reduces relations of reproduction to secondary status. Balkan, Berger, and Schmidt concentrate on "historical and dialectical materialism." Since social change is dialectical rather than evolutionary, "history is the perpetual disclosure and working out of . . . contradictory or conflicting class relations." Class conflict, structured by the "particular economic arrangements," creates inequities in wealth, power, and lifestyles. Consequently, the conflict between social classes "occurs over decisions as to how these various economic, political, and social resources are allocated" (1980, 12–13).

The most important determinant of class relations is the mode of production, which, following Marx, contains the forces and relations of production. The mode of production "forms the essential backbone . . . of a society" (ibid., 41). Following an economic base/superstructure paradigm, Balkan, Berger, and Schmidt (ibid.) state that "social institutions develop and operate in particular ways according to the nature of the mode of production they support and help to reproduce." In other words, "noneconomic institutions" (superstructure) develop to support and help reproduce the mode of production. Following Althusser (1971), they argue that these noneconomic institutions "do have a certain amount of autonomy" and take two forms—the state (executive and legislative bodies; courts and laws; army, police, and prisons) and civil society (ideologies, culture, family, religion, schools, arts, and media). Since they totally ignore the internal dynamics of reproduction as a codetermining element, they approach crime and deviance primarily through a class analysis (Balkan et al. 1980, 41–57).

Although Balkan, Berger, and Schmidt concentrate on the primacy of production, they do include a section (part IV), on women, gender, and crime. In their view, women engage in certain types of crimes due to their specific gender-role socialization under capitalism and, therefore, the resulting opportunities open to them. Sexist socialization underlies both women's involvement in certain kinds of crime and the crimes committed against women, such as rape, wife-beating, and forced sterilization (ibid., chs. 11 and 12).

These are definite advances, yet there are still problems. The primacy of class for Balkan, Berger, and Schmidt reduces gender to a subordinate status. In an historical analysis entitled "The Primary Role of Class: The 'Superexploitation of Women'," they see the condition of women as being dependent "upon the prevailing political-economic organization" of society (ibid., 207–10). They rely on Engels' analysis of the overthrow of "mother right":

> with the domestication of large animals there was a surplus of goods available for exchange. Private property marked the end of the maternal clan and kinship productive groups and the beginning of class society and the state. The property owner was the ruler of the household; women and other propertyless dependents worked to maintain and augment his property, while he was engaged in competitive production and exchange with other heads of households. Male dominance grew and patriarchy (the "law of the father") became the prevailing family form. [ibid., 207–8]

Like Engels, Balkan, Berger, and Schmidt fail to explain why women did not become the property owners and the rulers of the household since they were the primary producers in certain horticultural societies. Moreover, they seem unaware of the emergence of masculine appropriation of female labor and control of female sexuality in these horticultural societies. Clearly, Engels explanation of the rise of patriarchy does not explain why certain spaces are filled by women and others by men.

The authors go on, however, to connect superexploitation with the onset of industrial capitalism, in which production and therefore men were removed from the home and placed in the factory. Female dependence on male wage earners perpetuated masculine domination and subordinated the value of women's wageless household labor to zero. However, since women also eventually left the household to become wage laborers in low-paying jobs, they are "superexploited."

> An understanding of the condition of women in American society must consider women's relationship to the capitalist mode of production and the requirements and consequences of the capitalist family. Through both their vast amounts of unpaid domestic labor and their work in the wage-labor force, primarily in low-paying positions, women fill the needs of capitalism and provide a source of high profits. Women are thus "superexploited": They are members of the labor force receiving less

than the pay of male workers, and, in addition, they are responsible for the care of other working class members of their families. [ibid., 208]

For Balkan, Berger, and Schmidt, the sexual division of labor is functional to capital. Women's labor in both the home and labor market is understood as *only* serving the needs of capital, and not as serving the interests of men and mediating women's relationship to capitalism. The relationship between men and women does not need a specific analysis, as economic relations determine it. While it is true that the split between home and market is typical primarily of capitalist society, certain features of the sexual division of labor under capitalism have, as we have seen, been found in preclass and precapitalistic societies. Consequently, since these features are not exclusively functional to capital, a more comprehensive explanation is necessary (Jaggar 1983, 71). Balkan, Berger, and Schmidt fall into the trap that Heidi Hartmann (1981a, 3–4) has identified: "Most Marxist analysis of women's position take as their question the relationship of women to the economic system, rather than that of women to men, apparently assuming the latter will be explained in their discussion of the former." Looking at the oppression of women solely from an economic point of view does not fully explain the crimes against and by women, or the overall struggles between men and women in U.S. society. As Gayle Rubin (1975, 160) notes, understanding women's oppression as only an economic issue under capitalism does not "explain foot-binding, chastity belts, or any of the incredible array of Byzantine, fetishized indignities, let alone the more ordinary ones, which have been inflicted upon women in various times and places."

To overcome this problem, Balkan, Berger, and Schmidt discuss gender-role socialization, which arises, according to them, from a capitalist mode of production. Their analysis here helps us to understand why female criminality is less violent than male criminality, but it does not understand that gender-role socialization is not only the ideological result of a capitalist economic system, but is simultaneously rooted materially in patriarchal gender relations. Because Balkan, Berger, and Schmidt conceive of gender-appropriate traits only economically, they are unable to conceptualize the relations of reproduction. Consequently, following Marx and Engels, the position of women in capitalist society, rather than patriarchal capitalist society, "lays the foundation for a theory of women's criminality" (Balkan et al. 1980, 211). Very simply, according to these authors, in order for us to "understand the nature of female criminality, it is necessary to understand the ideology of sexism that legitimates the structure of the family under capitalism" (ibid., 216). Due to the needs of a capitalist society, "women's existence has been male defined and centered around family, sexuality, and home" (ibid.). Consequently,

Balkan, Berger, and Schmidt argue that crime by women—shoplifting and prostitution in adults, "promiscuity" and "incorrigibility" in juveniles—has reflected these conditions. When women commit violent crimes such as murder, their victims are family members, relatives, or lovers. Moreover, they are less likely to use guns and more likely to use household implements such as kitchen knives.

Furthermore, Balkan, Berger, and Schmidt consider "crimes against women," such as rape and wife-beating, to be the result of capitalist socialization. As they rightly show, rape and wife-beating allow the offender the opportunity to show his "manhood" and are thus acts of agression and contempt (ibid., 243). They derive this masculine "ideology," however, from capitalism, rather than root it in the structural inequality of male-female relations (patriarchy), which interacts with capitalist class relations.

Through their discussion of gender-role socialization, Balkan, Berger, and Schmidt have provided us with a much better understanding of crime, but they do not carry it far enough. First, their discussion centers around the separate ways men and women relate to capitalism and how patriarchy and masculine dominance are derived from the relations of production. Balkan, Berger, and Schmidt fail to recognize that the "mutual dependence of patriarchy and capitalism not only assumes the malleability of patriarchy to the needs of capitalism, but assumes the malleability of capitalism to the needs of patriarchy" (Eisenstein 1979, 27). Balkan, Berger, and Schmidt, by ignoring the second part of Eisenstein's apt formulation, flaw their overall understanding of the economy, family, and crime. Second, they limit their discussion of gender and crime only to crimes by women and crimes against women. What about homicide, assault, and robbery? Are gender-roles involved here, or is it only in crimes like rape and wife-beating that gender roles play an important part? For example, Balkan, Berger, and Schmidt's concentration on gender-role socialization in relation to exclusively "sexual crimes" is particularly apparent when they discuss working class crime and interpersonal violence, which they attribute *only* to economic structural characteristics. There is no attempt to integrate gender stratification and therefore patriarchy into their class analysis. Since their discussion concentrates solely on the relation between race, income, and street crime, they fail to show why *males* by far predominate as perpetrators of all forms of street crimes, and for that matter, more serious illegal activity like corporate crime. Thus, for Balkan, Berger, and Schmidt, rapists have gender roles but robbers and corporate criminals do not. This is what results when reproduction is omitted from theoretical consideration. In short, although Balkan, Berger, and Schmidt have produced an excellent Marxist criminological text, they follow in the footsteps of Marx and Engels insofar as they ignore gender stratification and reproduction, and therefore the other half of that most important materialist conception of society.

Julia and Herman Schwendinger

In 1983, the well-known Marxist criminologists Julia and Herman Schwendinger published a book entitled *Rape and Inequality.* This book, like the Balkan, Berger, and Schmidt work, subordinates gender relations to class relations. Here the authors attempt to explain the origin of sexual inequality while simultaneously undertaking a class analysis of rape. This work has, I believe, some serious problems centering around their failure to bring the reproductive sphere out of hiding. These problems occur primarily in three areas: their account of the rise of sexual inequality and violence toward women, their analysis of rape, and their failure to examine the so-called "socialist" societies.

In a section labeled "An Explanation of Rape" (ibid., 125–79), Julia and Herman Schwendinger make two important and controversial claims: (1) production for exchange historically is responsible for sexual inequality; (2) consequently, violence toward women is rooted in the mode of production. In this section the authors criticize the claim of many radical feminists that sexism is universal. Discussing Engels' *The Origin of the Family, Private Property, and the State,* they first attempt to account for the "Rise and Expansion of Sexual Inequality." While pointing out some of the limitations of Engels' work, Julia and Herman Schwendinger conclude that the rudiments of his premise are still valid for explaining the rise of sexual inequality.

> Engels theorized that within ancient communal societies the accumulation of wealth in private hands was stimulated by production for exchange and the creation of economic surpluses. Further developments involving war, population growth, and patrilineality increased private accumulation and *channeled it along male lines for posterity.* [emphasis added] [ibid., 129–30]

Like Engels, Julia and Herman Schwendinger, by ignoring women's labor and its appropriation by men, attribute the rise of sexual inequality to societies that produce for exchange and/or have antagonistic relations with neighboring groups, adding that

> some societies with sexual inequality are based on "lineage systems" that concentrate economic resources and surplus goods in the hands of male elders. Often the tribes are distinguished by patrilineal estates or individual male property ownership. Even though they are not yet class societies, exploitative developments move them in this direction. [ibid., 142].

However, they do not wonder why this is so. They ignore, or are unaware of the fact that, as noted in my discussion of Engels, males appropriated the labor power of women in certain horticultural societies even prior to the rise of social classes.

Julia and Herman Schwendinger's main point is that sexual inequality and the level of male violence in a society are determined primarily by class relations and that gender relations are secondary. Moreover, sexual violence is strongly tied to other forms of violence in the society as a whole (ibid., 184).

> Rape itself became associated with violent practices organized around broader aims: the subjugation of women and exploitation of tribes, classes, and other social groups. Violence became the focus of a seemingly endless struggle by individuals, classes and nations for power and property.

Consequently, the bulk of this book attempts to show that societies without commodity production are gender egalitarian; that is, women are considered equal to men in most aspects of societal life and that violence toward women is nonexistent. However, when these societies begin to produce for exchange (whether this pattern is imposed by a colonial power or arises voluntarily in the society), men control production while women, isolated in the home, produce for use to maintain the now more valuable, important male, who produces for exchange. Hence, inequality becomes closely tied to and rooted in the mode of production.

Julia and Herman Schwendinger discuss the changes that have taken place in *one* society, the !Kung Bushman of the Kalahari Desert, to support their thesis (ibid., 193–97). Using Patricia Draper's (1975) work on !Kung aboriginal foraging bands and sedentary villages, Julia and Herman Schwendinger argue that foraging (hunting and gathering) bands maintain high levels of sexual equality, that women have personal autonomy, that domestic chores and child-rearing activities are egalitarian, and that the people "are gentle and actively discourage any sign of harmful competition among males and violence between the sexes" (ibid., 194). This changes, however, when the !Kung relocate into sedentary villages with an economy characterized partly by commodity production, with males dominant. With this new division of labor, the authority of males increases, the status of women decreases, and violence toward women emerges (ibid., 194–97).

There are, however, problems with the Schwendingers' argument. Their thesis that sexual inequality arose primarily in those societies that produce for exchange appears to be historically inaccurate. Among feminist anthropologists today, the question whether sexual equality exists in hunting and gathering societies is extremely controversial. For instance, according to Eleanor Leacock (1981), the idea that these societies maintain sexual inequality results simply from an unconscious masculine bias found in Western anthropological research. Others, while not denying this, suggest that while women are not systematically exploited and degraded in most hunting and gathering societies, they are not entirely the social equals of men (Rosaldo and Lamphere 1974; Rubin 1975; Blumberg 1978; Collier and Rosaldo 1981; Shostak 1983). The evidence on the !Kung seems to support this latter view. The foraging bands, although considerably much more egalitarian than the sedentary villages, still have an unequal sexual division of labor. And although there exists nonexploitative relations and, therefore, a striking degree of equality between males and females, especially when compared to industrialized capitalist societies, men have the upper hand. !Kung women, as in most hunting and gathering societies, are the primary economic providers and spend much of their time "gathering" to provide food for their family. While performing this labor, women regulate their own work schedules, decide which foods to gather and where the gathering should take place, exclusively control the distribution of the food gathered, and derive much self-esteem from their important contribution to subsistence. However, the !Kung look upon the labor of women as different from the labor performed by men and its product (Shostak 1983, 241–42). In fact, in most hunting and gathering societies, there is a "sexual asymmetry" in the nature and organization of economic obligations resulting from the fact that women gather to feed their families, while men, in addition to feeding their families, hunt to distribute meat through the group according to specific rules (Collier and Rosaldo 1981, 281). As Lorna Marshall (1976, 97) reports of the !Kung,

> every able, adult woman is responsible for gathering for herself, her family, and her dependents. She may give to others as she wishes, but custom and expectation in !Kung society do not require that plant food be shared in a general distribution as meat is shared. This means that every able, adult woman must gather regularly.

Women do some hunting, for such small animals as lizards and tortoises, but only the meat of large animals is distributed to others according to specific rules. As Collier and Rosaldo (1981, 283) point out, this sexual division of labor and its resulting obligations, by involving men in a wider sphere of influence, provides them with an upper hand in !Kung society.

The preeminence of male labor and its product is clearly indicated by the rituals acted out in !Kung life. Women are excluded from the "big hunt" because of the belief that "femaleness negates hunting prowess" (Marshall 1976, 177). Women are also excluded from hunting rituals such as "the extremely important initiation rite for boys, the Rite of the First Kill, which is based on hunting and which must be performed before a boy may marry" (ibid., 178). This rite is performed twice for each boy—after he kills a large male animal and then again after he kills a large female animal. In addition, the !Kung describe many gathered foods as "things comparable to nothing" (with the exception of the mongongo nut), while "meat is so highly valued that it is often used as a synonym for 'food' " (Shostak 1983, 243). As Draper (1975, 82) notes, "All !Kung agree that meat is the most desirable, most prestigious food" even though the product of gathering is more important in the !Kung diet. Men provide women with their gathering tools but women are prohibited from handling men's hunting equipment (Shostak 1983, 243). For example, women, especially while menstruating, are not allowed to touch men's arrows (ibid., 239), and the hunter must not allow the milk of a lactating woman to touch him, as this "would destroy his hunting powers" (Marshall 1976, 177). No such rituals exist for gathering, and no prohibitions implicate men "as a negative influence on the success of women gatherers" (Shostak 1983, 244). In fact men do participate in some gathering and are as knowledgeable about plants as the women (ibid.). As Marshall (1976, 178) concludes, "I believe that the value put on hunting and the satisfaction of its success accrue to the enhancement of men's position in !Kung society."

Consequently, !Kung society's celebration of men and the product of their labor helps provide them with an upper hand. Women's rituals, on the other hand, celebrate their capacity for obtaining heterosexual ties with men (Collier and Rosaldo 1981, 303). !Kung women are scarified on their face and buttock, "for beauty," beginning around the age of twelve, the time when they begin attracting husbands (Marshall 1976, 41). In addition, a girl's first menstruation is celebrated with a rite that involves

> her seclusion and the staging of the sexually suggestive Eland Dance by
> other women. At the Eland Dance, sexually mature women remove their
> clothes and dramatize the power of their sexuality for energizing and
> rejuvenating adult men. Girl's puberty rituals do not seem to stress
> women's capacity for bearing children, and this lack of elaborate ritual
> concern for female fertility or maternity is reflected in the fact that
> women give birth in the bushes apart from the encampment, either
> alone or with their own mothers. [Collier and Rosaldo 1981, 303–4]

This cultural definition of men in terms of hunting and women in terms of sexual attractiveness is also reflected in parents desires for husbands and wives for their children. Marshall (1976, 267) reports, for example, that "parents of boys hope the girls to whom their sons are engaged will grow up to be good-looking, because, a man takes pride in a beautiful wife." On the other hand, the parents of a girl "want the boy to be responsible, kind to their daughter, and above all, . . . a good hunter" (ibid., 268).

!Kung rituals thus stress the skill and importance of men in !Kung society, and the sexual desirability of women. Hence, it seems reasonable to conclude, with Shostak (1983, 237), that men usually hold "positions of influence" in !Kung foraging bands and therefore have the upper hand. As Shostak (1983, 245) states, "!Kung women themselves refer to, and do not seem to reject, male dominance." While it is true that !Kung culture downplays many attitudes that encourage masculine dominance, men and women are not entirely social equals in !Kung society. And while !Kung women are not systematically exploited and oppressed in !Kung society, !Kung men "enjoy certain distinct advantages—in the way the culture values their activities, both economic and spiritual, and in their somewhat greater influence over decisions affecting the life of the group" (ibid., 243–44).

This conclusion becomes even more plausible when we consider the sexual division of labor in the family. While it is true that men spend considerable time hunting (and therefore traveling long distances), drawing water, repairing and making tools, and being involved in housework (food processing, cleaning, tending the fire, collecting firewood, and so on) (Lee 1979), women are responsible not only for gathering the food, but for the major share of the housework (approximately 15 hours per week for men and 22 hours per week for women), and approximately 90 percent of child care (Shostak 1983, 238; Lee 1979, 278, 451). In fact, as Draper (1975, 92) points out, men in !Kung foraging bands "unanimously eschew" certain aspects of child care. For example, a man seeing his child with a runny nose "will call out to his wife, "Ugh! Get rid of that snot.' " As Draper (ibid.) further reports,

> Men are also loath to clean up feces left by children. Usually the mother or an older child will scoop up the offending mess with a handful of leaves. If, however, a child's defecation has gone unnoticed by all except the father, he will call out to his wife to remove it.

The public nature of !Kung life means that much child care is shared, yet it is primarily the women who share in these duties, not the men. In fact, fathers rarely take sole responsibility for the child when the mother is absent (Lee 1979, 451). And although fathers may spend time playing with their children, and are many times intimately involved with them, they leave the "dirty work" to women.

In sum, the evidence indicates that men clearly have the upper hand in !Kung foraging bands. Indeed, most healers are men, and healers in !Kung society have more respect and status (Shostak 1983,

245). Moreover, while there are neither formal leaders nor political or legal institutions of authority in !Kung foraging bands, men's opinions carry the most weight (ibid.). Men not only are more vocal in group discussions but also step forward to contact other cultures (ibid.). As Draper (1975, 86) found in her field work, foraging men "have gained larger knowledge of the 'outside' world, for some young men have spent months, and even years, doing wage work at such towns as Ghanzi, Gobabis, and Windhoek. Women are less likely to have had these experiences."

While hunting and gathering societies like the !Kung have highly egalitarian political, economic, and gender relations, and no patriarchy as such, in !Kung foraging bands a sexual division of labor which gave men the upper hand was obviously apparent. As a result, when the !Kung relocated to villages and began producing for exchange, the men acquired the higher positions. What seems to have happened then is not, as Julia and Herman Schwendinger appear to argue, that a particular economic system gave rise to sexual inequality, but rather, that the economic system changed from production for use to production for exchange, in interaction with a preexisting sexual division of labor in which men had the upper hand. It is this interaction that *exacerbated* the condition of women. The problem with Julia and Herman Schwendinger's thesis is that it is economically reductionist. Instead of recognizing a reproductive sphere that has effects of its own on human development and organization, they simply relegate this sphere to secondary status.

In addition to these major problems, Julia and Herman Schwendinger inaccurately assume that !Kung foraging bands are nonviolent, for abundant evidence contradicts their argument. Marjorie Shostak (1983, 307), for example, reports that although most conflicts in !Kung hunting and gathering society are resolved at the verbal stage, "physical fights are nevertheless not uncommon." Most male-female fights are between husband and wife, with the husband usually the aggressor. When violent outbreaks take place, this will, in many instances

> rivet the attention and emotions of the entire community. People take sides, and long-buried resentments surface, provoking secondary arguments and fights, often remote from the original issue. Amid the pandemonium, someone may mention weapons, threatening, "I'm a man. I've got my arrows. I'm not afraid to die." If the brakes are not somehow applied, spears, clubs, knives, and poisoned arrows may enter the fray. [ibid]

According to Shostak (1983, 308), this wild, out-of-control type of violence is usually the province of !Kung men between the ages of twenty and fifty. In fact, over the fifty years previous to Shostak's research, all of the weapon-related deaths were caused by men.

Regarding husband-wife violence, Shostak tells a story of a recently married woman named Nai, who experienced her first menstruation, after which she was washed. Shostak (1983, 311) explains what happened next:

> Nai's husband started to bother her for sex. She refused, thinking "haven't I just been washed from my first menstruation? Why is this man saying we should make love now?" She refused because of those thoughts. But he kept bothering her.
>
> That's when it happened. One night he became so angry he grabbed her, and tried to take her by force. They struggled and he pushed her very hard. She fell down with great force, so great that her neck was broken—one of the bones even stood out so you could see it.

Others have recorded similar accounts of violence in !Kung foraging bands (Marshall 1976, ch. 9; Lee 1979, ch. 13). Richard Lee (1979, 371) found three levels of conflict amongst the !Kung: "talk"—or an argument; "fight"—an exchange of blows without weapons; and "deadly fight"—involving the use of spears, clubs, and poisoned arrows. Although most of the violence was between men, there were cases of marital violence. Lee (1979, 378) cites the case of a husband and wife whose dispute over a blanket ends with the man "thrashing his wife on the shoulders and back with a donkey whip."

Since marriages usually are arranged between an adult man and a teenage woman, the "man is physically larger and stronger; although the girl is protected by her family, the threat of his exercising his will or power against her—especially in sex—is always there" (Shostak 1983, 240). Thus, according to Shostak and others, wife-beating and other forms of violence occur, albeit rarely, amongst the !Kung. In assuming !Kung foraging bands are nonviolent, Julia and Herman Schwendinger have side-stepped the evidence. While the !Kung are considerably less violent than contemporary class societies, the persistence of some violence even in nonstate, production-for-use societies like the !Kung suggests the sources of violence do not depend solely on the relations of production.

Julia and Herman Schwendinger's analysis of rape is also questionable. First, using the most recent victimization surveys, they conclude that rape

> is not committed equally in all parts of the population. It is committed primarily by older adolescents and young adults. In addition, the social class of both rapists and their victims is skewed toward one end of the income scale. [Schwendinger and Schwendinger 1983, 212]

That is, rapists and their victims are found primarily in marginalized communities. The problem with this analysis is that it accepts without qualification the state definition of rape. This is rather surprising, since the Schwendingers have been outspoken critics of the state

definition of crime (Schwendinger and Schwendinger 1970). Victimization surveys only record evidence based on this definition of rape—
that is, forcible rape with the threat or actual use of physical violence.
Clearly, from a Marxist point of view, the type of rape the state
defines as criminal is the one marginalized men will most frequently
commit (see chapter 6). Furthermore, by concurring with this definition, Julia and Herman Schwendinger effectively narrow the scope of
their theoretical endeavor and ignore a large number of rapes,
namely those that involve force *without* the threat or actual use of
physical violence. Consequently, *Rape and Inequality* provides no analysis of rape in marriage or at the workplace. Since many of these
rapes do not fit the state definition of rape, they do not appear in
victimization surveys. While, over time, rape in marriage and at the
workplace *without* the threat or actual use of physical violence are
alienating and destructive, they are not, as a rule, as directly traumatic
and severely shocking as a violent attack. Many women raped at home
and in the workplace in the above fashion do not therefore interpret
the event as rape (as the state defines it) since they are not forced with
the threat, or actual use, of physical violence, and, in the case of wives,
their consent may normally not be required. Female employees and
wives may be forced into sexual relations by bosses and husbands who
are in the position to employ economic sanctions should the female
fail to submit. The Schwendingers' analysis covering only state-de-
fined rape, leaves untouched what is possibly the category that
includes the majority of all rapes (see chapter 6). Marginalized men
do not disproportionately commit the most of *all* rapes, as Julia and
Herman Schwendinger conclude, but do commit the most of a certain
type of rape, a type of rape that may in fact be the least prevalent.
Julia and Herman Schwendinger, in failing to understand the differences in rape, do not see its prevalence throughout the class structure.

   To be fair, I should point out that in chapter 3 of their book, the
Schwendingers do discuss different types of rape, including rape in
the family and what they call "sexual extortion," or rape at work;
unfortunately, this discussion is primarily descriptive rather than
analytic, while their analysis concentrates on violent physical rape by
marginalized males. Thus, toward the end of their book they write,
"Although we have emphasized rape by lower status men, we are
certainly aware that this crime as well as sexual extortion is committed
by middle- and upper-class males and known assailants, such as
employers, work superiors, husbands and other family members"
(ibid). But they present no theoretical explanation why middle and
upper class males engage in rape or why, when they do, it may be
different from that committed by marginalized men.

   Second, when they do analyze forcible rape with the threat or actual use of physical violence, their analysis only accounts for the incidence of violence toward women, not the specific forms that violence takes. Their discussion concentrates specifically on the capitalist mode of production, which, they rightly argue, continues to exacerbate the condition of women because it is not only a society that produces for exchange, but also an exploitative class society. In such a society, masculinity has become linked with violence and feminity with nonviolence, and all citizens perceive these stereotypes as natural. According to the authors, this "sexual fetishism of violence," along with men's contemptuous attitudes toward women leads, under capitalism, to violence against women (ibid., 197–210).

However, while this may help us understand violence in general and violence toward women in particular, still to be explained is why men use *sex* violently. Julia and Herman Schwendinger's thesis, as it stands now, can only account for the economic conditions that give rise to physical assaults toward women. Rape is a *violent sexual encounter*, rather than simply a violent encounter.

Finally, Julia and Herman Schwendinger ignore the *transitional* (so-called socialist) societies. Any analysis of the origins and changes in sexual equality/inequality as related to changes in *the mode of production* that fails to confront the experience of these transitional societies clearly lacks theoretical promise. If Julia and Herman Schwendinger were only concerned with sexual inequality and rape in capitalist societies, my objections would not be valid. Yet their work purports to explain sexual inequality *over time*, from foraging bands to capitalist economies. Today we also have in the world societies that are attempting to develop a clearly new mode of production. In many of these transitional societies, a market in labor power and an economy based on profit virtually do not exist. Even though they may retain certain features of capitalism, their mode of social and economic organization is qualitatively distinct from capitalism. Thus, if the mode of production is decisive for determining the position of women in a given society, then those claiming to be "socialist" (or whatever we wish to call them), should treat women differently. What does the evidence show?

Recently, there has been a large body of empirical work generated by feminists on the condition of women in the USSR, the Eastern European societies, China, Cuba, Nicaragua, and some societies of Southeast Africa (Randall 1974, 1982; Curtin 1975; Scott 1976; Atkinson et al. 1977; Kristera 1977; Boxer and Quataert 1978; Croce 1978; Stern 1978; Heitlinger 1979). Their evidence fundamentally challenges the Schwendingers' thesis. While in some of these societies the position of women has improved since prerevolutionary days, masculine dominance persists and is continually being reproduced. In most respects then, the condition of women in these societies is very similar to the position of women under capitalism: working primarily in postrevolutionary "pink collar ghettos," women hold those jobs in the society with the lowest pay, least mobility, and smallest social worth. Moreover, while women have entered professions previously limited to males in perhaps greater numbers, they concentrate at the lower- and, in some cases, mid-level of these professions and not in the elite; this "speaks of an identical process of structural and ideological discrimination" as that found under capitalism (Burstyn 1983b, 66). In these societies, women form less than 5 percent of the ruling cadres, and in some cases are virtually excluded from them (ibid., 67). Most importantly, women in these societies continue to face superexploitation; that is, like women under capitalism, "socialist" women face a double day of labor. Furthermore, in these transitional societies, "given the greater scarcity of consumer goods—from food and clothing to household appliances—women's second workday is more arduous, not less, than that of their counterparts in advanced capitalist countries" (ibid.). Judging by the evidence, the position of women under so-called "socialist" modes of production is strikingly similar to that under capitalist modes of production. As Varda Burstyn (1983b, 67) asks, if the mode of production is primary,

> how is it possible that the economic, social, sexual and political patterns characteristic of women's condition should be so strikingly, so depressingly simliar, not only to women's condition in capitalist countries, but across a range of societies which include highly industrialized, "advanced" political economies such as those of Hungary, Czechoslovakia and Poland and also quite agrarian, "backward" political economies such as Uzbekistan, Mongolia and the like? If bureaucratic rule has no distinctly masculinist or generic commitment, if it is precipitated independently out of the development of the productive forces in which there is no central and specific set of dynamics flowing from and reconstructing masculine dominance, if despite everything it should be possible to put politics in command to work towards the equalization of the sexes—how is it that these remarkably similar patterns of masculine dominance appear so uniformly across these societies?

Marxist explanations that fail to grant an autonomous and equal sphere in society to gender stratification and reproduction will be unable to account for these patterns. As a result, we can only conclude that *Rape and Inequality*, like the other Marxist work discussed, only partially illuminates gender relations while simultaneously reinforcing a framework which obscures masculine dominance and gender inequality.

2

Toward a
Socialist Feminist Criminology

I must now go beyond criticizing Marxist criminology for its masculine bias to outline the theoretical propositions for a socialist feminist criminology, a criminology that attempts to understand crime through a method encompassing production and reproduction simultaneously. I begin with a brief discussion of the current stage in the women's movement and its initial emphasis on liberalism and thus reformism. Because many women before long found this liberal perspective to be quite incompatible with their desires for liberation, more radical positions developed—in particular, radical and socialist feminism. I criticize the radical feminist position primarily because, though different in content, like Marxism, it is reductionist. I then go on to show how socialist feminism overcomes the limitations of both Marxist feminism and radical feminism. The chapter ends with an introduction to the socialist feminist perspective and how it may better help us understand crime.

Liberal and Radical Feminism

The contemporary feminist movement, which emerged in the 1960s, initially developed a liberal perspective on the condition of women in U.S. society. By the late 1960s this perspective had found political expression in the National Organization for Women and other groups. Following the theory of the civil rights movement, the liberal feminist movement identified as its major goal extending equal rights to women. For liberal feminism, women are oppressed simply because they are discriminated against on the basis of sex and therefore deprived of the same opportunities as men and kept outside the mainstream of society (politics, business, finance, medicine, law, and so forth). Consequently, if "the problem is that women are in some sense 'out,' then it can be solved by letting them 'in' " (Ehrenreich and English 1978, 19). The goal of liberal feminism is to allow women to leave the "private world," so that they can exercise their skills in the "public world." The liberal feminist "program is one of assimilation, with ancillary changes (day care, for example) as necessary to promote women's rapid integration into what has been the world of men" (ibid.). In their eagerness to get women into the world of men, however, liberal feminists have not challenged the structure of work to see how it came to be and whom it serves. Additionally, by concentrating on moving women out of the house and into the labor market, liberal feminism denigrated women's traditional work (childcare, housework, and nurturance), thereby alienating many women from a feminist consciousness (Jaggar 1983, 186–90). Finally, liberal feminism is unable to explain

> the emergence of gender inequality, nor can it account, other than by analogy, for effects of race and class stratification on the conditions of women's lives. Its analysis for change is limited to issues of equal opportunity and individual choice. As a political ethic, it insists upon individual liberty and challenges any social, political, or economic practice that discriminates against persons on the basis of group or individual characteristics. It remains for more radical perspectives to explain the causal conditions of women's oppression and its relationship to race and class oppression. [Andersen 1983, 260]

Radical feminism was the first "radical perspective" to challenge the liberal feminist philosophy and practice by criticizing liberal feminists for being too simplistic. Concentrating on "equal opportunity," radical feminists argued, would allow only *some* women to become "equal" to men, but would not transform the conditions in society that produce the *overall* unequal relations between men and women. Instead, radical feminism suggested examining structural conditions and the psychological orientations they produce. For radical feminists, patriarchy is an independent and autonomous political force. While Marxists emphasized the structural conditions in the economy as the cause of masculine dominance, radical feminists see masculine power and privilege as the "root cause" of *all* social relations. Thus, according to radical feminists, the most fundamental relations in a society are not rooted in class relations, but in patriarchy, which is primary; all other social relations are secondary and derive from male-female relations (see, for example, Daly 1978). History is an everchanging struggle of men for power and domination over women. This is the dialectic of sex (Firestone 1970). As Kate Millett (1970, 25) suggested, patriarchy is based on two basic principles: "male shall dominate female," and "elder male shall dominate younger." For radical feminists, men have the power as *men*, and society is organized into "sexual spheres" (Eisenstein 1979, 16). The battle lines throughout history are "drawn between men and women, rather than between bourgeoisie and proletariat, and the determining relations are of reproduction, not production" (ibid., 17).

A major problem with radical feminism is that it assumes universal patriarchy. However, as indicated in chapter 1, while hunting and gathering societies were most likely characterized by a sexual division of labor that gave men the upper hand, patriarchy, in the sense of a full-fledged systematic and institutionalized masculine control of the labor power and sexuality of women, clearly did not exist. This leads us to the second major problem with radical feminism, which is related to—indeed a product of—the first: radical feminism is reductionist in the same way that Marxism is. Radical feminists separate the sexual and economic spheres and replace capitalism with patriarchy as the primary oppressive system. While radical feminists see the economic system of capitalism as being problematic for women, its oppressive characteristics are driven and therefore molded by patriarchy. However, and as Zillah Eisenstein (1979, 21) has shown, this is a false dichotomy.

> today the two systems support each other. They are mutually dependent. This relationship only gets distorted when one tries to define it in causal and dichotomized terms. The effect of this dichotomization is the theoretical assertion that sexual oppression is primary oppression. . . . To say that sexual oppression is primary is to sever the real connections of everyday life. Is this not what Marx did himself by focusing on class exploitation as the primary contradiction?

This does not mean, however, that radical feminism has made no contributions. Radical feminists have shown the importance of patriarchy as a system we must consider in order to comprehend men's and women's positions in society. By drawing our attention to social relations between men and women, radical feminists have added an important dimension to our understanding of oppression.

Socialist Feminism

Socialist feminists synthesize some aspects of radical feminism and Marxism into a theory that gives priority to neither production nor reproduction, but views them as equal, interacting and co-reproducing each other. Socialist feminists point to the need to understand how production and reproduction interact to determine the "social organization under which the people of a particular historical epoch live." Production and reproduction are so inextricably intertwined that they are inseparable (Jaggar 1983). A full understanding of production requires a recognition of how it is structured by reproduction and conversely, a full understanding of reproduction requires a recognition of how it is affected by production. In addition to the premise that reproduction structures society equally with production, socialist feminists argue that an individual's life experiences are shaped by both class and gender. The social experience of men and women are different just as class experiences are. This differing social experience shapes and limits the lives of both men and women. Consequently, the sexual division of labor becomes crucial, as it, in conjunction with class position, helps determine how men and women conceive the world and act upon it.

In order to understand society, and therefore "criminality," we need to comprehend how both production and reproduction interact to affect one's life. The reason for this is simple. As pointed out earlier in the Introduction, all societies satisfy human needs through the reproduction of the species via procreation, socialization, and daily maintenance, as well as through the production and consumption of goods. To satisfy these needs, labor is required within each sphere. While Marxism recognizes the labor in the production sphere, socialist feminism recognizes the socially necessary labor performed in both production and reproduction. Production and reproduction organize different aspects of human labor. All societies need food, shelter, and clothing. Consequently, in every society people must organize themselves into social relations to satisfy those needs. These relations are, of course, termed relations of production, since they organize human interaction to produce needed or desired goods. On the other hand, in all societies, people also have the need to reproduce, obtain sexual release, experience affection, socialize the young, and maintain their daily lives. Consequently, in every society, people organize themselves into social relations to satisfy those needs. These relations can be termed relations of reproduction. Relations of both production and reproduction have varied historically, but in contemporary U.S. society, relations of production take the form of capitalist class relations and relations of reproduction take the form of patriarchal gender relations.

All human adults, male and female, are capable of virtually all types of productive and reproductive labor (except childbirth). Still, production and reproduction must be identified and studied as distinct spheres of labor, distinct but related. Production and reproduction are simultaneous, interdependent modes of social relations that constitute the most fundamental activities in society.

Beyond this, both "production and reproduction relations embody *relations of power* which define them" (Eisenstein 1979, 21). Therefore, to understand production and reproduction in any given historical context, we need to grasp the power relations that give them shape.

Socialist feminists analyze power relations in the reproductive sphere as part of the power relations in the productive sphere and vice versa, rather than cut off from each other, to understand how interdependent and interconnected these power relations are (ibid.). Moreover, seeing the interconnected nature of *power* is essential for understanding crime in patriarchal capitalism.

As I have shown, Marxist criminology concentrates its historical explanation of power relations in terms of production, and therefore reduces the power relations associated with reproduction to the production sphere and consequently misses the interconnectedness between relations of production and reproduction. Far from being autonomous, power relations are interconnected and mutually dependent (ibid.).

Since at least certain horticultural societies, in the spheres of both production and reproduction, one group has appropriated the labor of subordinate groups. The appropriating group has (1) defined what work should be done and how it should be performed, (2) benefited disproportionately from the labor (both productive and reproductive) of the subordinate groups, and (3) used the labor performed by subordinate groups to consolidate and extend its control over those groups (Jaggar 1983, 136). As a result, historically there has been both productive and reproductive oppression expressed through "both material and ideological dimensions" (Eisenstein 1979, 22–26). Oppression reflects a much more complex reality never envisioned by Marx. It also reflects the hierarchical power relations of the sexual division of labor and society (ibid.).

I will attempt to delineate a system of oppression that involves the mutual dependence and interarticulation of production and reproduction. At any given moment of human activity, relations of both production and reproduction are present. For example, the factory under patriarchal capitalism not only maintains relations of production but also relations of reproduction (male- and female-defined jobs). The family, in the same society, not only reproduces the species but also is economic in nature (engages in consumption). Similarly, as I will show, crime and its social control simultaneously reflect both relations of production and reproduction. Thus, to understand any societal formation, human interaction, or activity within a society, we need to comprehend the interrelation of both forms of relations. As Rosalind Petchesky (1979, 376–77) expresses the socialist feminist view:

> "Production" and "reproduction," . . . far from being separate territories like the moon and the sun or the kitchen and the shop, are really intimately related modes that reverberate upon one another and frequently occur in the same social, physical, and even psychic spaces. . . . Not only

do reproduction and kinship, or the family, have their own, historically determined, products, material techniques, modes of organization, and power relationships, but reproduction and kinship are themselves integrally related to the social relations of production and the state; they reshape these relations all the time.

For criminology, the important aspect of the relations of production and reproduction is that their interaction leads to specific patterns of social involvement. By employing human powers to satisfy needs, relations of production and reproduction develop into linked institutions that significantly affect how members of society think and act and what each is capable of doing. Analyzing both production and reproduction gives us a more thorough understanding of how and why people in different class and gender locations act as they do in particular societies.

For many years after Marx's death, Marxists held the "social superstructure" to be rigidly determined by the "economic base." Today, this "economic determinism" is breaking down, as most Marxists acknowledge that the superstructure has considerable autonomy. Marxist criminologists, following this interpretation, argue that production determines the superstructure only in that it sets limits to the form. Greenberg (1981, 15) makes this clear in *Crime and Capitalism:*

> To say that the relations of production are a foundation on which legal and political structures "rise" is not to say that these structures are *determined* by the foundation, or base. The foundation of a building does not uniquely specify the form of the upper stories, but it does set limits.
> Thus, the characterization of Marxism as a form of "economic determinism" is a caricature. . . . the legal, political, and other institutions of a society, as well as its "forms of consciousness," have a dynamic of their own. They evolve in a manner that is related to, but not reducible to the economy.

Socialist feminism accepts this view, reinterprets it, and adds to it. Socialist feminism views the "base" of society as a historically changing system of organizing reproduction, in interaction with a system of production. The base entails a dualistic system—production and reproduction—interacting dialectically. The interpenetration and interconnection between production and reproduction most pervasively influences the culture or "superstructure" of society—that is, its legal, political, religious, aesthetic, and philosophic forms—and therefore is most important in setting limits to what forms can ultimately exist in a society. These superstructural institutions interact with one another as well as the base. Consequently, we have dialectical interaction *within* both the "base" and "superstructure," as well as *between* them.

In addition, socialist feminists point to the important fact that when we engage in particular activities to satisfy needs, we also create a consciousness and personality structure (character structure) that endures beyond the social activities that shaped it. Character structure is an internalized pattern of behavior, a daily organized habit, experienced in terms of identity, which reflects the dominance/subordination relations found in production and reproduction. Although people, as both creatures and creators of society, have the capacity to make themselves, they are not free to do so as they might like. Unless they undertake consciously to change themselves, individuals are restrained by the character structures they have previously developed by interacting in the institutional structures of production and reproduction. As Wilhelm Reich (1970, 44) stated, character structure "represents the specific way of an individual" and is an expression of his or her "total past."

And finally, since the oppression of women and of the working class is intimately related through the interaction of production and reproduction, the material base of society *as a whole* needs to be transformed to end that oppression. The institutions of society must be transformed to create a *socialist feminist* society, not just a socialist society.

Capitalism, Patriarchy, and Crime

Since the system of production in contemporary U.S. society is *capitalist* and the system of reproduction is *patriarchy,* we must look at each more closely to uncover their basic elements, to observe how they interconnect and how understanding this interaction helps us to comprehend crime in the United States.

Marxism is a theory with tremendous analytic power for understanding relations of production under capitalism. We know, from using Marxist social theory, that capitalist societies are driven by the demands of accumulation. By far the most important aspect of this process is production oriented around exchange, rather than use. Under capitalism, production is driven and shaped by the profit imperative, and profits result because those who own and control the productive sphere (capital) can exploit labor power. The accumulation of capital simultaneously transforms the social structure and relations of production. The concept of social class is central. Historically, capitalism has maintained four classes: the bourgeoisie (capitalists), the petty bourgeoisie (artisans, professionals, and small business people), the proletariate (workers), and the lumpenproletariat (impoverished, non- or sporadically employed). Of these four, the working class and capitalist class are by far the most important.

That the foundation of class analysis under capitalism is in the relations of production helps us understand why the capitalist class and working class are the most important. The capitalist class owns the means of production and employs land, labor, and capital to pursue profit making and accumulate wealth. To support itself, the working class sells its labor power to the capitalist class for wages. These relations of production are inherently *exploitative,* since the capitalist class makes its profits by paying less in wages than the value of what the working class actually produces. These relations are also essentially power relations. In capitalist societies, the capitalist class exercises power over all other classes by compelling members of those classes to work for its own benefit. The capitalist class has an objective interest in maintaining a social structure that reinforces and increases its power, while the working class has an objective interest in eliminating these power differentials. Consequently, conflict is inherent in the class structure of capitalism. As such, capitalism creates a social system with irreconcilable class antagonisms.

What maintains this class rule are both repressive and ideological institutions of the "superstructure" not directly based in production. The capitalist class is served by, and so controls, at least indirectly, the means of organized violence represented by the state—the military and criminal justice system. Through its preeminent influence on the state, the capitalist class is able to repress behaviors that challenge the status quo. Other institutions, like the educational system and the mainstream media, expound an ideology supporting the status quo. Overall, then, relations of production under capitalism have both material and ideological dimensions.

Patriarchy is likewise a set of social relations of power, in which men control the labor power and sexuality of women. It is this control—both in the home and labor market—that provides the material base of patriarchy. However, patriarchy is also a system of hierarchical power relations that provides control not only of men over women but also among men; for some men receive more benefits from women's labor than other men. For example, within each social class men accrue privileges over women in the home. However, capitalist class men gain privileges over *all* women since they control not only some women's labor power in the home, but they also benefit from exploiting women's labor power in the labor market. This shows how interdependent reproduction and production are in patriarchal capitalism.

The sexual division of labor is of utmost importance here. Varda Burstyn (1983b, 53–56) has identified three important features of the sexual division of labor under patriarchal relations of reproduction.

First, the nature of the labor performed by men and women is different. While men have, under patriarchy, labored primarily in the productive realm, women have labored in both the productive and reproductive spheres. As such, women's labor is not only different from men's, but it is substantially more extensive, and men-as-a-group have appropriated that labor to themselves, even if the extent of that labor has varied by class.

The second feature of the sexual division of labor is masculine control over women's sexuality. What is important here is normative heterosexuality "as the major psycho-sexual organizing principle" of patriarchal gender relations, "with its attendant subordination of women's right to erotic pleasure as well as masculine control of children and property" (ibid., 54). The "propagation of the species," in Engels' words, is socially determined. As Levi-Strauss (1971, 348) has shown, the sexual division of labor "is nothing else than a device to institute a reciprocal state of dependency between the sexes." In other words, since biologically there are many different forms of sexual expression, without some controls, specific social forms of species propagation become difficult. The sexual division of labor, as a social invention, divides the sexes into two mutually exclusive categories, creating gender, and enjoining heterosexual marriage for economic survival and biological reproduction. Gayle Rubin (1975, 179) has extended Levi-Strauss' argument, reasoning that the necessity to engender in order to guarantee heterosexual marriage and thus biological reproduction, leads us to question the "naturalness" of any form of sexual expression, including heterosexuality. For Rubin (1975, 180), the sexual division of labor "is implicated in both aspects of gender—male and female it creates them, and it creates them heterosexual." Consequently, the sexual division of labor has historically rested upon the enforcement of normative heterosexuality.

In hunting and gathering societies women tend to have control over their own sexuality, despite the existence of heterosexual marriage relations. However, and as shown in chapter 1, with the development of masculine appropriation of female labor power in certain horticultural societies, women became affiliated and controlled wives, who began to lose control over their sexuality. The condition of women is aggravated in agrarian societies, as

> virginity is typically required and the negative sanctions for non-marital sex of any kind can be horrendous for the woman. She is breeding children for a male-dominated family group, and any suspicions concerning paternity would be very awkward where there was property to be transmitted. [Blumberg 1978, 52]

Moreover, here we begin to find the world's strictest and most bizarre practices of secluding women and controlling their sexuality, such as, veils, foot-binding, chastity belts, *purdah* (where women are not allowed out of the house), as well as "double standard monogamy," eventually leading to punishments for female adultery.

Today, normative heterosexuality, institutionalized in patriarchal gender relations, tends to force women into motherhood and reinforce double standard monogamy, which both restricts their sexual freedom and makes it easier for men to control their productive and reproductive labor. Normative heterosexuality helps to legitimate the ideology that women are dependent on men for their sexual and economic well-being, denigrates women's relationships with other women, and subjects them to continued domination by men. Moreover, economic survival for most women means learning to present themselves as sexual beings. As Alison Jaggar (1983, 308–9) points out,

> male superiors penalize women who seem to be "punishing" or defying men through their appearance; much of women's paid work is sexualized; and, in the end, the best chance of economic security for most women remains the sale of their sexuality in marriage. . . . [Women] are expected to titillate male sexuality in situations that are not overtly sexual and in overtly sexual situations, they are expected to fascinate, to arouse and to satisfy men. In short, men rather than women control the expression of women's sexuality: women's sexuality is developed for men's enjoyment rather than for women's.

The third and final feature of the sexual division of labor outlined by Burstyn is that men control the economic, religious, political, and military systems of power in society. Women's exclusion from these positions is fundamentally parallel to their relegation to primary responsibility for reproductive labor. This exclusion is a major reason why women are relatively powerless to centrally change the first two aspects of the sexual division of labor.

Since patriarchal relations then are essentially power relations, men exercise power over women by appropriating women's labor power and controlling their sexuality. Consequently, conflict, just as in class relations, is inherent in a patriarchal system.

Patriarchal rule is maintained not only by the family and the economic system, but also by the state and ideological institutions of the "superstructure." Since males control the state, behaviors that tend to call into question patriarchy are repressed. Other institutions, like the educational system and the mainstream media, ideologically support patriarchy. Overall then, relations of reproduction under patriarchy, like relations of production, have both material and ideological dimensions.

The Interaction of Capitalism and Patriarchy

It is very important not to underestimate the importance of either capitalist or patriarchal social relations. While both are somewhat autonomous, they are also highly interdependent. Capitalist social relations become prevalent in patriarchy and patriarchal relations are a part of capitalism. In other words, the interlocking institutions of capitalism and patriarchy condition each other. Consequently, we do not live in simply a "capitalist" society, but rather a "patriarchal capitalist" society.

The last chapter argued that an incipient patriarchy emerged within certain horticultural societies. This growth of patriarchal gender relations continued into early capitalist development as a central element of continuity, namely, by its "organization through the power, privilege, and authority of the ruling class father, replicated in miniature within the households of the laboring classes" (Burstyn 1983b, 56). In other words, while several modes of production have been prevalent during this time period, in terms of reproduction, patriarchy (although organized differently in different eras) has been the major form of organizing masculine domination. Ehrenreich and English (1978, 6–7) describe preindustrial patriarchy:

> authority over the family is vested in the elder males, or male. He, the father, makes the decisions which control the family's work, purchases, marriages. Under the rule of the father, women have no complex choices to make, no questions as to their nature or destiny: the rule is simply obedience. . . . The patriarchal order of the household is magnified in the governance of village, church, nation. At home was the father, in church was the priest or minister, at the top were the "town fathers," the local nobility, or as they put it in Puritan society, "the nursing fathers of the commonwealth," and above all was "God the Father."

With the development of capitalist industrialization and the proletarianization of the working classes, however, capitalism interacted with patriarchy, resulting in some major contradications between the two systems of social relations. As capitalists began to organize production on a large scale, it was removed from the home. Whole families—working class men, women, and children—had to labor long hours outside the home to survive. The productive resources of the home (women and children) previously controlled by the husband/father, now left the home and entered the wage labor market. While this might possibly have undermined familial patriarchy, it is clear that working class men appropriated for themselves the major positions as wage laborers (breadwinners) outside the home. As Heidi Hartmann (1979, 217) has shown, masculine control over women's labor was altered by the wage system, but not eliminated.

In the labor market the dominant position of men was maintained by sex-ordered job segregation. Women's jobs were lower paid, considered less skilled, and often involved less exercise of authority or control. Men acted to enforce job segregation in the labor market; they utilized trade-union associations and strengthened the domestic division of labor which required women to do housework, child care, and related chores. Women's subordinate position in the labor market reinforced their subordinate position in the family, and that in turn reinforced their labor market position.

By 1840 in England, however, the wage labor of the working class family outside the home began to change, as male factory workers lobbied for an eight-hour day of work for children under age thirteen, and disallowing the employment of children under the age of nine. One effect of the subsequent child labor laws was to create difficulties with child care for parents (ibid., 217–18). This situation caused problems for the reproduction of the working class, since with both adults in the paid labor force children could not be trained and supervised. Consequently, male workers and the upper classes began to recommend that women, in addition to children, be removed from wage labor in the factories. Male-controlled unions fought for and won "protective legislation" for women, limiting the number of hours they could work. Moreover, males denied women training for skilled work and eventually drove them out of male-controlled trade unions (ibid., 226). As Heidi Hartmann (1979, 219) makes clear, excluding women from factories and unions and denying them skills is explained not solely by the needs of capitalism, but also "by patriarchal relations between men and women: men wanted to assure that women would continue to perform the appropriate tasks at home." Consequently, for the upper layers of the white working class, a "family wage" developed that was sufficient to allow women to stay home, raise the children, and maintain the family. In this way, rather than having all family members working in the labor force, the male appropriated to himself, once again, both the position of breadwinner in the labor market and the labor of women in the home. This is not to imply that men operated consciously to subjugate women. Rather, operating within an agriculturally based patriarchal context, working class males resisted the destruction of the patriarchal family unit and attempted to ameliorate the oppressive nature of the wage labor system on "their women." In addition, while many women resisted the family wage system, many others felt that the workplace was a desperate and dangerous place for them and their children, so they, along with their husbands, supported the family wage system. In short, the workplace was reorganized along patriarchal lines—clearly exhibiting the ability of patriarchy to reproduce itself even when relations of production alter.

The family wage, resulting from the partnership between patriarchy and capitalism, likewise developed in the United States, where it was supported not only by working class men who wanted "their women" out of the factories, but also by "a chorus of concern . . . from reformers, ministers, conservative feminists, doctors, and other representatives of bourgeois morality, all bent on 'preserving' the family" (Zaretsky 1978, 211). By the end of the Progressive Era (1900–1917), state policy toward the family supported the idea of a family wage, entailing both a husband solely supporting his family and a full-time mother in the home. These policies, as Zaretsky (ibid., 212) makes clear, "not only reflected the outlook of the bourgeoisie but also the aspirations of both men and women within the working class."

The family wage system, then, validated the husband/father as the sole breadwinner earning enough to maintain children and a wife who did not labor outside the home. The family wage system was partly economic in that it corresponded to capitalist needs for a more stable and healthy work force, a reserve army of labor ready to be drawn into production, and a healthier working class from which to draw the military. Yet it also maintained, across the class structure, masculine domination and consequently masculine appropriation of female labor in the home. Thus, the family wage system not only demonstrates the crucial interaction of patriarchy and capitalism in this society, but it also exhibits the complications that emerge from this interaction. While working class and capitalist class men are antagonistic toward one another regarding the labor-capital relation, they in fact cooperate to maintain their privileged position over women in patriarchal capitalism (Sokoloff 1980, 172). However, a conflict between working and capitalist class men occurred over the use of women's labor power. Capitalist men needed an abundant supply of labor such as women provide at low wages, but this might possibly lower working class male wages. Working class men, on the other hand, want "their women" at home to service them personally and maintain the family. Thus antagonisms result between working and capitalist men over the allocation of women's labor power (Hartmann 1981a, 19). However, both classes of men simultaneously cooperate to maintain patriarchy and their privileged position over women. The family wage serves both classes of men's interests. As Natalie J. Sokoloff (1980, 173) notes:

> It provides the individual working class male with an inexpensive servant who artfully stretches the budget and typically lives at a lower standard of living than her husband. She not only cares for his needs but also relieves him of caring for his children's needs. He need not do unwaged and devalued reproduction of labor power. Moreover, her economic dependence gives him greater power in their relations. It is not an equal exchange between them. Finally, without her, he cannot sell his labor

power to the capitalist. But part of his labor power includes her labor power, too.

Capitalist men also benefit from the exploitation of their wives, which allows them to devote the largest part of their time to their career, while exploiting "the surplus value of male workers without having to pay fully for their reproduction and maintenance since this is done through the hidden work of their wives" (ibid.).

The family wage system was stabilized materially and ideologically up to World War II. However, with the economic developments of the postwar period, the full contradictions between capitalism and patriarchy have, as Varda Burstyn (1983b, 62) argues, "really begun to explode." The family wage system and the breadwinner power of the male have been undermined. Increased inflation, unreliable wages, and increasing individual expectations and material demands stimulated by advertising have compelled working class families to rely on two wages to maintain the adequate standard of living previously obtainable by a single male breadwinner. In addition, capital's ever-increasing search for new areas of development has resulted in an expansion of service sectors and clerical work. Consequently, these two developments created the conditions for many women once again to move out of the home and into wage labor. Women have been drawn, as a reserve army of labor, out of the home to fill the needs of capital. Working outside the home, women have been segregated into "nurturing" jobs—clerical, service, nursing, school teaching, and cleaning of all kinds. Thus, the sexual division of labor reappears in the labor market, where women generally do the same type of labor they do in the home. Job segregation by sex maintains patriarchy under capitalism since it preserves a lower status for women and channels them generally into low-wage positions (see chapter 4). Women today are paid approximately half what men earn, and this differential wage aids, "in *defining* women's work as secondary to men's at the same time it necessitates women's actual continued economic dependence on men. The sexual division of labor in the labor market and elsewhere should be understood as a manifestation of patriarchy which serves to perpetuate it" (Hartmann 1981a, 26). This economic dependence reinforces the need for most women to marry and thus to be supported by the husband's ever-decreasing family wage. Even if women work as wage laborers, they still do the major share of unpaid labor in the home (see chapter 4). Consequently, men continue to benefit from higher wages in the labor market and the work women do in the home. The sex-segregated labor market allows men a more powerful economic position and simultaneously ensures women's dependence on men and their sub-orindate position in the home. As Hartmann (1979, 208) concludes:

> Thus, the hierarchical domestic division of labor is perpetuated by the labor market, and vice versa. This process is the present outcome of the continuing interaction of two interlocking systems, capitalism and patri-archy. Patriarchy, far from being vanquished by capitalism, is still very virile; it shapes the form modern capitalism takes, just as the develop-ment of capitalism has transformed patriarchal institutions. The result-ing mutual accommodation between patriarchy and capitalism has cre-ated a vicious circle for women.

Women's labor continues to be an important element in men's domination of women. Even though there exists an increasing tend-ency to dissolve the traditional patriarchal nuclear family (see chapter 4), which diminishes somewhat exploitation of domestic labor on an individual basis (by the husband/father), women's labor continues to be appropriated. In short, women as the so-called "nurturers" have now entered the paid labor force. What exists today is a "publiciza-tion" of the previously privatized labor of women, because even women who live single most of their lives have their labor power appropriated through the work they do in the labor force (Burstyn 1983b, 64).

For single men it is quite different, since their high wage (relative to women—for we cannot forget that most men's labor power is also appropriated) enables them to purchase their nurturance in the labor market. Most women rarely have this opportunity (as shown in chapter 4), since they do not receive a "family wage," even if they are the "head" of their household. As is increasingly the case, women are responsible for maintaining themselves and their children and at the same time are unable to purchase services outside the home, even if they are full-time wage laborers. Consequently, and contrary to popular belief, throughout the sixties and seventies and into the eighties, the condition of women, as well as that of the working class, has actually worsened.

Capitalism, Patriarchy, and Gender

Under patriarchal capitalism, gender is rooted materially in the sexual division of labor and, therefore, in the activities men and women perform in the home and labor market. We are shaped "woman" and "man." This is in part what Engels meant when he talked of "the production of human beings themselves."

One's gender is also related to normative heterosexuality. All Western patriarchal capitalist societies have a hierarchical system of sexual value, with marital, reproductive heterosexuals alone at the top, followed by unmarried heterosexuals, those with a preference for solitary sexuality, lesbians and gay males, prostitutes, transvestites, and sado-masochists (Rubin 1984, 279). Heterosexuals are rewarded with certified mental health, respectability, legality, social and physical mobility, institutional support, and material benefits, while those whose sexual preference is other than heterosexual are presumed to be mentally ill, disreputable, and criminal; their social and physical mobility is restricted; they have no institutional support; and they face economic sanctions (ibid.). Normative heterosexuality, then, creates a sexual ideology that "there is one best way to do it, and that everyone should do it that way" (ibid., 283).

Under these conditions—patriarchal capitalist division of labor and normative heterosexuality—gender develops in the United States. Most men and women develop sex-specific stereotyped behaviors based on "feminine" and "masculine" behavioral styles. A masculine character structure—under patriarchal capitalism the most important and desirable—requires self-confidence, independence, boldness, responsibility, competitiveness, a drive for dominance, and aggression/violence. These are likewise the dominant values of a "capitalist ideology." As Michael Silverstein (1977, 178) makes clear, men's drive for dominance is the psychic engine of a capitalist society.

> [t]hose with real power, ruling class, white males, in order to perpetuate the existing social structure and thus ensure their continued control, use their control of the educational, communication, entertainment, and religious institutions to create men who seek a positive self-image in their power over others. Thus, they have at their disposal middle class men motivated to operate the organizational machinery of capitalism by a desire to achieve power, and working class men who can be reconciled to their real powerlessness by personal power over their women and the possibility of successful competition for personal power with rivals of their own class. In addition, white working class men are given at least a vicarious power over third-world peoples.

In addition to this drive for dominance, the masculine role in such a system centers around earning money and providing material security for *his* family. The ideal masculine identity is invested in men's work and occupational duties outside the parameters of the home and family.

The ideal female character structure necessitates patience, understanding, sensitivity, passivity, dependence, and nurturance/nonviolence. The female role centers around functions reflecting these characteristics, specifically in the family. As mothers, women provide support, nurturance, and services to their husbands and children. Women are expected to—and of course many do—evaluate their self-worth "by their success in emotionally and materially supporting a man in his struggle for power, rather than acting as competitors themselves" (ibid.). (The rise of feminism, however, attests to how much this expectation has been breaking down.) Outside the home, as I have noted, women work in nurturing and servicing positions such as secretary, nurse, or elementary school teacher. Sexism, the ideology that women are inferior to men, is institutionalized in a patriarchal capitalist system and obviously benefits men.

One word of caution about gender development needs to be pointed out. I do not hold that individuals are oversocialized by patriarchal capitalism. Although we are, in a sense, "created" through socialization, we are simultaneously "creatures" who have the power to change our behavior—within certain limits. Consequently, in this society individuals take on different degrees of gender-role character structures. However, we can say that the male and female stereotypes described above are widely accepted by most of the population. Hence, comprehending each system of social relations and the behavior of individuals in society requires understanding the dynamics of the interaction of patriarchy and capitalism. It is time now to turn to a general theoretical outline for understanding crime under patriarchal capitalism.

Crime in Patriarchal Capitalism

As I have shown, patriarchal capitalism creates two basic groups: a *powerless* group, comprising women and the working class, and a *powerful* group, made up of men and the capitalist class. Within patriarchal capitalism, individuals are affected structurally by their class and gender position in *interaction*. Social behavior is socially regulated. Individuals are enmeshed in class and gender structures that organize the way people think about their circumstances and devise solutions to act upon them. Gender and class shape one's possibilities. The conditions individuals confront and the manner in which they choose to "handle" those conditions are socially regulated. Just as conforming behavior is socially regulated and intimately related to one's class/gender status, so is nonconforming behavior. Just as there are gender-appropriate and class-appropriate forms of conforming behavior, so there are gender- and class-appropriate forms of nonconforming behavior. Criminality is related, then, to the interaction of patriarchy and capitalism and the structural possibilities this interaction creates.

The major premise of a socialist feminist understanding of crime is therefore twofold: First, to comprehend criminality (of both the powerless and the powerful) and its social control (by the powerful), we need to consider simultaneously patriarchy and capitalism and their effects on human behavior. And second, from a socialist feminist perspective, *power,* in terms of gender and class, is central for understanding serious forms of criminality. It is the powerful (in both the gender and class spheres) who do the most damage to society, not, as is commonly supposed, the disadvantaged, poor, and subordinate. The interaction of gender and class creates positions of power and powerlessness in the gender/class hierarchy, resulting in different types and degrees of criminality and varying opportunities for engaging in them. Just as the powerful have more legitimate opportunities, so they have more illegitimate opportunities. The capitalist class and men in general have a greater opportunity to obtain high quality education, lucrative jobs, and overall social status. Yet they also have a greater opportunity than the powerless to engage in criminality not only more often, but also in a way that is more harmful to society. We can say, then, that criminality is strongly related to the distribution of power within the division of labor in both the market *and* home. Types of criminality are only possible when particular resources are available. Individuals make use of these resources to act upon their position in the gender/class hierarchy. For the powerless (the working class and women), criminality represents a form of both *resistance* and *accommodation* to their oppressed and powerless position. Crimes of the powerful (the capitalist class and men) serve to maintain their *domination* over and *control* of the powerless. While neither of these motives may necessarily be conscious, their objective result represents resistance/accommodation or domination/control, depending on one's position in the gender/class hierarchy. The acting out of resistance/accommodation and domination/control is constrained by one's possibilities.

Females, subordinate and powerless in the gender/class hierarchy (although some females do have more power than other females, and in some cases, more than some males), do not predominate in any form of *serious* (felony) criminality in patriarchal capitalism. Official statistics, self-report studies, and victimization surveys all report that females commit far fewer street crimes (murder, assault, robbery, burglary, larceny/theft, auto theft, and arson) than do males (Box 1983, 168–69). Moreover, females rarely engage in certain other forms of criminality, such as corporate crime (see chapter 5).

Females, by reason of their subordinate position in patriarchal capitalism, commit the least serious crimes for a number of reasons. First, of course, most of the serious acts commonly understood as criminal, as well as those that are not, are "masculine" in nature. That is, the most serious harms in society demonstrate, as Oakley (1972, 72) observed, "physical strength, a certain kind of aggressiveness, visible and external proof of achievement, whether legal or illegal—these are facets of the ideal male personality and also much of criminal behavior." Second, low female criminality is related to primarily womens subordinate position in patriarchal capitalism. Female subordination in the family means young women are more closely supervised—mainly by their mothers—than their brothers (Hagen et al. 1979, 34). This creates a cycle of subordination and powerlessness that isolates women within the family and therefore away from certain types of serious crime. Therefore females spend more of their lives within the confines of the nuclear family, isolated in the home. As Hagan, Simpson, and Gillis (1979, 34) found in their research, "in the world of crime and delinquency, as in the world of work, women are denied full access to the public sphere through a socialization sequence that moves from mother to daughter in a cycle that is self-renewing." Tove Stang Dahl and Annika Snare (1978) agree, arguing that women in patriarchal capitalist societies are "coerced into privacy," making it less likely they will be involved in crime. Being segregated in the nuclear family, women

> are hindered from having their own personal life due to lack of mobility, cash and free time. In particular a housewife with small children can not regulate her own time. With the important qualification in mind that in society at large loss of autonomy and choice are class-bound factors, one can propose that through material and ideological bonds, women are kept "out of circulation," if we mean by that a life in the public sector where men (of the ruling class) are now in control. [ibid., 22]

Young females and mothers are thus less likely to come into contact with the resources required to engage in serious "illegalities."

A third reason why females commit less serious crime is also related to female subordination. We find, worldwide, that

> women form 52 percent of the world's population, perform two-thirds of the world's labor, receive one-tenth of the world's wages, and own less than one-hundreth of its property . . . women form less than 5 percent of the world's top governmental cadres and . . . something like the same proportion, or perhaps even less, in terms of their presence in the upper echelons of the church hierarchies and the positions of authority within the military. [Burstyn 1983b, 55]

The fact that females are subordinate and therefore less powerful in economic, religious, political, and military institutions worldwide means that females have less opportunity to engage in serious criminality. If we concentrate on the economy in the United States, we find that those females who do work outside the home typically fill the lowest paying and most menial jobs (see chapter 4 for an elaboration of this), while males are highly overrepresented in powerful economic positions where the most serious forms of work-related crimes are found (Box 1983, 181). Thus, while more females are entering into wage labor, they are simultaneously being segregated into the "pink collar ghetto," and away from those positions where the most socially, physically, and economically harmful behaviors are prevalent (see chapter 5).

And finally, since illegitimate opportunities for females are patriarchically controlled, females play a very subordinate role. In teenage gangs, for instance (chapter 3), the females who are recruited remain hidden and powerless, spending their time nurturing the demands of the male leaders rather than planning and executing serious forms of criminality. In addition, many females in this society evaluate their self-worth by how well they nurture a man—their "duty" is not to compete with men, even in the illegitimate marketplace. Power, therefore, is once again an important determinant of one's opportunity for serious criminality.

When women do engage in "antisocial" behavior, it is related to their oppressive and powerless position in both the home and labor market. Women confined to the home may reach the point where they can no longer endure the continued hardships of domination and therefore turn to isolated and self-destructive forms of "deviance" not normally considered criminal: alcoholism, drug addiction, mental illness, and suicide. This type of privatized *resistance* against their subordinate and powerless position in patriarchal capitalist society is one of the most pervasive forms of "antisocial" behavior engaged in by women (see chapter 4).

When females engage in criminality, it likewise reflects their subordinate position in the gender/class hierarchy. As shown in chapter 4, because of their deteriorating economic position in patriarchal capitalism, women most often engage in the less serious, nonviolent forms of theft, such as shoplifting, fraud, and embezzlement, as well as other economic crimes like prostitution. Such crimes are a form of *accommodation* to their oppressed and powerless position in patriarchal capitalism.

Males, on the other hand, perpetrate the most serious crimes in this society. Crime is associated with power. Since men have more power than women, men have far more opportunities to engage in crime. Their particular crimes are related to the opportunities their gender/class position allow. Working class men, for instance, while relatively powerless vis-à-vis capitalist and middle-class men, hold within their class more powerful positions than women and as a result predominate in all forms of serious criminality specific to their class—that is, street crime. While they share with females of their class many limits on their opportunities to resist their oppressive conditions, their patriarchal position within the working class provides working class males options for criminality not available to working class women. Chapter 3 discusses the influence of patriarchal capitalism on, and the *resistance* by, marginalized males, and how this structures their pre-dominance in the crimes most feared by the public—one-on-one forms of interpersonal violence such as homicide, assault, and rob-bery. *unemployed/displaced*

Capitalist class males, like their powerful counterparts, commit the most crime in their class, as well as in the society as a whole. By reason of their doubly powerful position (both in terms of gender and class) their criminality is by far the most horrendous, destructive, and harmful to society and its members. Chapter 5 discusses the criminal-ity of powerful males and how in a patriarchal capitalist society corporate crime helps to maintain and continue capital accumulation, and therefore the economic and patriarchal *dominance and control* by males from the capitalist class or their middle-class surrogates.

Finally, under patriarchal capitalism, males in all social classes are powerful since men have power over women. Their powerful position allows some men to engage in crimes specifically *as men* to maintain their dominant position. Primarily directed at women and children, subordinate and powerless individuals, crimes such as rape and wife-beating are forms of *domination and control* of the powerless. Chapter 6 exhibits the connection between these behaviors and patriarchal capitalism.

The remainder of this book is devoted to using this theoretical perspective to help us understand crimes by both the powerless and powerful in patriarchal capitalism. Before that, however, it is impor-tant to understand how patriarchal capitalism is maintained and continues to proliferate.

Maintaining Patriarchal Capitalism

Capitalism and patriarchy are institutionalized in other spheres of society. As pointed out above, the superstructure maintains institu-tions—not directly related to production and reproduction—that help to maintain patriarchal capitalism. This section briefly discusses the state and one important ideological institution, the media.

The state is more than the mediator of class conflict and therefore the "enforcer" for the ruling class. The state, and therefore the social control of crime, must also be studied as an arena where conflicts, other than class conflicts, are fought out. The state is influenced by at least one other sphere—reproduction—while simultaneously influ-encing both production and reproduction. The state helps to main-tain capitalist relations of production by, for example, subsidizing corporations through tax laws and aiding in different ways the accumulation of capital. Yet the state also helps to maintain patriarchy by passing laws and policies that support masculine dominance. For example, as Zaretsky (1978) and many others have shown, state policies enforced the family wage, therefore allowing men a privileged position in the labor market while isolating women in the home.

In addition, the state through various activities, ensures that all women are subject to a patriarchal social order. As Varda Burstyn (1983b, 64) has shown, the state has become,

> for large numbers of women, especially mothers, drawn now from the petty bourgeoisie and the proletariat as well as the chronically poor, the great collective father-figure, a new representative of men-as-a-group, but now a new kind of group, totally divorced, as it were, from these women in terms of kinship and mutual aid, a bureaucratic, impersonal pyramid of a group of men, who have taken the place of all those absent fathers.

Consequently, policies delineating social welfare systems, education, family courts, and reproduction are all under the control of men, even though they primarily affect women and children (Brown 1981). The state has taken over the control and domination of women as "private patriarchy" in individual households deteriorates.

Historical research also points to the importance of understanding production and reproduction in order to understand the state. In hunting and gathering societies, there is no formal authority or government to exert control over others. The generally egalitarian nature of these societies (at least in comparison with patriarchal capitalist societies) means that little crime exists. There is no pressure amongst the people, for instance, to acquire greater amounts of material goods, and individuals can see themselves as valued and worthwhile members of their community. As Michalowski (1985, 65) has shown, this "type of self-affirmation provides a strong motivation to support the community and its rules and to avoid behaviors that would threaten this sense of value and belonging." When community rules are violated, responsibility for this deviant behavior is viewed as collective. Since both the offender and the victim are involved in resolving the trouble, potential violators of community rules recognize "that at some point they will have to confront, not some abstract system of justice, but those whom they have directly harmed. This may be a greater restraint on deviant behavior than any abstract legal threat" (ibid.). Forms of resolving conflicts in such nonstate societies range from members of the group intervening to end the conflict, to blood revenge (the victim's kin kills the murderer or one of his or her kin), retribution (returning the offender an equivalent harm), ritual satisfaction (such as public ridicule), and restitution (payment made to the victim or his or her kin) (ibid., 55–56).

Though within hunting and gathering societies there exist both male and female networks with their own rituals and rites of passage, men and women tend to participate equally in the political sphere. Yet when gender stratification gets under way in certain horticultural societies, and eventually becomes exacerbated and institutionalized in agrarian societies,

> women's autonomous public political participation becomes increasingly curtailed as men's decision-making power increases and their social, religious, and military authority comes to dominate and finally exclude women entirely from power in the political sphere. Such an evolution is associated with the increase in warfare, in turn a product of a combination of factors: expanding population, surplus production, protection of goods for exchange, desire for human (above all female) labor power, struggles with invading groups, the need to migrate, and the like. [Burstyn 1983a, 30]

In addition, according to Rosalind Petchesky (1979, 384), in the course of state development, antiwomen ideologies helped to resolve social disorder among men's networks arising from such things as class divisions, militarism, and warfare. Men resolved disorder "by unifying groups of men across class lines around the abstract notion of 'citizenship.' " Petchesky (1979, 385) concludes that antiwomen ideologies and

> institutions help to legitimate the bourgeois political ideology of "liberty and equality" for all males, serving thus to secure national (male) unity, loyalty, and military service, among other things. The ideology of legitimate and illegitimate birth itself not only functions as one prop of patriarchal control over the means of reproduction . . . it also helps to elevate and mystify the very notion of citizen.

One key effect is that male allegiance shifts away from the family and kinship group and toward the abstract state; that is, to draw men away from a more domestically focused life, women are devalued.

Moreover, recent work indicates that throughout each stage of capitalism, the state has mediated and regulated "capitalism's needs for a given form of labour power and surplus extraction in such a way as to retain masculine privilege and control"—that is, patriarchy in society as a whole (Burstyn 1983b, 57). The state, from its beginning, has acted to maintain not only class, but gender relations as well. Political power reflects both class and gender divisions; it is ruling class *men* who dominate the political decision-making apparatus in the United States.

The patriarchal and capitalist nature of the state is clearly evident in the criminalization process. Abundant evidence reveals that criminal laws are in fact ideological constructs, which do not, as we have been told, attempt to protect society from the most harmful behav-

iors. On the contrary, the criminal law criminalizes only some harmful behaviors—namely, those disproportionately committed by the
powerless—while excluding others—those committed by the powerful against the powerless. This does not mean, however, that the law is
simply a mirror image of the interests of the powerful. Rather, the
"criminalization of conduct" reflects not only basic contradictions in
the social structure but also attempts by state managers (who are
disproportionately men) to deal with the conflicts engendered by
those contradictions (Chambliss and Seidman 1982, ch. 6). However,
since the powerful hold an upper hand in the legislative process
(through lobbying and other means), the shape and content of the law
reflects their interests significantly more than those of the powerless.
As a result, criminal law tends to reflect the interests of both the
capitalist class and men in general, since they have more power to
influence legislation. Still, the legislation that does emerge represents
the *conflict* between powerful and powerless groups (capitalist class
versus working class; men versus women)—not just the interests and
ideologies of the capitalist class and men. For example, the state
definition of "homicide" and "assault" includes *only* those acts which
involve one-on-one killings or injuries to persons—that is, the murder
or injuring of a police officer, prison guard, or of someone during the
commission of a felony, or of an acquaintance in an argument. This
law obviously does protect a number of people, capitalist and worker,
man and woman. It does not, however, include other *avoidable* killings
and assaults that may result from

> (1) the production of faulty consumer merchandise (e.g. defective auto-
> mobiles, flammable children's clothing, and botulism in canned foods);
> (2) the existence of working conditions (e.g. black-lung) . . . (3) the
> implementation of governmental policies (e.g. pollution and war) and (4)
> the transgression of more abstract moral laws (e.g. malnutrition, starva-
> tion, and exposure). [Hepburn 1977, 80]

Furthermore, the criminal law does not define forced sterilization
and unsafe contraception as "criminal" even though they kill or injure
many women yearly (see chapter 5). Furthermore, it does not define
as "murder" death due to industrial chemicals, wastes, and food
additives and preservatives, which kill approximately 300,000 persons
each year (Reiman 1979, 67–82).

The same argument can be made with the crime of theft. While it
includes various kinds of one-on-one forms of stealing, it excludes
sweatshops, which exploit the labor of women by systematically violating minimum wage laws and overtime pay regulations. Furthermore,
it excludes deceptive practices by corporations and advertisers, corporate tax loopholes, price-fixing, and corporate fraud (see chapter 5).

Regarding sexual exploitation, the criminal law includes only one kind of rape—namely, the insertion of a penis into a vagina by the threat or actual use of physical violence. It excludes, in most instances, forcible sexual intercourse between husband and wife. It excludes forcible sexual intercourse because of economic power, and it excludes the forced insertion of any other instrument than a penis (see chapter 6 and Box 1983, 10).

The point should be clear. The criminal law encourages us to view certain behaviors and acts as criminal while hiding others by either ignoring them altogether or relegating them to "adjudication" in what I call the "Regulatory Agency System" (see chapters 5 and 6). Moreover, while the criminal laws against murder, assault, rape, and robbery do, in a sense, protect us all, this protection is not equal. The criminal law defines those harmful behaviors readily accessible to the powerless (the working class and women) as criminal, while simultaneously hiding from the masses the avoidable harmful behaviors readily accessible to the powerful (the capitalist class and men) that are imposed *on the powerless*. The powerless are seen as the "dangerous" individuals, attention is diverted away from the powerful, and the patriarchal capitalist social order is reproduced. The criminal law, in serving the interests of the capitalist class and men, subjects them to less social control and provides them with much more opportunity to engage in criminality.

Regarding ideological institutions, Balkan, Berger, and Schmidt (1980, 44) have summarized studies that clearly indicate the class bias of the media. The media also helps to maintain patriarchy by portraying men and women as stereotypes. As Margaret Andersen (1983, 215–16) has shown:

—on television women are more likely depicted in family rather than work roles, while men are usually seen in high status positions in which they dominate women;

—during "prime time" women tend to be characters in comedies and men in "serious" dramas, thus suggesting that men, but not women, are to be taken seriously;

—approximately 75 percent of all television ads using women are for products found in the kitchen or bathroom;

—childrens cartoons include fewer women than do adult shows, and when women do appear they are likely to be comical, located in family roles, or victims of male violence;

—children who watch the most television tend to have the most stereotypic gender values;

—in the "news," women are underrepresented as reporters, and as reporters are more likely to report on the "soft' news;

—news about women is rare, and even then most likely to celebrate traditional gender values.

Similar evidence could be presented with regard to newspapers and magazines. The important point, however, is that the media, as an ideological institution, not only maintains a class society, but a patriarchal one as well.

In reference to nonconforming behavior, the media exposes chiefly those crimes committed by the powerless while practically ignoring the harmful behaviors of the powerful. Prime time crime dramas rarely, if ever, focus on, for example, corporate crime, wife-beating, or rape in executive suites. Rather, *Kojak, Starsky and Hutch, Hill Street Blues* and other crime programs center their attention on one-on-one crimes like murder, robbery, and theft, and potray the criminals as members of powerless groups. The same holds true for news coverage (television, radio, and newspapers) and popular films. The media effectively create the impression for the U.S. public that the most dangerous and criminal individuals are the powerless.

Throughout society, the state and ideological institutions help to maintain patriarchal capitalism. Repressive and ideological institutions are necessary for the capitalist class and men to maintain domination over the working class and women.

3

Powerless Men and
Violent Street Crime

In November 1984, Benjamin Wilson Jr., 17, rated one of the best high school basketball players in this country, was shot and killed by two other young black males as he walked near his high school. This killing accented the epidemic of violence being perpetrated on marginalized communities. As Salim Muwakkil (1984, 8) reported, statistically this "incident was nothing unusual; it merely underlined the distressing fact that young black men have become their own worst enemies." The purpose of this chapter is to analyze why, in patriarchal capitalism, powerless men in general have become "their own worst enemies."

Violent street crime has deeply affected the way most people in the United States live—people today particularly fear murder, assault, robbery, and rape. (This chapter discusses only the first three; rape will be analyzed in chapter 6). Approximately four out of every ten individuals in this country say they are concerned about their safety in the community and fear being home alone or being by themselves in the center of the city (Pollock and Rosenblat 1984, 34). Again, four out of every ten individuals fear specific violent acts, such as murder and robbery, and in particular, approximately one in six people fear being murdered (ibid.). In addition, six out of ten individuals keep their doors locked while riding or sitting in cars; six out of ten telephone a friend or relative to advise that they have returned home safely; and eight out of ten protect their homes by constantly keeping doors locked and asking people to identify themselves before permitting entry (ibid., 35). Obviously, large numbers of us, particularly those living in marginalized communities, feel they are living in a war zone, and on the losing end at that.

This fear is primarily caused by the media. Because magazines, newspapers, and television focus on dramatic violent crimes like murder, assault, and robbery, people come to fear these acts and simultaneously develop a distorted view of crime as overwhelmingly violent. For instance, there are many more crimes of theft (larceny, autotheft, and burglary) than murders and robbery. Moreover, the

51

chance of being killed by a stranger is only about one-tenth the chance of dying in an automobile accident and about one-third that of dying in an accidental fall (Silberman 1978, 6). This does not mean, however, that violent crime in this country is not a problem, or that people have a "false consciousness" about violent street crime. The United States has the highest level of violent street crime in the industrialized world (Currie 1982a, 26), and the majority of individuals are rightly concerned about this pervasive violence.

Who Commits Violent Street Crime?

The public's perception of the "typical violent criminal" is colored by the way the media publicizes those who are processed through the criminal justice system and who therefore fill our nation's prisons. According to official statistics, those imprisoned for violent street crimes are overwhelmingly male and primarily between the ages of eighteen and twenty-four. While the official unemployment rate (outside of prison) hovers around 8 percent, approximately 65 percent of all inmates had no income during the twelve months prior to their arrest, and almost 90 percent made less than $2,000 annually. Those who worked prior to arrest were generally unskilled and semiskilled laborers. Moreover, while approximately 11 percent of the United States population is black, close to 50 percent of the prison population is black. Consequently, it is young, marginalized males, usually a minority, whom the public fears most and considers the dangerous criminals (Sheldon 1982, 39–50).

However, there are at least two problems with this perception. As shown in the last chapter, the criminal law defines only certain kinds of violence as criminal—namely one-on-one forms of murder, assault, and robbery, which are the types of violence young, marginalized minority males primarily engage in. The criminal law excludes certain types of avoidable killings, injuries, and thefts engaged in by powerful white males, such as maintaining hazardous working conditions or producing unsafe products (see chapter 5 for an elaboration of this). Consequently, the public's perception of what serious violent crime is—and who the violent criminals are—is determined first by what the state defines as violent and what types of violence it overlooks. Second, recent self-report studies and victimization surveys conclude that there is more street violence than is indicated by the official statistics—that is, those statistics based on who is arrested, prosecuted, convicted, and incarcerated. These crimes are much more frequent and are committed by a wider variety of people than was previously thought (Platt 1978, 21–29). In addition, while these studies and surveys conclude that *violent street crimes are more likely to be committed by young, unemployed minority males,* their *contribution to violence* is nowhere near as high as that indicated by arrest and prison statistics, which tend to make them seem solely responsible for these crimes. In fact, violent street crimes seem to be spread (albeit unevenly) throughout the male population, through all social classes and races (Reiman 1979, 1984; Schwendinger and Schwendinger 1985). Why, then, are young marginalized minority males so overrepresented in arrest and prison statistics? When males from all social classes and races come into contact with the criminal justice system *for the same criminal behavior,* young marginalized minority males are the most likely to be arrested, prosecuted, convicted, and sentenced to prison for long terms (Reiman 1979, 1984). As Jeffery Reiman (1979, 128) concludes after examining a large quantity of research:

> At every stage, starting with the very definitions of crime and progressing through the stages of investigation, arrest, charging, conviction, and sentencing, the *system weeds out the wealthy.* . . . Among those acts defined as "crimes," the system is more likely to investigate and detect, arrest and charge, convict and sentence a lower class individual than a middle or upper class individual who has committed *the same offense, if not a worse one!*

Moreover, it is marginalized *minority* males, especially black males, who are processed through the criminal justice system (Sheldon 1982). For example, blacks receive substantially longer prison terms than whites convicted of the same crimes, even when the black person is a first-time offender and the white person a second- or third-time offender (Parenti 1983, 149).

Consequently, the criminal justice system has both declared war on young marginalized minority males and created the "typical criminal" for us. The state's war on minority males entails much more than disproportionately arresting and prosecuting these individuals. In addition, they die at the hands of the police. In a typical year, between 2 and 4 percent of all homicides in the United States are the result of police shootings (Binder and Scharf 1982; Sherman and Langworthy 1979), and the number of police homicides has been increasing since the late 1960s (Takagi 1974; Harring et al. 1977). And, more important, a large body of research reports that minority males (especially blacks), are much more likely to be killed by the police than are whites (Robin 1963; Harring et al. 1977; Milton 1977; Kobler 1975; Meyer 1980; Fyfe 1982). While some may argue that minority males are killed because they are disproportionately violent offenders, evidence belies this conclusion. First, the police themselves, in their own study, have shown that approximately 40 percent of police killings occurred when no criminal activity was taking place (Sheldon 1982, 155). Second, individuals are many times killed by the police even when there is no threat of death or severe injury. Kobler (1975, 188) for instance, found in his study of police killings that 30 percent of the victims were either involved in no criminal activity or in a misdemeanor such as a traffic violation. Another 27 percent were found to be involved in property crimes. And third, of individuals involved in criminal activity with no threat of death or severe injury, blacks are killed more often than whites. For example, Fyfe (1982, 720), after examining cases of *property* offenders killed by the police, found that blacks who were *unarmed and nonassaultive* were killed eighteen times as often as whites.

In warring on minority males, the state and its criminal justice system have reinforced the prevalent belief that the most dangerous social evils are violent street crimes and that young marginalized minority males are the violent criminals in our society. Since the law defines the violent behaviors of these youth as criminal, and since the police direct their activities toward these youth, and since the courts generally convict these youth and sentence them to the longest prison terms, it appears that these youth must be the most dangerous members of society, who need to be controlled with repressive force. The criminal justice system thus functions in two important ways: First, it effectively publicizes the view that crimes engaged in by young marginalized minority males are the most violent and that these dangerous individuals are responsible for the real harms in U.S. society. Second, it exaggerates the involvement of these youths in serious forms of violence—other youth, of other social classes and races, are also involved in violent street crimes. Additionally, powerful adult white men engage in much more serious forms of violence than all youth (see chapter 5), but the criminal justice system effectively diverts attention from the powerful and the harm they produce, while focusing on the powerless, especially minority youth.

Nevertheless, these youth are overrepresented in violent street crimes and their behaviors do cause much fear and suffering in this society, especially in marginalized communities. It is thus important to understand why these crimes occur and how they can be controlled. While chapter 7 discusses how these behaviors can be more effectively controlled, the remainder of this chapter attempts to show how patriarchal capitalism provides the conditions favorable for the involvement of these youth in violent street crime.

Capitalism, Marginalization, and Violent Street Crime

While the evidence indicates that minority male youth are responsible for a higher incidence of violent street crime, Tony Platt (1978, 30) points out that "this does not mean that crime is simply a racial phenomenon," street crime has historically been concentrated in "the marginalized sectors of the labor force and in the demoralized layers of the working class, irrespective of skin color or ethnic origin." Since Blacks, Chicanos, Native Americans, and Puerto Ricans are disproportionately marginalized, they are also disproportionately the offenders *and* victims of violent street crimes (ibid.). Studies confirm that racial minorities are overrepresented in street crime primarily because they are marginalized (Shaw and McKay 1942; Fleisher 1966; Green 1970; Lofton and Hill 1974; Beasly and Antunes 1974; Calvin 1981).

U.S. capitalism has developed into two main labor market sectors: a monopoloy or *core* sector and a competitive or *peripheral* sector. Two important phenomena formed this stratification of the labor force: (1) conscious strategies of labor market stratification on the part of those who own capital; (2) the uneven development of capital itself (Edwards et al. 1978). Today, this division in the labor market continues to be reproduced. Growth in the monopoly or core sector tends to produce both surplus capital (surplus goods or surplus productive capacity) and surplus population (technological unemployment) (O'Connor 1973). This occurs in a capitalist economy chiefly because accumulation, or growth of production in the core sector of the economy relies upon increases in productive output per worker and technical progress, rather than on the growth of employment (ibid.). Since accumulation is the foundation of the capitalist mode of production, mechanization of core sector industries both limits employment and persistently produces a surplus because of a deficiency in demand. Employment fails to increase as rapidly as manufactured products, so the labor needed by the core sector industries, as a proportion of the total labor force, shrinks. As a result, labor connected with scientifically and technologically advanced industries diminishes, to produce a *relative* surplus population. Furthermore, finding new jobs in the core sector becomes increasingly difficult. Those affected, primarily people of color, youth, and women, compose the *absolute* surplus population (ibid., 26). Consequently, the peripheral sector of the economy is composed of workers who are "not needed" in the core sector (relative surplus population) as well as those who are entering the labor force for the first time (absolute surplus population). A portion of this peripheral sector (approximately 30 percent of the labor force) is marginalized. That is, they are unemployed, underemployed, or working full or part-time in low-wage menial jobs. Those in the marginalized surplus population can hardly maintain adequate living conditions (Balkan et al. 1980, 53). Thus, people of color, youth, and women compose the economically and politically powerless. I will concentrate here, however, on marginalized male youth, as they are disproportionately involved in violent street crime.

Because of the inherent mechanisms of a capitalist economic system—and the racism affecting minority youth—poverty and unemployment are common in powerless communities. Recent employment data reveal the employment problems facing male minority youth. From 1950 to the mid 1970s the participation of black youth sixteen to nineteen years of age in the labor force declined a little over 33 percentage points (Greenberg 1977, 197), while the white teenage labor force participation rate declined by approximately 5 percentage points (Manpower Report 1976, 30). Labor force participation rates provide an assessment of the deteriorating job opportunities for all youth while also indicating racial differences.

For our discussion, probably the most significant aspect of unemployment, however, comes under the heading of "reasons for unemployment." Table 3.1 shows the reasons for unemployment for teenagers sixteen to nineteen years of age during 1969, 1974, 1977, and 1981. The total unemployment rate has continuously increased throughout this period. However, for each year the largest percentage of unemployment was due to *reentrants* and *new entrants* in the labor force. In 1969, 9.0 percent of the teenage unemployment rate was due to the influx of individuals who had never worked plus those who had reentered the labor force. By 1981 these figures had increased to 13.5 percent, while 4.3 percent of the unemployment rate was due to losing a job.

These patterns demonstrate two important points: First, the U.S. Capitalist economy shows a persistent and growing incapacity to absorb new entrants into the labor force (the private sector cannot

Table 3.1   Unemployment Rates, for Teenagers by Reason for Unemployment, 1969, 1974, 1977, 1981

Reason	1969[a]	1974	1977	1981
Lost last job	1.8	3.1	3.4	4.3
Left last job	1.5	2.0	1.7	1.8
Reentrants	4.2	4.9	5.1	5.4
New entrants	4.8	6.0	7.6	8.1
Total unemployment	12.2	16.0	17.7	19.6

[a]This column is from the 1978 edition (p. 72) of the source below.
Source: Employment and Training Report of the President (Washington, D.C.: U.S. Government Printing Office, 1982), 202.

expand employment to keep pace with such new entrants). Second, by reason of the core sector's inability to absorb living labor and the subsequent generation of surplus labor, young entrants into the labor market are especially confined to the "competitive" sector of the economy (low wage, menial labor). As a result, youth, in particular, experience the basic problems of workers in this sector—specifically a high employment turnover rate as the elevated rate of "reentry" for youth shows. In short, a population of redundant youth results because the monopoly sector of the economy creates both surplus productive capacity and surplus population; this, in turn, generates an inability to absorb many of the new entrants into this sector and "low job attachment" among workers in the competitive sector.

Due to racism in U.S. society, black youth are hardest hit by marginalization. By 1980, 34.9 percent of black male teenagers were "officially" unemployed as compared to 14.6 percent of white male youth (U.S. Commission on Civil Rights 1982, 51). By 1983, however, the "official" unemployment rate for all teenagers, but black teenagers in particular, had increased considerably. As table 3.2 shows, black men and women teenagers had the highest unemployment rate (48.8 and 48.2 respectively), while white men and women had the lowest (20.2 and 18.3 respectively).

In many ghetto communities today the "unofficial" unemployment rate for black youth reaches 80 percent (Marable 1983, 61). In short, *all* youth, but black youth in particular, have become *marginalized,* and their means of subsistence taken away. They are, without a doubt, a major component of the economically powerless in U.S. society, and economic powerlessness relates directly to street crime. Research has consistently shown that economic inequality is significantly related to street crimes (Shaw and McKay 1942, Henry and Short 1954, Glascr

---

Table 3.2. Unemployment Rates for Teenagers by Race and Sex, 1983

Teenagers	Rate (percent)
Black men	48.8
Black women	48.2
Hispanic men	29.4
Hispanic women	28.7
White men	20.2
White women	18.3

Source: Twenty Facts on Women Workers (Washington D.C.: U.S. Department of Labor, Women's Bureau, 1984), 2.

and Rice 1959, Schmid 1960, Reiss and Rhodes 1961, Green 1970, Phillips et al. 1972, Loftin and Hill 1974, Beasley and Antunes 1974, Brenner 1976, Jankovic 1977, Greenberg 1977a, Yeager 1979, Braithwaite 1979a, Humphries and Wallace 1980, Calvin 1981). Moreover, in a very important recent study, Blau and Blau (1982) suggest that violent crime rates depend significantly upon economic inequality, particularly between races. From data on the 125 largest metropolitan areas in the U.S., they concluded that economic inequality substantially increases rates of violent street crime and that racial socioeconomic inequalities in particular "are a major source of much criminal violence" (ibid., 126). And finally, Elliott Currie (1985, 146), after examining a variety of different types of studies, concluded that "economic and racial inequality affect not only the extent of crime but also its seriousness and violence. The relationship tends to be astonishingly linear—the worse the deprivation, the worse the crime."

Patriarchy, Collectivity, and Violent Street Crime

Examining the dynamics of capitalism as they interact with racism is the first step in understanding why marginalized adolescent males are overrepresented in violent street crimes. The second is to examine the elements of the reproductive sphere to see how patriarchy interacts with capitalism and racism to give rise to specific types of crime. It is *males*, rather than females, who are disproportionately the offenders and victims of violent street crimes. Consequently, to understand these behaviors, class, race, and gender must be addressed.

While these male youth are *economically* powerless, they remain *powerful* in terms of gender. Since crime is associated with power, men have more opportunities to engage in crime than women as they have the power. For example, their position of power first of all enables young males in this society to be free of the restraints of the household and that provides them with more opportunities to engage in collective and individual types of criminality. While adult and young females in patriarchal capitalist societies tend to spend a portion of their time isolated from each other, adolescent males typically engage in a high degree of interaction (Cloward and Piven 1979, 659). Consequently, analyzing masculine power in patriarchal capitalism is essential for understanding the types of crimes young marginalized males engage in and how this power allows them certain opportunities not allowed to females. It is these material conditions—unemployment, more freedom (relative to females), and collectivity—that helps us to understand marginalized male criminality. Since marginalized males experience high unemployment, and because they are adolescents and therefore lack places of their own in which to congregate, they generally aggregate on the street. Thus, marginalized male criminality takes the form of street crime, as opposed to occupational crime. Marginalized males as *men* commit the greatest amount and most serious forms of street crimes because their gender/class position makes this type of criminality accessible.

The second aspect of the reproductive sphere that makes street crime more likely for the marginalized male is gender development. It is here where we begin to discover why street crime by young males takes a violent form. As discussed in chapter 2, gender development is rooted materially in the sexual division of labor and normative heterosexuality. Two important elements of gender development in U.S. society result from these material conditions; both masculinity and power are linked with aggression/violence while femininity and powerlessness are linked with nonviolence. Throughout our society, from the realm of TV dramas to childrens story books, violence is associated with power and males, and for some youth this association is reinforced as part of family life. As a result, most young males come to identify the connection between masculinity-power-aggression-violence as part of their own developing male identities. In patriarchical culture, men validate their masculinity through aggression/violence.

The linking of masculinity with violence and feminity with nonviolence found in patriarchal culture is conducive to violent street crime as Herman and Julia Schwendinger (1985, 161) rightly argue.

> Under these conditions, women undergo early childhood experiences that reduce their engagement in most antisocial forms of conduct. The differential in regard to violence, however, is most significant. Women act far less violently than men, whose character structures are more closely aligned with the exploitative requirements and industrialization of the capitalist mode of production. Also, men retain a monopoly over weapons and training for war, and these relationships reinforce male aggression. Consequently, it is not surprising that with respect to crimes based on personal victimization, such as robbery, assault, and rape, female criminality can hardly be compared to criminality among men.

But as we have seen, these crimes are not committed equally across class lines. While violence—ranging from mere tolerance and acceptance to engaging in violent acts—tends to be a part of most male youth social formations at all class levels, marginalized males tend to engage in more extreme forms of violence (robbery, assault, murder) than other youth (ibid., 168). As discussed below, marginalized males collectively make up an urban masculine street culture that has the potential for creating interpersonal violent situations. This does not mean, however, that *all* marginalized males automatically engage in violence. The fact is, *most marginalized men do not commit violent acts*, and most of those who do, after adolescence, maintain reasonably law-abiding adult lives. However, certain conditions, related to capitalism, racism, and patriarchy, increase within this street culture the *tendency* for this *type* of violence—homicides, assaults, and robberies—to occur. I will discuss three of these conditions: the reliance on property crimes for survival, exploitative individualism, and male bonding.

Property Crimes, Survival, and Violence

As we have seen, economic conditions for marginalized male youth are unusually desperate and degrading. In addition, a number of powerless adolescent males reject hard labor for low wages even when its *available*. As Bell Hooks (1981, 76) states regarding black men,

> Despite the fact that the American capitalist economic structure forces many black men to be unemployed, there are some black men who would rather not work "shit" jobs with endless hassles and little monetary reward if they can survive without them; these men do not have doubts about their masculinity. To many of them, a low paying menial job is more an attack on their masculinity than no job at all.

These individuals refuse alienating labor for "the man." They would much rather take their chances on the street than work at "shit jobs" (Hall et al. 1978, 353). For many powerless black youth, the "promised land effect" (Gordon 1971b, 62) is real. Their parents and grandparents continued to search for better times and yet were constantly disillusioned in not finding the "promised land." Consequently, these youth have come to believe that their escape from poverty is totally closed off. Their generation, like the one before it, had grown up with racism, and therefore segregation, as a fact of life (Hall et al. 1978, 354). Racism in both the labor market and in black-white relations cannot be explained away as a temporary condition, as it was to their elders. In their experience things *do not* improve with time; U.S. society *remains* constantly racist, and their economic condition will *remain* the same no matter how hard they work. As Claude Brown (1965, 8) stated over twenty years ago in his book *Manchild in the Promised Land,*

> The children of these disillusioned colored pioneers inherited the total lot of their parents—the disappointments, the anger. To add to their misery, they had little hope of deliverance. For where does one run to when he's already in the promised land?

And it has not changed for those young black men who make up the male teenage population in U.S. ghettos. In point of fact, it has probably become worse. A fifteen-year old Brooklyn "street kid" describes the differences between those who maintain "hope" and those who have come to experience the "promised land effect."

> In Brooklyn you fall into one of two categories when you start growing up . . . First, there's the minority of the minority, the "ducks," or "suckers." These are the kids who go to school every day. They even want to go to college. Imagine that! School after high school! . . . They're wasting their lives waiting for a dream that won't come true.
>
> The ducks are usually the ones getting beat up on by the majority group—the "hard rocks." If you're a real hard rock you have no worries, no cares. Getting high is as easy as breathing. You just rip off some duck . . . You don't bother going to school; its not necessary.
>
> Hard rocks do what they want to do when they want to do it. When a hard rock goes to prison it builds up his reputation.
>
> He develops a bravado, that's like a long sad joke. But it's all lies and excuses. It's a hustle to keep ahead of the fact that he's going nowhere.
> [cited in Browning 1982, 30]

In short, the interaction of capitalism and racism in U.S. society has resulted in "shit jobs," unemployment, and the promised land effect for young powerless males.

Moreover, these youth are now experiencing a renewed marshalling of white hatred, which finds its extreme expression in racial violence not only by the police, but the white citizenry as well. Today there is increasing brutal violence against racial minorities, primarily blacks. A few examples will suffice.

—In 1981, a Rochester white man was indicted for criminality and he boasted about the blacks he had killed (Browning 1981, 37).

—In March 1981, a nineteen-year old black youth was lynched in Mobile, Alabama (Marable 1983, 233).

—In May 1981, the tortured body of a black man was found floating down a river in Cleveland, Mississippi. His genitals had been hacked off and the coroner reported finding his penis in his stomach (ibid.).

—In January 1981, a forty-five-year old black man was lynched in Tallahatchie County, Mississippi (ibid.).

—In February 1981, a thirty-two year old black man was lynched. He had been badly beaten in the head and face, his hands were tied behind him, and he had been shot point-blank in the head (ibid., 234).

In 1980, the Subcommittee on Crime of the U.S. House of Representatives began to investigate this widespread violence. In their report, *Increasing Violence Against Minorities,* the subcommittee pointed to renewed anti-black attacks by not only individuals, but also by groups like the Ku Klux Klan. The report concluded that there "is abundant evidence of a marked increase in the incidence of criminal violence directed against minority groups" (U.S. House of Representatives, 1980, 2).

As a result of their high unemployment, the types of jobs available to them, and their understanding that racism is here to stay (the "promised land effect" and increasing white racist violence), combined with their masculine socialization and position in society as males (relative freedom from parental restraint), a large number of young powerless males search out alternative "roles" that allow both masculine expression and survival. One solution is found in the street culture. Here a life develops for those whose future has no meaning, for those who are "going nowhere." Urban marginalized youth, especially males, make up a street culture that provides an alternative to routine labor for "the man." This urban street culture becomes an answer to badly paid demeaning labor, unemployment, and racism.

Jean-Paul Sartre's (1963) discussion of "the project" not only helps us comprehend the street culture but also adds to our understanding of the interaction of patriarchy, racism, and capitalism. For Sartre, people make history, on the basis of prior conditions (for our purposes, class, gender, and race) to be sure, but *people* make it, not prior conditions. As Sartre (ibid., 87) goes on, "these conditions exist, and it is they, they alone which can furnish a direction and a material reality to changes which are in preparation; but the movement of human *praxis* goes beyond them while conserving them." What Sartre affirms is the explicitness of the human act "which transforms the world on the basis of given conditions" (ibid., 91). The project, for Sartre, then is behavior that is determined by the present factors that condition it, as well as the future or nonfuture that is visualized: "The most rudimentary behavior must be determined both in relation to the real and present factors which condition it and in relation to a certain object, still to come, which it is trying to bring into being. This is what we call the *project*" (ibid.). For Sartre, at any given historical period there are what he calls a "field of possibles." The material conditions of existence (in contemporary U.S. society, white supremacy, patriarchy, and capitalism) circumscribe an individual's field of possibilities. Young powerless males are circumscribed or limited by poverty and patriarchy and often by racism. These individuals, according to Sartre (ibid., 95), are "defined negatively by the sum total of possibles which are impossible for [them]; that is, by a future more or less blocked off. For the underprivileged classes, each cultural, technical, or material enrichment of society represents a diminution, an impoverishment; the future is almost entirely barred." What Sartre points to is the social-psychological effects of marginalization on the powerless. The life of young marginalized males is defined not by what is possible, but by what is impossible. They are in effect denied their humanity; they undergo, in Sartre's words, a "subjective impoverishment" (ibid., 95–96). They go beyond the subjective to the objective. To the individual male in a marginalized community, his lack of future reflects the fate of his class (and race) (Takagi 1982, 45–47).

Consequently, the street culture is *in part* the result of a collective awareness of a future that is, in terms of social possibilities, almost "entirely barred." It is a form of *resistance* limited by class, racism, and patriarchal relations. Individuals become aware of their position in society by perceiving what future is possible for them (ibid., 46). For young marginalized males in the street culture, rebellion has become both a collective solution to their "prohibitions" and a "style" that takes the form of voluntary unemployment *and* street crime. These are the "field of possibles" for resisting class and racial domination. However, as Mike Brake (1980, 133) has pointed out for black youth,

> consciousness and motives do not work so that crime is chosen as a
> political revenge. Black youth drifts, then develops a collective definition
> of a collectively experienced situation which draws on their anger and
> hostility about racism. Crime becomes a simple survival strategy, and is
> not a real solution, but is brutalizing and destructive.

The roots of violent street crime by the powerless are not found in a political consciousness of young marginalized males but rather in *material conditions:* poverty, racism, a negated future, and the power accorded males in patriarchal capitalism.

This latter aspect—the power accorded males in patriarchal capitalism—is important. While marginalized males are limited by their race and class, they have power in terms of gender, at least relative to females of their race and class. The street culture consequently allows an alternative confirmation of masculinity, as other avenues of masculine expression (that is, "the job") are closed off. Not surprisingly, females are mostly excluded and for a number of reasons. The first is related to what has already been discussed—the material conditions of patriarchy and the power it provides young males. (Parents tend to control young females' spare time more closely than that of young males; the patriarchal arrangements in this society supports a higher degree of interaction amongst males; and young males are freer to explore the outside world and are thus much in contact with other young males.) Consequently, young male criminality is much more likely than female criminality to be collective. Second, the street culture, because of its emphasis on aggression/violence, does not agree with female gender-role socialization, so females choose peripheral roles. And third, males simply do not want females involved because to them females are emotional, unreliable, untrustworthy, weak, and physically inept; this is not the type of person to take along on an armed robbery (Box 1983, 182).

Females who are included in the street culture are usually, but not always, invisible (kept out of sight), powerless, and pushed by masculine dominance to the periphery of social activity. Treated as sex objects, they are expected to nurture the demands of the males. Consequently, males dominate in street cultures because patriarchy creates the conditions for them to have the *power* to dominate, while young females are deemed subordinate and *powerless*. Thus, while some young females do participate in the street culture, their participation is defined by males. As a result young females cannot use the street culture to explore a female-defined identity. A recent study, *The Girls in the Gang* by Anne Campbell (1984, 242–43), found that

> Females must accept the range of roles within the gang that might be available to them in society at large. The traditional structure of the nuclear family is firmly duplicated in the gang. In straight society the central, pivotal figure is the male. His status in the world of societal and material success is the critical factor, while the woman supports, nurtures, and sustains him. The gang parodies this state of affairs, without even the economic infrastructure to sustain it, for the male rarely works and often it is the female who receives a more stable income through welfare. Nevertheless, the males constitute the true gang! Gang feuds are begun and continued by males; females take part as a token of their allegiance to the men.

Additionally, males control and exploit the female member's sexuality. While male members are often allowed to "turn tricks" for money and admit to engagements with male transsexual prostitutes, when "dykes" are discovered, they are "multiply raped and thrown out of the club" (ibid., 245). Women are expected to be heterosexual as this helps to perpetuate masculine control and dominance. Overall, the range of possibilities open to female gang members are dictated and controlled by males.

Furthermore, the street culture is also macho in form. That is, since the powerless urban male street culture emphasizes expressions of aggression/violence, the property crimes marginalized males engage in for survival (that is robberies) reflect, and reproduce, this emphasis. Their aggressive crimes often entail the actual or possible confrontation with another member of the marginalized labor force. Moreover, participation in property crimes like robbery drastically increases the possibilities of other kinds of violence, and this has important implications for the comparatively higher homicide and assault rate by young marginalized males as against males from other classes. For instance, robbery is normally committed by "gangs" or "teams" of young marginalized males. Often, these group robberies result in more violence not simply because violence is a necessary adjunct to "pulling it off" (without a weapon the chances for a successful robbery diminish), but also because "the guys" are looking on or participating. The robbery and subsequent use of violence, provide the ideal opportunity for members of the street culture to display their toughness and maleness, to validate their masculinity both individual and collective. This clearly increases the possibilities of homicide. In 1984, 9.3 percent of all homicides occurred in the course of a robbery, while 18.0 percent occurred in the course of a felony (FBI 1985, 12). Consequently, while marginalized males must many times rely on property crimes to survive, as males, they choose masculine types of crimes (like robbery), which often lead to more extreme forms of violence. Although marginalized males choose robbery because it is the most *available* option within their class, it simultaneously provides a mechanism for masculine expression and validation. As Erik Olin Wright (1973, 16) argues, robbery can help to satisfy not only the individuals need for material survival, but also for power and domination. "In the act of committing a crime, an individual who is otherwise powerless can, for a moment at least, hold considerable power in his own hands. This is especially true for a crime like armed robbery in which the robber directly confronts his victim."

And most robberies are armed robberies. In 1984, approximately 36 percent of all robberies involved the use of a firearm; 13 percent knives or some form of cutting instrument; and 10 percent, some other form of weapon. For the remaining 41 percent, the offender used "strong arm tactics" (FBI 1985, 18).

This possession and use of lethal weapons by marginalized males probably explains why so many street crimes result in homicide. Young males coming of age in marginalized communities must exhibit their courage and fearlessness to their male peers in the street culture. The macho street culture demands that these young males *show* that they are not afraid of violent acts. As Bell Hooks (1981, 104) states of the ghetto, "Carrying a gun and being prepared to use it are the ways they [young black males] publicly assert their 'masculine' strength . . . After all, sexist socialization has been encouraging them all their lives to feel they are 'unmanned' if they cannot commit violent acts." The interaction of class and gender encourages the possession of weapons as a means of indicating that one is a "man." It is a way of showing "the guys" one's manliness. As such, in 1984 we find that firearms were used in about three of every five murders, and firearm victims were primarily between the ages fifteen and thirty (FBI 1985, 10). In 1986, it was reported that handguns were used in approximately 71 percent of the homicides involving young black males (Sargent 1986, C3).

Thus, for marginalized males, property crimes such as robbery provide a mechanism for both survival and masculine expression and validation. By reason of their class position, robbery is one of the few options for solving economic problems. But in addition to that, males predominate in robbery, not only because it provides an alternative for masculine expression and validation, but because they have the power within their class. The marginalized street culture's reliance on violent property crimes helps create the conditions for forms of violence more extreme than those usually found in other youth social formations.

Exploitative Individualism

Clearly, the macho street culture provides young marginalized males with alternatives (like armed robbery) for masculine validation and survival that may lead to altercations with other members of the street culture and greatly increase the possibilities of homicide and assaults. But beyond this, the conditions of marginalization create an intense exploitative individualism that adds to street crime and violence.

First of all, production relations organized capitalistically (based on competition and exploitation) generate very individualistic and exploitative character structures in all social classes. As Michael Parenti (1980, 41) makes clear,

> Our peers are potentially ones enemies; their success can cause us envy and anxiety, and their failures bring secret feelings of relief. The ability or desire to work collectively with others is much retarded. Competitive efforts are primarily directed against those of the same class or those below, a condition that suits the interests of those at the top.

Those who accept this competitive individualism are lead amorally to "objectify and exploit people as things. They adopt a callous and instrumental indifference to suffering" (Schwendinger and Schwendinger 1983, 204). When large numbers of people are marginalized from economic activity and then congregate in the inner city, the social life of a community deteriorates to produce a brutal street life filled with individual exploitation. When the productive foundations underpinning social life are destroyed (marginalization), life becomes both chaotic and hostile to all feelings of community and other people's welfare (Humphries 1979, 235). In short, marginalization exacerbates exploitative individualism. As Judah Hill (1975, 85) notes, the life style of the street

> creates an intense form of individualism. In an economic mode of cheating, stealing, extorting, exploiting, drugging, gambling, and lying, survival and success go to the most ruthless and clever. Trust is a dangerous hang-up. Each individual is constantly at war with everyone else.

In such an environment, most are forced to think only of fulfilling their own needs the best way possible. A form of ruthless, egotistic, exploitative individualism becomes the norm for the macho street culture. People relate to each other as competitors and strangers. Takagi and Platt (1978, 24) have shown that, under the conditions of severe marginalization, "individualism replaces reciprocity as the basis of social relations" and people become tools to be exploited for an individual's selfish advantage. Street crime reflects this exploitative individualism, and, as Julia and Herman Schwendinger (1983, 205) note, it is particularly those youth from the marginalized labor force who

> depict and live in a world of *givers* and *takers;* and the takers are accorded superior status. These criminals assume that successful persons justifiably achieve their positions in life primarily through the manipulation of less powerful beings. They are convinced that people are at each other's throats unceasingly in a game of life that has no moral rules. Society is seen as a jungle in which the powerful and exploitative individual has a greater chance of survival.

These individuals view social reality in the following manner:

> It's *fuck-your-buddy-week*, fifty-two weeks of the year.
> Do unto [exploit] others as they would do unto you—*only do it first.*
> If I don't cop [steal] it, somebody else will.
> You know, man, *everybody's* got their little games. [ibid.]

Exploitative individualism and amassing large numbers of people in the inner city creates certain situational factors linked to violent street crimes. Since many youth spend their time mainly on the street—"hanging out" on corners or in front of bars—there are more opportunities for public encounters, confrontations, and exploitation. One observer describes the way marginalized male youth typically pass their time.

> As an example of the city's unemployed and under-employed black teenagers, Cleo is far from unique. That becomes clear after three weeks of hanging out with other Cleo's on street corners, in chilly, dark housing-projects, parking lots, and on rocky, red clay clearings that pass for basketball courts and baseball diamonds. There the acrid, depressing stench of cheap marijuana blends with the gloom of corroding lives.
> Black teenagers in housing projects like Dalton Village, Earle Village and Boulevard Homes, sitting in groups on cars or concrete apartment steps, are mistrustful of strangers, fearful of police harassment, angry, idle, frustrated, not really sure if they are criminals, as adults say they are, or the victims. [cited in Liazos 1982, 321]

The street environment provides opportunity for confrontation, even armed robbery. Many homicides by marginalized male youth begin as impromptu quarrels that grow into aggravated assaults. As stated earlier, *most* marginalized males do not commit violent acts. However, as large numbers of people amass in inner city areas, frequently encounter each other in the streets, possess weapons, and are violently aggressive, exploitatively individualistic, and indifferent to other people's welfare, the *tendency* for street violence rises, and minor altercations—for *some* youth—easily turn into injury or death, as the following extreme example illustrates:

> Well, we were in the show and he was with his girl and there was a lot of crowd around, you know, just around. And I asked his girl for a piece of candy and he jumps up and smacks me in the face with a cap. Well, I could whip him. By me whipping him I take the cap and hit him in the face. He grabbed me around the throat again so I pushed him against the wall again and I hit about three or four times and he said, "Now I'm going to kill you," and he stuck his hand in his pocket. Well I went in mine and I was just a little faster than he was and I cut his throat. [cited in Rainwater 1970, 289]

In the marginalized street culture an individual's status is recognized and continually reaffirmed by periodic confrontation. For men, violence and exploitation are positive aand fulfilling expressions of masculinity; they are rewarding acts.

Male Bonding

Despite the exploitative individualism of patriarchal capitalism, males in all social classes form close, specialized relationships with one another. For marginalized males, this male bonding occurs in the street gang, where assurance of one's masculinity can be found through ritually rejecting femininity. Male bonding does not so much entail "having friends," as exhibiting one's masculinity before others. As Stoltenberg (1977, 75–76) writes:

> Male bonding is institutionalized learned behavior whereby men recognize and reinforce one another's *bona fide* membership in the male gender class . . . male bonding is how men learn from each other that they are entitled under patriarchy to power in the culture. Male bonding is how men get that power and male bonding is how it is kept. Therefore men enforce a taboo against unbonding.

Male bonding thus provides the competitive arena in which an individual proves himself a man among men. Participating in gang violence becomes a way for powerless males to prove their masculinity. In communities with marginalized populations we "find a greater proportion of peer groups that subscribe to violent macho ideals" (Schwendinger and Schwendinger 1983, 205).

In inner city areas where gang violence exists, a large percentage of homicides involve violence between gangs. In the middle 1970s, about one quarter of all teenage homicides in cities troubled with gang violence were found to be gang related (Miller 1975, 31). By 1980 there were approximately 2,200 gangs with 96,000 members in 300 cities and towns in this country. During the period 1967–1980, sixty of these cities alone recorded 3,400 gang-related homicides (U.S. Department of Justice 1981, 84). Many youth gangs transport weapons across state lines to other gang members (ibid.) and the increased quality and sophistication of weapons has increased serious gang violence. The switch blade "rumble" has ben replaced by "ambushes" in which automatic rifles, shotguns, Molotov cocktails, and even bazookas are used (Curtis 1975, 54).

Gang violence is based on an explicit concern with masculine expression and validation. Struggling for supremacy with other marginalized males is a way to gain recognition and reward for one's masculinity. As one member of the "Savage Nomads," a gang in the South Bronx, stated:

> I been raised in the gangs. Like my brothers were, only they're in jail now and one got on junk (heroin) so my mother said he's dead. Gangs are like families. Like brothers and sisters all together. We rumble because you have to show blood. Blood is strength. In the Bronx, there's a lot of blood. [cited in Browning 1981, 36]

The two main reasons for gang warfare are masculine defined— maintaining or gaining status ("rep") and protecting one's territory ("turf"). Gangs define status or reputation as the ability to stand up to violent physical confrontations. To make and maintain a "reputation," gang members need violent encounters. One gang member explained "rep":

> We got a lot of challenges, which gave us some headway, cause that meant a lot of fights was on our own ground. Now, a rival gang when they just outright challenge you, always wanted to use you as a stepping stone, just like boxers do. They figure if they could chalk up a lot of wins in gang fights, then they'd be in a better position to fight somebody big. [cited in Allen 1978, 46]

In the macho street culture, males gain status, reputation, and self-respect through gang violence, which often results in homicides and assaults.

Another important aspect of intergang relations is "turf," or the territory the gang controls. Within a neighborhood, a gang's own particular territory is closely marked and guarded to apparent absurdity. Defining the gang and the perimeters of gang activity, turf in fact serves as a boundary between gangs and consequently an area of status and thus possible conflict. Territory, as an area for defense, also becomes an area for intergang violence. Apparently becoming the dominant form of intergang violence is the "foray," in which small numbers of a particular gang make raids on a rival gang. Walter B. Miller (1975, 38) describes the foray:

> This pattern, logically called "guerilla warfare," and by other terms, involves relatively small (five to ten) raiding parties, frequently motorized, reconnoitering in search of rivals, and engaging in combat, if contact is made. Forays are seldom announced, and count on surprise for their success. . . . Since the raiding parties almost always carry firearms, such engagements frequently involve serious injuries and sometimes death.

Intergang forays occur in attempts to raise or maintain status. By "beating up" or killing a number of rival gang members, one gang raises its status at the expense of another. This provokes the other gang to retaliate, resulting in further violence. This cycle "ends only when one gang becomes so strong as to be able to coerce others to its ranks" (Sanders 1981, 204). Male bonding and consequently gang warfare increases homicides and assaults in marginalized communities.

Due to white-supremacist patriarchal capitalism and the power it makes available to males, many powerless males commit violent property crimes to survive, acquire an exploitative individualistic ideology, and bond with each other into violent peer group formations—all of which increase the possibilities for homicides and assaults. Some marginalized males adapt to their *economic and racial* powerlessness by engaging in, and hoping to succeed at, competition for *personal* power with rivals of their own class, race, and gender. For these marginalized males, the personal power struggle with other marginalized males becomes a mechanism for exhibiting and confirming masculinity. Many powerless males express their masculinity not through a job but through the macho street culture—not through organizational or corporate dominance, but street gang dominance. As Tolson (1977, 40–46) notes, the young marginalized male progressing through adolescence is very aware of the street culture and the appropriate "style" (behavior) that guarantees his social acceptability. The marginalized male expresses himself through a "collective toughness, a masculine performance" observed and cheered by his "buddies." Members of the macho street culture have and maintain a strong sense of honor. As he must constantly prove his masculinity, an individual's reputation is always at stake. Tolson (ibid., 43) further observes that for "support and recognition, a sense of position and social status," the marginalized male remains bound to the world of the street. Throughout his adolescence, the marginalized male is extremely "concerned with the physical presence he is able to maintain, as a force to be reckoned with." He must learn to be "one of the gang." Powerless masculinity becomes a "performance." As a member of the street culture, he learns to reproduce the expectations of his audience (ibid.). In short, while the street culture is a basis for *resistance*, it simultaneously results in an *accommodation* to a society that is capitalist, patriarchal, and racist.

In conclusion, marginalized males commit those serious street crimes most feared by the public, and these acts are the result of the interaction between their position in the gender hierarchy (power) and their location in the class and race hierarchy (powerlessness). The following chapter discusses females, and how their powerlessness in *both* the gender and class hierarchies affects the types of crimes they commit.

4

Women, Powerlessness, and Nonviolent Crime

In the late 1930s, Virginia Woolf (1938, 74) eloquently captured the condition of women in patriarchal capitalism:

> Behind us lies the patriarchal system; the private house, with its nullity, its immorality, its hypocrisy, its servility. Before us lies the public world, the professional system, with its possessiveness, its jealousy, its pugnacity, its greed. The one shuts us up like slaves in a harem; the other forces us to circle, like caterpillars head to tail, round and round the mulberry tree, the sacred tree, of property. It is a choice of evils, each is bad.

For Virginia Woolf, women are powerless and oppressed in both the reproductive and productive spheres of society. This chapter looks specifically at some of the effects of oppression and powerlessness in both the home and labor market, and how they help to generate specific forms of criminality on the part of women. The chapter begins by looking at mothers/housewives in the home, whose structural position in society is often responsible for privatized forms of self-destruction. The remainder of the chapter discusses both the relationship between the women's movement and female crime and the major kinds of crime women commit. Overall, patriarchy and capitalism, in interaction, are the primary source of women's "antisocial" behaviors.

Mothers/Housewives, Alienation, and Privatized Modes of Self-Destruction

Marx developed the concept of "alienation" primarily to describe the condition of wage laborers in a capitalist society. The capitalist organization of work disguises the link between humans and things and humans and other humans by making it appear that they are all separate. Since workers do not control their labor power, they become alienated from the products of their own labor, from their coworkers, (who they come to see as competitors), and their own creative potential. Under capitalism, workers come to seem alien and opposed to each other when, in fact, they are dialectically related. Consequently, workers are alienated from the process and product of their labor.

Like workers, many mothers and/or housewives, since they do not control their labor power and sexuality, are also alienated. As elaborated in chapter 2, work in the reproductive sphere is *necessary* labor for the survival of individuals and society. However, due to patriarchal relations of reproduction in this society, women primarily perform this necessary labor, whose product is appropriated by men. This social relationship between men and women in the reproductive sphere, and the alienation it entails for mothers/housewives, has important implications regarding the type of antisocial behavior these women engage in.

Just as the wage labor workplace is an arena of conflict, so is the family. Patriarchal gender relations means that men and women are engaged in different activities and therefore have different and inherently conflicting interests. This does not mean that families do not simultaneously have strong emotional ties of closeness and sensuality. Obviously they do. Still the patriarchal family has inevitable conflicts that relate to the "antisocial" behavior of the powerless—mothers/housewives.

Since the family maintains *material* social relations, it is important to identify what work is performed by individuals involved in this social process, discover who has the power, and consider how it all relates to crime and deviance. Members of families are members of genders and so have different interests related directly to patriarchal capitalism. For instance, all family members have an interest in the size of the family income. Yet since the father/husband, in most cases, is the primary breadwinner, while the mother/housewife, even though she may work outside the home, performs the majority of household labor (see below), the differing types of labor and, therefore, interests create power differentials, tension, and conflict. Clearly the father/husband has the power in this relationship and therefore controls (not always consciously) the labor power and sexuality of others. The material base of patriarchy is masculine control over the labor power and sexuality of women, both within and outside of the home. Men's appropriation of the labor power and sexuality of women in the home causes women's alienation and consequently rebellious behavior.

Earlier it was pointed out that patriarchy was perpetuated under capitalism. Men, by becoming the primary breadwinners (wage laborers), also retained the ability to appropriate the labor power of their wives, who became primarily housewives and mothers. In this capacity, women's labor takes care of family members' basic needs, socializes new members of the society, and sustains male workers by enabling them to return to work. Female labor in the home is appropriated therefore primarily by both men and the capitalist class. Thus, although under capitalism men lost some of their patriarchal control to the capitalist class, in the family men primarily control and therefore benefit from the labor power of women.

Within the last fifteen years, however, dramatic changes in the family have taken place. Only approximately 10 percent of all U.S. households consist of a husband and wife with two or more children at home and the husband as the sole breadwinner (Petchesky 1984, 246). Moreover, as fertility is delayed or declines, and more and more women work during pregnancy and childrearing years, active motherhood is shrinking as a part of most women's lives (ibid.). Nonetheless, men still control and, therefore, benefit from the labor power of women in the home. The evidence clearly indicates that patriarchy is thriving even as these demographic changes occur.

The contemporary full-time mother/housewife works approximately fifty-seven hours per week doing such things as preparing and cleaning up after meals, laundry, house cleaning, caring for children and other family members, shopping, and keeping household records (Hartmann 1981b). In contrast, men spend approximately eleven hours per week on housework. Although the father/husband does do *some* work around the house, the sexual division of labor defines not only who will do most of the work, but also what kinds. Male members of the family usually perform "public" domestic labor—such as mowing the lawn, taking the garbage out, raking leaves, and some shopping. For mothers and daughters, their domestic labor is "privatized," entailing such things as, childcare, preparing meals, washing and drying dishes, cleaning the house, and doing the laundry (Andersen 1983, 100). Reproductive work is consequently gendered, and men have appropriated for themselves leisure (relaxing, out-of-doors) types of domestic labor. In addition to this, the full-time mother/housewife is expected to be "on duty" all day long, every season of the year, while the father/husband is not (Dahl and Snare 1978, 17).

A good indication of the operation of patriarchy in the home is the amount of labor performed by women *who are also wage laborers*. Husbands of wives who are wage laborers, studies tell us, do not spend more time on reproductive labor than husbands whose wives do not work outside the home (Hartmann 1981b). While these women end up doing less housework, it is not because men "pitch in," but because they do not have the time. As Heidi Hartmann (1981b, 381) has concluded after examining extensive research,

> Women are apparently not, for the most part, able to translate their wages into reduced work weeks, either by buying sufficient substitute products or labor or by getting their husbands to do appreciably more

housework. In the absence of patriarchy, we would expect to find an equal sharing of wage work and housework; we find no such thing.

In addition, when there are children in the household, the burden of housework increases dramatically; that is, the labor of the mother increases under such conditions, but not the domestic labor performed by men (ibid.). In families with a child under one year old, a mother who does not work outside the home spends about seventy hours a week on reproductive labor, thirty hours of which is devoted to the child (ibid.). While husbands in these families spend about five hours per week in child care, they end up spending less on other types of reproductive labor, so their total household labor remains constant (ibid.).

Finally, evidence also shows that the total time women spend on housework has not declined since the 1920s (Berch 1982, 97; Vanek 1978). As a result, women who work as wage laborers (as they increasingly do), have the longest total work weeks while men have the shortest (Hartmann 1981b, 392). The result is that more and more women are being subjected to the "double burden," which creates the condition for superexploitation, generating conflict and moving women to rebel and protest their condition. However, the way they act out this protest is significantly related to their overall position in patriarchal capitalism.

In patriarchal capitalism, women's reproductive labor power is controlled by the father/husband, who appropriates it so as to pursue his own interests. Women perform labor for men, nurture their survival needs, while the father/husband pursues leisure.

> He reads the evening paper and his wife fixes dinner. He watches the news or an informative television show and she washes the dishes. He retires to his study (or his office or his shop or a soft chair) and she manages the children. Men gain leisure time at the expense of the oppression of women. This is a very fundamental privilege which accrues to the division of labor (or lack of division) in the home. [Newton 1973, 121]

In short, since women do not control their labor power, they, like wage laborers, are alienated from the process and product of their labor (Jaggar 1983, 307–17).

Childrearing and the institution of motherhood in U.S. society provide a prime example. Since the full-time mother/housewife is isolated in the home most of her waking hours, while the husband is away pursuing "his career," she alone must provide all the childrearing work. Prior to the isolation of women under patriarchal capitalism, childrearing, though still in the hands of women, was an extended-family affair. Now that it has become the work primarily of one individual—the mother—the amount of time spent on child care has increased. And many women with children work as wage labor-ers; in 1977, for example, 51 percent of all women with children worked outside the home (Baxandall 1979). By 1983, however, about 61 percent of all mothers with children worked in the wage labor force (U.S. Department of Labor 1984, 3). For women who work outside the home, exclusive responsibility for both child care and other reproductive labor creates the condition for superexploitation.

Sole responsibility for child care creates terribly alienated and oppressive conditions for women. While childrearing *per se* need not be oppressive, the institution of motherhood, as organized under patriarchal capitalism, contributes to the material and ideological oppression of women. First, as Alison Jaggar (1983, 256–57) argues, in patriarchal capitalist societies, women tend to be forced into motherhood. Patriarchal relations in U.S. society often deprives young women of adequate contraceptive information; and when contraception is provided, it is in the form of unreliable and danger-ous devices. Moreover, young women, especially poor women, have limited access to abortions. What's worse, under patriarchal relations women are encouraged to engage in intercourse as their primary means of emotional and sexual satisfaction. Thus, on the one hand, women are not provided with adequate birth control, while on the other, they are encouraged to engage in intercourse. In addition, women are taught that they can only achieve true fulfillment and genuine respect through motherhood, and today's economic realities (see below) impel women into marriage and eventually motherhood. Second, although young girls are socialized to become mothers, they are not prepared for the isolation in the home that mothering often entails. As Jessie Bernard (1975) has pointed out, when women marry, they end up being involved in a role reversal syndrome. Since they are now wives and mothers, they must cease being dependent and become responsible for the care of both the husband and chil-dren. Consequently, motherhood may easily become a mixture of satisfaction and pleasure on the one hand, and on the other hand, anger, frustration, and bitterness (Rich 1976). Third, ultimately many mothers, since they do the majority of housework as well as childcare, come to experience the "tired mother syndrome" (Jones 1970). In addition to the tremendous workload placed on her, the mother, especially when caring for infants, ends up missing sleep.

> [c]hildren differ, some cry more, some cry less, some cry almost all the time. If you have never, in some period of your life, been awakened and required to function at one in the morning, and again at three, then maybe at seven, or some such schedule, you can't imagine the agony of it. [ibid., 57]

As a result of these working conditions, a new mother's

muscles ache and they respond with further pain when touched. She is generally cold and unable to get warm. Her reflexes are off. She startles easily, ducks moving shadows, and bumps into stationary objects. Her reading rate takes a precipitous drop. She stutters and stammers, groping for words to express her thoughts, sounding barely coherent— somewhat drunk. She can't bring her mind to focus. She is in a fog. In response to all the aforementioned symptoms she is always close to tears. [ibid.]

Clearly, as Alison Jaggar (1983, 313) argues in response to the above description, the condition of many new mothers parallels that of the alienated wage laborer, whose work, as Marx put it, "mortifies his body and ruins his mind." And fourth, women's control over their labor—that is, childrearing—has been reduced drastically by the emergence in the twentieth century of the masculine-dominated "science" of child development (ibid., 311). This "scientific childrearing" creates an ideology that "the child is a product which has to be produced according to exact specifications," and "that mothers are ignorant of how to rear children and have to be instructed by experts" (ibid., 312). This clearly alienates mothers from childrearing.

> Although mothers are not paid for rearing their own children, the increasing subjection of the domestic childrearing process to scientific control suggests that mothers' experience is parallel in this respect to the experience of wage laborers and provides one reason for characterizing mothers' work as alienated. [ibid.].

In addition to being alienated from their domestic labor, many mothers/housewives develop their sexuality for the husbands enjoyment, rather than their own. A "good" mother/housewife finds satisfaction in the satisfaction of others and so places her own needs second. As a result, in the sexual sphere, many mothers/housewives ignore sexual incompatibilities and fake orgasms to nurture a man's sense of self (Ferguson 1979, 299). In fact, approximately seventy percent of "women do not experience orgasm regularly as a result of intercourse" (Hite 1980, 229). Frequently, mothers/housewives are alienated not only from the process and product of their domestic labor, but their sexuality as well.

Because of their alienation, mothers/housewives become overwhelmed by their isolation, by the amount of their labor, by the way it is appropriated, by the repetition, role reversal, tiredness, by "scientific" control over them, and finally by unequal sexual exchange. It becomes very difficult for them to assert their own needs, since their time is devoted to others, and they have no economic power with which to demand equal sexual satisfaction (Ferguson 1979, 300). The mother's needs become subordinate to the needs of the father/

husband and the children. Mothers, anxiety-ridden over their condition, find that they are experiencing a "problem that has no name"
(Friedan 1963). Because of their gender role socialization, which
teaches them from a very young age to "put up" with what they have
and are experiencing, they endure their oppression as long as possible.

Finally, those who can no longer endure resist and rebel against
their conditions, though the form of rebellion differs according to
historical conditions. In the Victorian Era, resistance to these oppressive conditions manifested itself as "hysteria,"—a means of gaining
some control over their sexuality (by avoiding the male) and temporary power over husbands and doctors (Ehrenreich and English 1978,
38–44). Today, women act out this resistance differently, yet it is still
related to their powerless position in patriarchal capitalism. Those
mothers/housewives who do not work in the labor market and are
isolated in the home cannot readily engage in collective forms of
deviation, or of course, occupational crimes. As Dahl and Snare
(1978, 16) point out, full-time mothers/housewives are "severely restricted in their mobility both because of their specific family duties
and, as a consequence, their lack of money. The concept of *immobility*
is thus imbodied in the nuclear family and the marriage contract." For
all mothers/housewives, their gender position precludes masculine
forms of response to their oppression—that is, aggression and violence. Thus, their powerlessness restricts the antisocial possibilities
available to mothers/housewives who choose to rebel against their
alienation. Consequently, today, many mothers/housewives involve
themselves in privatized forms of self-destructive "deviance" not
normally considered criminal—alcoholism, drug addiction, mental
illness, and suicide—as a private rebellion against their subordinate,
powerless, and alienated position in patriarchal capitalist society. Not
surprisingly, research on depression indicates that married women
are more often depressed than single women, housewives more
depressed than working women, and "supermothers" more depressed than other women (Andersen 1983, 50). Full-time mothers/
housewives are more likely to use psychoactive drugs to alter moods
than are women who work outside the home (Sandmaier 1980, 111).
Usually in response to marital problems, females attempt or commit
suicides as a "wish to kill her spouse or children—a retroflexed anger
or 'cry for help,' " rather than through a sincere wish to die (Maris
1969, 97). And finally, as Procek (1981, 29) argues, mothers/house-
wives may take on a "sick role" (mental illness) as a response to their
powerlessness in the family; "womens' mental illness is the form taken
by their power struggle within the personal space of the family."

By reason of their powerlessness in this society, the only option of many mothers/housewives is what Cloward and Piven (1979, 660) call "hidden protest"—privatized forms of self-destruction. Their unhappiness reflects their overall discontent with their alienated labor and sexuality. As Carol Smart (1976, 149) has noted, the untenable nature of the traditional female role "produces a high incidence of breakdown among women."

In addition, since women have historically been the primary providers of childcare, patriarchal ideology has rationalized this by arguing that women are childlike themselves; they are characterized as weak, emotional beings who are irrational and unable to take care of themselves (Jaggar 1983, 256). Hence, some women come to think of themselves as impulsive and deficient in self-control. Therefore, when they are unable to cope any longer with oppressive conditions, many will turn to those behaviors that reflect this belief—namely, privatized modes of self-destruction.

The Women's Movement and Female Crime

I have established so far two important aspects of female "deviance." First, females' subordinate position (powerlessness) in patriarchal capitalism means that they commit less serious crimes than males (see also Box 1983, ch. 5). And second, privatized forms of self-destruction correlate with the powerlessness of mothers/housewives under patriarchal capitalism. Still to be explained, however, are the crimes females commit. Some have attempted to attribute *increasing* female criminality to the effects of the women's movement *on women*. That is, these theorists assume first that women are clearly becoming "liberated" from masculine domination and second that they are therefore committing more crimes (Adler 1975, Simon 1975). Specifically it is argued, as women enter the labor force, their rate of *occupationally related* property offenses will increase relative to men (Simon 1975). Moreover, since the women's movement has eroded traditional gender roles, the resulting "masculinization of female behavior" leads to substantial increases in crimes of violence by females (Adler 1975). Indeed, a quick glance at the official statistics reveals support for this thesis. Regarding property crimes, the rate for females has increased faster than that for males, and the gap in male-female crime rates for property offenses has narrowed substantially since 1960. However, while the percent of the female contribution has doubled for property crimes since 1960, the sharpest increases have occurred for nonviolent forms of theft (Steffensmeier 1981). Contrary to the "liberation thesis," the bulk of these increases are found in nonoccupationally related crimes, such as shoplifting and minor forms of fraud (check and welfare frauds) (ibid.). Moreover, the bulk of these female property offenders are adolescents who have had little, if any, contact with the labor market (Miller 1983, 60).

What about crimes of violence? According to the most recent evidence, since 1960 female crimes of violence against the person have increased absolutely but not relative to the rate for males. Recent studies in the United States and Great Britain tend to indicate that this absolute increase can be explained in the changed attitudes of those who label females criminal—the public, police, judges, and prosecutors (Box and Hale 1983; Hindelang 1979; Bernstein et al. 1979; Chesney-Lind 1978). The public is now more willing to report violent female offenders, the police more likely to arrest, prosecutors more willing to prosecute, and judges and juries more prepared to convict. Thus, what this evidence indicates is that while female violent behavior has changed very little, the response of the public, police, prosecutors, courts, and juries may well have been affected.

Rather than "liberation" causing more females to be violent, the changing position of women in society affects the attitudes of those who label females criminal. As one feminist criminologist has noted, "the police, social workers and other agents of social control are more ready to define deviant behavior by women and girls as violent or 'masculine' because of apparent changes in the social and economic position of women in society" (Smart 1976, 73). Increasingly, those females who do not act in a "feminine" way—that is, those whose behavior indicates an erosion of traditional female gender-roles—are viewed as stereotypically nontraditional and therefore deserving of punishment.

The criminal justice system deals with females as it does with marginalized males: its task is to control nontraditional behavior. Publicizing and exaggerating women's involvement in serious crime and linking it to the women's movement serves to deligitimize the general expansion of women into nontraditional roles in several ways. First, since criminal justice personnel are more likely today to label a female engaged in violence as a criminal, female involvement in serious crime is exaggerated. Second, just as the state publicizes female involvement in criminality, it hides the criminality of *powerful males*. The overall contribution by women to serious crime is thereby magnified. Third, black and poor females in particular are publicized as increasingly dangerous. As with male offenders, racism and class bias in the criminal justice system results in more black and poor females being imprisoned than their white counterparts who have committed similar crimes (Lewis 1981). Thus, the criminal involvement of black lower class women—those least powerful in U.S. society—is substantially exaggerated by the *normal* functioning of the criminal justice system.

Overall, no evidence confirms the assumption that the women's movement has stimulated female crime. Indeed, as Steffensmeier (1981, 54) has concluded after analyzing an abundance of evidence,

> The new female criminal is more a social invention than an empirical reality and that the proposed relationship between the women's movement and crime is, indeed, tenuous and even vacuous. Women are still typically non-violent, petty property offenders.

Instead, there is a publicization and exaggeration of the crimes females commit, which renders women more easily controlled by the masculine-dominated state.

Still to be explained however is why females today are increasingly involved in nonoccupationally related crimes and embezzlement.

Nonoccupational Crimes and Embezzlement

There are specific age differences between the two major categories of crimes females commit. For larceny/theft, arrest rates peak at ages fifteen and sixteen and then drop off rapidly. For fraud and embezzlement, the arrest rate peaks somewhat later, at twenty-two to twenty-five, and declines with age, but much more slowly (FBI 1985, U.S. Bureau of the Census 1983). Let's look at these crimes to see why increasingly females are involved in these behaviors and why these age differences occur.

Nonoccupational Crimes: Larceny/Theft and Fraud

David Greenberg (1977a) has provided probably the most comprehensive analysis of why teenage youth engage in nonviolent forms of theft. What Greenberg argues is that, during the transition from childhood to adolescence in capitalist societies, attachments to parents are weakened while simultaneously a heightened sensitivity to peers and their evaluations takes place. "Popularity" and being attached to the right groups becomes the central issue for youth. Yet the detachment of youth from the family, along with the emergence of advertising directed toward a teenage market, has pressured teenage youth to engage in a hedonistic, consumption-oriented social life. As Greenberg (1977a, 196) states, in addition to personal assets and skills, participating in teenage social life requires money "to purchase clothing, cosmetics, cigarettes, alcoholic beverages, narcotics, phonograph records, transistor radios, gasoline for cars and motorcycles, tickets to films and concerts, meals in restaurants, and for gambling." Yet increasingly youth are finding it difficult to finance their social activities because of the continuing decline in teenage employment and labor force participation. While the last chapter discussed the employment problems facing youth today, this is a long-run problem that began to develop as early as the nineteenth century.

The surplus of youthful labor that began to appear around the turn of the century was a major concern for corporate capital. Prior to 1880, children formed an integral part of the labor force in agriculture, manufacturing, and mining. In the nineteenth century, labor scarcity in the United States elevated the demand for cheap youthful labor. The earliest cotton mill in the United States was operated solely by youthful labor. A journalist visiting this cotton mill early in the nineteenth century stated:

> All processes of turning cotton from its rough into every variety of marketable thread state . . . are here performed by machinery operating by waterwheels, assisted only by children from four to ten years old, and one superintendent. [cited in Lebergott 1964, 50]

In 1820, 43 percent of all textile workers in Massachusetts, 47 percent in Connecticut, and 55 percent in Rhode Island were children (ibid.). As the factory system grew, it "reached out" for youthful labor. By the 1830s, between 50 and 60 percent of all labor throughout the country was provided by children ten to fifteen years of age (ibid., 51). However, since the 1840s, the proportion of child labor in manufacturing and mining has continuously and prominently declined, with even a mild decline in agriculture from 1880 to 1910. Furthermore, the overall ratio of child labor in all occupations plunged by two-thirds between 1910 and 1930. The long-run, permanent decline of youthful employment and labor-force participation increased most rapidly in the latter part of the nineteenth century and early years of the twentieth century. Even though the gainfully employed population quadrupled from 1870 to 1930, the number of gainfully employed workers in the ten to fifteen-year-old age bracket declined drastically (Greenberg 1977a, 196). Furthermore, there seems to be no association between fertility changes and adolescent worker rates during this time period (Lebergott 1964, 54–56).

The decline in child labor since the 1840s reflects the needs of both capitalism and patriarchy. First, a market for such labor fell as those newly formed monopolistic industries underwent rapid technological change. The declining employment of children in factories, mines, and agriculture as a result of monopolization was a major contribution to a youthful surplus labor problem. However, in addition, as we saw in chapter 2, during this time male factory workers lobbied to exclude children from the workplace, eventually creating the male-dominated "family wage" and masculine control in both the workplace and the home. As a result, the interaction of patriarchy and capitalism continually developed a surplus of youthful labor in the

United States and caused unemployment and sharply diminishing labor force participation rates for teenage males and females, especially minority youth (see chapter 3 for specific rates). The increase in larceny/theft among teenage females is attributed, as Greenberg (1977a, 197) concludes, to "a response to the disjunction between the desire to participate in social activities with peers and the absence of legitimate sources of funds needed to finance this participation." In other words, the interaction of patriarchy and capitalism has created the conditions for the inability of females to finance their increasingly costly social life. Full or part-time employment once funded such a social life, itself embedded more within a cross-generational community life. Theft now serves as an alternative (ibid.).

But why do teenage females engage in nonviolent theft, and why do they steal what they do? The vast majority (almost 80 percent) of female arrests for larceny/theft are for shoplifting (Cameron 1964, 125). Shoplifting is not a "masculine" crime, since, unlike burglary or robbery, it does not involve a possible or real confrontation with another. Moreover, shoplifting reflects the traditional feminine role of women as consumers, "since it is not unusual or suspicious for women to shop at various stores throughout the day" (Steffensmeier 1981, 53). Even more important, shoplifting provides the opportunity to satisfy women's ornamental role, which derives from the patriarchal notion of females as sexual objects. Females are supposed to compete with other females in looks to "catch a man." And, the items adolescent females steal, like cosmetics and clothes for personal use, reflect their need for ornaments to participate in peer group social activities (Greenberg 1977a, 198).

Since in patriarchal capitalist society women and young girls do not have control over their sexuality, they learn to present themselves first as sexual beings for men, as everything else becomes secondary. Women develop their sexuality for men's enjoyment rather than for their own (Jaggar 1983, 308). Women, therefore, spend large amounts of time and money on cosmetics, clothes, and other elements deemed necessary to please men. Thus young girls learn early in life that their identity is primarily related to their sexuality, and its expression must satisfy men. They learn that since marriage is their career, they must prepare for it. As Frith (1978, 66) argues,

> marriage is a girl's career and the source of the constraints on her leisure. This argument can be pushed further: a girl's leisure is her work. It is leisure activities that are the setting for the start of her career, for the attraction of a man suitable for marriage.

Not surprisingly, females steal those items that help them to progress in their "career."

The effects of sexual objectification go beyond the simple dichot-omy between the "objectifier" (the male) and the "objectified" (the female). As Sandra Bartky (1982, 131–32) has shown, normative heterosexuality and masculine control of female sexuality encourages the development of what she calls "feminine narcissism." In patriar-chal capitalist society

> objectifier and objectified can be one and the same person: a woman can become a sex object for herself, taking toward her own person the atti-tude of the man. She will then take erotic satisfaction in her physical self, reveling in her body as a beautiful object to be gazed at and decorated.

Females learn that male observers will constantly appraise them and that their life prospects depend on those appraisals. Consequently, as women learn to appraise themselves first, they develop a dual femi-nine consciousness wherein "the gaze of the Other" is internalized so that a woman becomes "at once seer and seen, appraiser and the thing appraised" (ibid., 134).

Capitalism, of course, plays upon this feminine narcissism by con-stantly producing and displaying to women commodities alleged to create perfect female beauty. Since the female body is portrayed as constantly needing transformation (ibid., 135), young females strongly desire commodities such as cosmetics and clothes that can make these changes.

Increases in larceny/theft by adolescent females in this society can therefore be attributed to their deteriorating economic position, their gender-role socialization, normative heterosexuality, and the mascu-line control of female sexuality. Thus, the interaction of patriarchy and capitalism leads to the high rate of shoplifting by adolescent females. As shown in the last chapter, teenage females, especially those of color, experience one of the highest unemployment rates because capitalism, interacting with patriarchy, has determined that youth would be marginalized, and patriarchy (plus racism for minor-ity females) has determined that teenage females would be one of the most severely marginalized. In the face of escalating costs of social life, patriarchal gender role socialization, alienation from their sexu-ality, and low labor force participation rates, the "field of possibilities" for young female adolescents is narrowed and larceny/theft increases.

In the case of fraud, why are the total arrests for women and men nearly equal and why is this crime also age specific? The answer to this question is found in the interaction of capitalism and patriarchy, which creates acute economic problems for women, while leaving them fewer options for survival. Many women turn to gender-specific illegal options, such as fraud, to put food on the table. Let's look at the economic realities facing women today that lead them increasingly into fraud.

First, the increase in fraud can be attributed to the "feminization of poverty." Today there are approximately 32 million poverty-stricken people in the United States. Of the adult members of this group, two out of three are women, and women head half of all poor families (Stallard et al. 1983, 6). Moreover, for each year between 1969 and 1978, an additional 100,000 women and children fell below the poverty level, and in both 1979 and 1980 another 150,000 entered the poverty rolls (ibid.). In fact, poor, female-headed households are the fastest growing type of family in the country. This fact led the President's National Advisory Council on Economic Opportunity in September 1981 to conclude,

> All other things being equal, if the proportion of the poor in female household families were to continue to increase at the same rate as it did from 1967 to 1978, the poverty population would be composed soley of women and their children before the year 2000. [cited in ibid., 7]

That poverty today is both a class and gender issue helps explain why most females incarcerated in prison are heads of families and the sole support of their children (U.S. General Accounting Office 1979, 10). Mann (1984, 95–96) estimates that 50–80 percent of incarcerated female offenders are mothers. Crime, for many female heads of households, becomes the only option for family survival.

Women's unemployment rates are one reason for the feminization of poverty and, thus, the increasing rate of fraud by females. Female "official" unemployment rates have been consistently higher than male rates. For example, "officially" in 1949, 5.9 percent of males were unemployed while 6.0 percent of all females and 7.9 percent of black females were unemployed. By 1978 women's unemployment became quite bleak. For males, it actually decreased to 5.2 percent, while for all women it rose to 7.2 percent and black females to 13.1 percent (Birch 1982, 17). By 1983, the unemployment rate for adult black women was 16.5 percent, while for white women it was 6.9 percent (U.S. Department of Labor 1984, 2). Moreover, while female teenagers have the highest unemployment rate of all women, the second highest unemployment rates and the prime working ages (twenty to twenty-four), are also the peak ages for involvement in fraud. For white women in March 1980, 7.2 percent were unemployed in this age bracket, while the black female unemployment rate shot up to a shocking 21.7 percent for these ages (U.S. Commission on Civil Rights 1982, 51). This partially helps us explain why black women show a higher crime rate than white women (Lewis 1981). In addition, for both male and female workers, the average period of unemployment has lengthened considerably, while the duration of unemployment benefits has shortened. Consequently, more than half of those unemployed do not receive any benefits whatsoever (Stallard et al. 1983, 45). The situation is exacerbated for women, since they are less often eligible for unemployment compensation than men and do not, many times, receive insurance or union benefits (Schlozman 1979, 96).

The root cause of this feminization of poverty is the "family wage" system discussed in chapter 2. The family wage system, which benefited primarily white working class and middle class men, operated to take jobs away from women, or when women did work, to keep them from higher wage jobs by segregating them in the secondary labor market. Women have been defined as inferior workers available only for low-paying occupations or secondary workers who must stop working to provide jobs for men. This ideology has resultingly legitimated systematic wage and labor force participation discrimination against women. Thus, the "family wage" system, which in the earlier days of this century did provide—for a short time period and for selected layers of women—some sort of economic security, today has impoverished women. The medium family income for all families in 1980 was $21,021. For female-headed households, the median family income was $11,908 for white households, and $7,425 for black households (U.S. Department of Commerce 1981, 55). By 1981, black single mothers average yearly income declined to $6,907 (Glick 1981). By comparison, in the same year, male-headed households with no woman present had a median income of $18,731 for whites and $12,557 for blacks (U.S. Department of Commerce 1981, 55). Furthermore, in 1980 almost 33 percent of all female-headed households lived below the "official" poverty level, in that year—$8,414. And, 25.7 percent of white female-headed households were below the poverty line, while 49.4 percent of black female-headed households were poor (ibid.).

Although the *absolute* dollar amount of median income has increased from 1960 to 1979 for all families, when the *real* value of the dollar is controlled for, family incomes have in fact declined (Currie et al. 1980, 21). Indeed, after paying for necessities, a family's disposable income declined approximately 5 percent between 1973 and 1979 (ibid.). As a result, families today maintain living standards only by increasing labor outside the home. Between 1969 and 1978, those families with two wages were able to maintain themselves about 6 percent above the cost of living (ibid.). However, one-wage families fell approximately 7 percent behind the cost of living. Consequently, for female-headed households, maintaining a living has become desperate, and, as pointed out earlier, it is these women, primarily black female heads of households (Lewis 1981, 97), who are filling U.S. prisons.

As a result of unemployment, many women are forced onto welfare to survive. Not surprisingly, 93 percent of all welfare recipients are women and children (Stallard et al. 1983, 30). Moreover, approximately 4 million women and 8 million children receive Aid to Families with Dependent Children (AFDC) (ibid., 31). Yet "the 'real value' of AFDC benefits (taking inflation into account) declined 29 percent between 1969 and 1981" (ibid.). As Stallard, Ehrenreich, and Sklar (1983, 31) go on to state, "Payments are so low nationwide that in only three states do AFDC benefits *plus* foodstamps bring a household *up to* the poverty threshold." Consequently, many women and children in this society are hungry.

Considering these economic realities for women, it should not be hard to see why more women are being arrested for fraud. The "official" fraud rate peaks at the twenty- to twenty-four-year-old age group (FBI 1985, 177), which, as stated earlier, is the age group experiencing the second highest unemployment rate for women; and most women arrested for fraud are involved in petty offenses such as passing bad checks and welfare fraud (Hoffman-Bustamante 1973, 127). Women's increasing involvement in fraud is a consequence of the feminization of poverty under patriarchal capitalism. Capitalism creates marginalized populations, while patriarchy determines that women, in particular minority women, will be most severely marginalized.

In addition, as the female labor force participation rate increases, women's unemployment rate also increases. Because of patriarchy, women seeking employment are largely limited to "feminine" occupations of the secondary labor market (see below). This market becomes saturated, and women's unemployment increases along with their increasing labor force participation (Niemi and Lloyd 1975, 198). Moreover, racism interacts with this condition so that employing greater numbers of white women depresses the marketability of minority women. As a result, many women, particularly minority women, experience unbearable economic problems. It is hardly surprising that female property crime began to increase around the mid-to-late 1960s (at least according to official statistics) (Miller 1983), a time when the unemployment rate for women, relative to men, increased dramatically (Niemi and Lloyd 1975, 199). Many women turn to gender-specific illegal options (that is, *nonviolent* options, such as fraud rather than robbery or burglary) as an *accommodation* to their gender/class position.

Embezzlement

The "liberation" thesis would seem correct with regard to embezzlement, since as more women enter wage labor they come into contact with the temptation to take "from the till." However, what the "liberation" theorists ignore is the *type of work* made available to women under patriarchal capitalism. As stated in chapter 2, and repeated above, women who find work in the paid labor market are not only paid less than a "family wage," they are also locked into deadend jobs paying very low wages. In other words, as women's labor force participation rate increases, occupational segregation depresses their relative wages (Niemi and Lloyd 1975, 200). This makes it difficult for a single woman to survive and almost impossible for one with children. Since single women working outside the home are not paid a "family wage," they cannot afford the outside services single men can. As a result, "social speedup" occurs for these women, because "leisure time" declines severely while "work time" increases tremendously (Currie et al. 1980, 21). These women are solely responsible for work both in and outside the home. And the time women spend on unpaid household labor has not declined since 1920, when it was first measured (Vanek 1978, 395). These additional burdens may be related to higher rates of both fraud and embezzlement. As women experience increasing economic pressure and personal stress, they may be forced to write bad checks or "take a little from the till."

Women's economic position helps to explain the increased attraction of crimes like embezzlement, and the sexual division of labor in patriarchal capitalism determines the *type* of embezzlement women are most likely to commit. Although women account for one-third of all embezzlers, they are largely petty embezzlers. For example, 70 percent of those who embezzle over $1,000 are males, while 81 percent of those embezzling between $1 and $150 are women (Datesman and Scarpitti 1980). This petty nature of women's embezzlement is related to their subordinate position in the sexual division of labor of patriarchal capitalism. For the most part, women are not employed in positions in which they handle large quantities of money, but are occupationally segregated into "pink collar ghetto" employment—such as clerical work, domestic work, restaurant and food service, retail sales, and light assembly work (Howe 1977, 83). The women who make up the majority of workers in these positions are systematically underpaid. Indeed, there is a fundamental difference between male and female poverty: "for men, poverty is often the consequence of unemployment, and a job is generally an effective remedy, while female poverty often exists even when a woman works full time" (Stallard et al. 1983, 9).

Within the pink collar ghetto, women are usually found in clerical and service work—*low-wage sectors of the economy.* Women comprise approximately 75 percent of all clerical workers and about 40 percent of all service workers (U.S. Department of Labor 1982). It is estimated that by the end of the century the percent of women clerical workers will rise to around 90 percent (Olesen and Katsuranis 1978, 87). In the late nineteenth century, clerical work was highly paid and prestigious, a skilled trade entailing shorthand, writing, and accounting; it was the monopoly of males. However, as offices were mechanized, clerical work eventually became "proletarianized" and less skilled workers were needed. Consequently, women were introduced into the offices, wages were lowered, and the prestige associated with office work declined (Braverman 1974, 293–358). Capitalists were provided with a large female labor market from the home, while patriarchy helped to make sure that this source of labor remained cheap. Similarly, approximately 70 percent of all new private sector jobs created between 1973 and 1980 were low paid, mostly "pink collar" jobs such as retail, clerical, and service sector positions (Stallard et al. 1983, 23); as a result, the United States "is moving toward a structure of employment even more dominated by jobs that are badly paid, unchanging, and unproductive" (ibid., 25). Proletarianization, deindustrialization, and overseas investments have all reduced the number of semiskilled and skilled positions. Under patriarchal capitalism, the continuing "degradation of labor" determines that since the unskilled poorly paid positions are reserved for women, their economic condition will worsen, and their embezzlement rate will increase. Indeed, at about the same time that women began to enter the labor force once again and thus the pink collar ghetto, female property crimes began to increase (Miller 1983).

In sum, because women are subject (just like powerless males discussed in the last chapter) to the marginalization process inherent in patriarchal capitalism, many females experience high unemployment rates and poverty conditions. When these females do find a job, it is in the pink collar ghetto, where working conditions are poor, job security minimal, and wages very low. This "feminine marginalization" can be explained only by the interaction of patriarchy and capitalism. Capitalism creates a dual labor market while patriarchy determines who will fill the subordinate position in that market. Consequently, women experience severe economic problems. For many, the only option for solving their economic problems is gender specific crime like shoplifting, petty fraud, and minor embezzlement, which becomes an *accommodation* to their powerless position in the gender/class hierarchy. As one woman who survives by supplementing her welfare checks with crime put it, "We break the rules out of need. We are resisting enforced poverty" (Twopines 1985, 50).

Prostitution

As I have shown, females' increasing economic problems seem to lead to increasing amounts of *less serious* forms of criminality, like nonviolent forms of theft. However, while more women are turning to illegal property crimes, many turn to other forms of "criminality," such as prostitution, to accommodate their gender/class position. Why then do some women turn to prostitution?

First, many women reject both unemployment and the "shit jobs" available to them. Studies reveal that women turn to prostitution because it is financially more advantageous than the employment that is available for women in the legitimate wage labor force. Esselstyn (1968, 129) sums up the economic lure of prostitution: "Women are attracted to prostitution in contemporary America because the income is high and because it affords an opportunity to earn more, buy more, and live better than would be possible by any other plausible alternative." When Esselstyn mentions that the pay is high, she means, of course, in the relative sense. As one woman pointed out:

> I worked for $1.67 from February to April, $1.67 at Marc's Big Boy (a fast food chain), and I think that was really against my constitutional rights. But I didn't have no choice. I need a job and I grab it. And I thought: "I'm not gonna work for $1.67"; I'm not I told 'em . . . I said: "Damn. This is 1979. What is this here?" It was a trip. They don't know what they doin' to these young women with their job 'cause . . . it don't make 'em workin' any harder; it don't. It makes 'em want to get it faster. You might meet somebody you're waiting on one day, gives you a wink and telephone number . . . or come on up to his apartment, or: "I got a better position for you upstairs." I did. [cited in Miller 1986, 82]

Other studies confirm that most prostitutes are motivated by a desire for money and material goods (James 1976), which, due to patriarchy in the paid labor force, they find increasingly difficult to obtain.

Nevertheless, women elect prostitution for more than mere survival. As Karen Rosenblum (1975, 177) makes clear in her study of prostitution, the "specific precipitating factors . . . can be identified simply as independence and money." In other words, in addition to material security, independence is a precipitating factor associated with prostitution, and several other studies support this conclusion (Benjamin and Masters 1964; Esselstyn 1968; Miller 1986). For example, Eleanor Miller (1986, 140), in her recently published book *Street Woman,* concludes that prostitutes in their own way have a degree of independence, excitement, and autonomy in their work that similarly qualified persons who labor in the world of legal work rarely enjoy. Housewifery and the jobs available in the "pink collar ghetto" are routine, confining, and seriously alienating. Interviews with prostitutes show that many feel "overt hatred of routine, confining jobs" (Greenwald 1970, 202). One prostitute put it this way: "You don't have certain hours you have to work. You can go to work when you want, leave when you want . . . you don't have a boss hanging over you, you're independent" (James 1982, 302). In short, prostitution becomes a way for some women to reject their predetermined position in patriarchal capitalism and the authoritarian structure of pink collar positions.

Prostitution exists not only for economic reasons; in fact it is possible as an *accommodation* because in U.S. society patriarchy has defined women's value as primarily sexual. In patriarchal capitalist society, where masculine control of women's sexuality and heterosexuality is the norm, the conditions are ripe for prostitution. In such a society, males are socialized to have an uncontrollable sexual "drive" whereas females are supposed to be sexually seductive and meet the sexual needs of men. Under this type of sexual ideology, prostitution becomes a "natural" option for solving economic problems. Prostitution is the simple extension of what all women are supposed to do: nurture men and take care of men's sexual desires in return for economic security. Prostitution rests upon and reinforces masculine control of female sexuality.

While the majority of prostitutes enter into prostitution for the above reasons, they live very different kinds of lives. Balkan, Berger, and Schmidt (1980, 258) make the point that prostitution as a business is stratified along class lines:

> Call girls, often used by businessmen, for a night on the town and impressing their colleagues, are usually white, young, attractive, better educated, and earn more money for their time. On the other hand, streetwalkers are usually working-class, minority, older, poor women. Not only do they make less money, they are often subjected to harassment by law-enforcement officials.

As a result of the class character of prostitution, many have suggested that prostitutes compete with and distrust each other (Bryan 1965). While this may be true across class lines (Sheehy 1973, 33–35), it is often not the case within class-specific prostitution subcultures. Prostitutes within these groups tend to work together and rely on each other for safety and support. Far from exploiting each other, they are emotionally and financially interdependent (Rosenblum 1975, 180). Moreover, and contrary to public opinion, not all prostitutes rely on pimps. As one study found, some

> prostitutes laugh at the notion of having a pimp and say that they only
> use men to give them back-up protection. The men, on the other hand,
> thought they were pimps, even though the women did not think so.
> [Andersen 1983, 184]

This does not mean prostitutes do not rely on pimps, for the majority
do. In patriarchal culture, women learn to feel incomplete if they do
not have "a man." Thus, many prostitutes turn to pimps for protection and to take care of business. This is a response to the structure of
power in gender relations, where men are supposed to negotiate the
"rough spots." The pimp then lives off the earnings of the prostitute
and acts as her agent and/or companion. Although the prostitute can
earn more than she would in the legitimate labor force, she receives
only a fraction of the revenue she earns because the bulk of her
income goes to the pimp, hotel owners, and the police in payoffs. Like
the legitimate labor market, the "prostitution market" is segregated by
sex and under masculine control. Males appropriate the labor of
female prostitutes, which in turn reproduces their dependency.

Men may control usually fewer than three prostitutes. If a male has
two or three females working for him, they are referred to on the
street as "wives-in-law," who not only prostitute, but also may "bust
paper" (commit forgery) and "boost" (shoplift) for their "man," and,
of course, prepare his meals and do the housework (Miller 1986, 37–
38). Moreover, as all women learn, their socialized need for men is
reinforced by the fact that a woman's status is defined by the man she
is with. Thus, a prostitute may attempt to hook up with a "high class"
pimp to raise her status in the subculture of prostitution (James 1982,
304). The pimp provides companionship, someone to live and be with
in return for the prostitute's earnings. As one prostitute defined her
relationship with a pimp, it meant "just knowing that you have
somebody there all the time, not just for protection, just someone you
can go to" (ibid., 304). Actually, many times the prostitute-pimp
relationship is not that different from "normal" male-female relationships in patriarchal capitalism. Indeed, normative heterosexuality
simplifies the task of the pimp.

However, a relationship between a prostitute and a pimp may result
in *forced* prostitution and female sexual slavery, with the women no
longer engaging in prostitution "for her own benefit," but as a sexual
slave for the pimp. Some women who turn to prostitution do not
realize until later that they cannot get out. When prostitutes attempt
to leave their pimps, many are physically brutalized and tortured
(Barry 1979, 79). The following is what happened to a sixteen-year-
old when she attempted to leave.

> Well, first he put his foot in my face which broke my nose and knocked
> me out and I got out the door—we lived on the third floor of this build-
> ing and I couldn't get out the door in time before he caught me and

there was just punches in the face and he had long fingernails which scarred up my body pretty much and kicking because I kept falling on the floor from being hit in the head. . . . I finally got out the door and was running out the middle of the street and he was trying to drag me into the place again when the police came. [cited in ibid., 79]

For some males, the pimp lifestyle is a survival strategy which is both exciting and rewarding for them as males. Street pimps are usually marginalized men who choose pimping in preference to routine labor for "the man." They rely on women for their livelihood, but their brutal control of women testifies to their masculinity. The misogynistic treatment of women by pimps is clearly exemplified in biographies of pimp life (Malcolm X 1965; Iceberg Slim 1967). These biographies and other studies show that the most "masculine" aspect of pimp life is impressing others by subjecting the female to exclusive control. In many instances the female becomes a sexual slave. As Christina and Richard Milner (1972, 52–53) point out in their study of pimping:

First and foremost, the pimp must be in complete control of his women; this control is made conspicuous to others by a series of little rituals which express symbolically his woman's attitude. When in the company of others she must take special pains to treat him with absolute deference and respect. She must light his cigarettes, respond to his every whim immediately, and never, never, contradict him. In fact, a ho (prostitute) is strictly not supposed to speak in the company of pimps unless spoken to.

The prostitute/pimp relationship is the ultimate consequence of a patriarchal capitalist social order where men are *powerful* and women *powerless*, and where men are socialized to dominate women, and women are taught to defer to and subordinate themselves to the male. This is further exemplified by the fact that pimps, many times, support each other's violence toward "their ho." In their study, Christina and Richard Milner (ibid., 56) discuss how a pimp took one of "his" prostitutes (who was also a dancer) into the dancer's dressing room and "began to shout at her and slap her around." It was loud enough for everyone in the bar to hear, and "the six pimps sitting at the back of the bar near the dressing room began to clap and whistle loudly," seemingly for the current dancer, "but in reality to cover the noise of the beating from the ears of the straight customers." When the pimp emerged from the dressing room and joined the others he exclaimed, "Well, I took care of that bitch." Then they all began to joke around. In contrast, when the prostitute emerged, not "one of them (pimps) felt it proper to comfort her in any way." By reason of women's powerlessness in patriarchal capitalism, it becomes very difficult for the prostitute to escape such conditions, and the violence becomes a means of "disciplining" the prostitute.

Prostitution and International
Patriarchal Capitalism

Patriarchal capitalism is international in scope, and, consequently, so is prostitution. As transnational corporations (and therefore patriarchal capitalism) have expanded around the world, so has prostitution. A prime example is East Asia, where transnationals spread quickly in the 1960s, first to Hong Kong and Taiwan, next to South Korea, Singapore, and Malaysia (Fuentes and Ehrenreich 1983, 8). Between 1960 and 1969, investment in offshore manufacturing by U.S. corporations increased from $11.1 billion to $29.5 billion (ibid.). By the mid-1970s, Thailand and the Philippines were added to the list (ibid.). Eighty to ninety percent of these corporations' light assembly workers are women, who are subjected to crowded and unsanitary boarding houses, extremely low wages, and severe health hazards (ibid. 12, 16-25). Consequently, as transnational investment has grown, so has the number of women involved in prostitution. In Thailand in 1957, for example, there were 20,000 prostitutes; by 1982 the figure had reached 700,000 (500,000 of which are in Bangkok), or about 10 percent of all Thai women between the ages of fifteen and thirty. In the Philippines and South Korea over 200,000 prostitutes operate (Gay 1985, 34).

In East Asia, many women enter into prostitution to survive the feminization of poverty. Fuentes and Ehrenreich (1983, 26) discuss one such case:

> For Noi, a 20-year old Thai woman, prostitution provides a desperately needed second income. "I get 25 *baht* per day" [then worth less than $1.50] working in a battery factory, she explains. "But this is not enough to cover my expenses. How could this be enough to pay for my food, my bus ticket and other expenses? And I can tell you I am thrifty. I have to find work at night so that I can send money to my parents." Many other prostitutes are former factory workers, desperate for employment, or young women who came to the cities looking for factory work they never found.

Many women also enter into prostitution in preference to the hazardous working conditions in the factories. As one woman stated, "You get cancer working in factories, we get abortion and VD working as prostitutes"(cited in Gay 1985, 34).

Transnational investment in Asia has pushed these nations to the aggressive export of goods produced in the cities, with a corresponding reduction in agricultural investment, resulting in the impoverishment of the people who live off the land. In a typical rural village in Thailand, for instance, approximately one-third of the families have no land and three-quarters have less than the two acres needed for subsistance. As a result, many "send their daughters to Bangkok to work as prostitutes" (ibid., 34). Many young girls are actually "sold for a few dollars by their impoverished parents to save the family from hunger" (Lenze 1979, 7).

In South Korea, prostitution is big business, with revenues up to $270 million a year (Fuentes and Ehrenreich 1983, 26). Much of this comes from *kisaeng* (prostitute) brothel tours, which attract business-men primarily, but also tourists, as customers. Often subsidized by his own company, a businessman can obtain a "chartered tour of two nights and three days" for "no more than $200—including the price of sex" (Yayori 1977, 20). South Korea, as a result has become known as a "male paradise" catering to "transnational businessmen, U.S. military personnel and government officials. Transnational corpora-tions and banks have invested heavily in the hotels, agencies, and transportation systems that support *kisaeng* tourism" (Fuentes and Ehrenreich 1983, 26). As Yayori Matsui (1984, 69) concludes, "With the profits reaped by paying minuscule wages to workers, foreign businessmen buy the bodies of South Korean women. *Kisaeng* tours epitomize the ugly relationship between economic and sexual exploi-tation."

Conditions are similar in the Philippines. Cynthia Enloe (1983, 37) describes the "typical life cycle of a Filipino prostitute."

> A teenage girl grows up in a poor rural family which has failed in its
> struggle to hold on to land which could produce a sufficient income to
> sustain the family. The girl may have suffered sexual abuse by male
> adults in the family. To help her family pay off its rising debts, she is sent
> off to Manila. Sometimes the girl goes in the custody of an adult who
> promises her parents she will be trained for an income producing job in
> the city. She may start working as a domestic servant, still hoping to find
> work in one of Manila's many Japanese or American owned garment or
> microelectronic factories, whose managers are known to favor young
> girls on their assembly lines, but eventually she is put to work as a prosti-
> tute. She hits her peak right at the start, working in the city's expensive
> international hotels where Western men stay on their business trips.

According to one study, between 70 and 80 percent of male tourists from Japan, the United States, Australia, and Western Europe, travel-ing to the above Asian countries, "do so solely for the purpose of sexual entertainment" (Gay 1985, 34).

In sum, some women turn to prostitution in the face of economic marginalization, caused by the interaction of patriarchy and capital-ism, because of (1) unemployment, the types of jobs available to them, the low pay, and the dangerous working conditions, and (2) patriar-chal ideology, which emphasizes nurturing men, "taking care" of their sexual needs, and working for them. Prostitution then provides a rational alternative to the "feminization of poverty." Many women, because of their subordinate and powerless position in patriarchal capitalism, turn to this alternative as an *accommodation* to their economic problems. Moreover, the prostitution business is controlled by men because of their relative power vis-à-vis women, which is exercised through economic, physical, and state sanctions.

Female Sexuality, Crime, and the State

It is not only the prostitution business, however, which is controlled by men and serves their interests. The "social control" of prostitution is also masculine-dominated and likewise serves the interests of men. Earlier it was noted that the criminal justice system publicizes to the U.S. population the crimes females commit, and prostitution is a prime example. In many states, two main types of laws affect our perception of prostitution: those against loitering with the intent to commit prostitution, and those against offering or agreeing to an act of prostitution (James 1982, 295). A woman convicted of the latter is subject to future arrests for "loitering as a known prostitute." If she is seen in an area "known to be inhabited by prostitutes," she also incurs the risk of arrest for loitering (ibid.). The law does not, of course, require the arrest of "known customers." In this way, the law clearly discriminates against women, and creates the impression that it is the *female prostitute*, rather than the *male customer*, who is guilty of agreeing to an act of prostitution.

In many states the laws against prostitution apply only to women and not to men. Neither males who prostitute themselves nor males who patronize male or female prostitutes are criminalized (Tong 1984, 55). While a number of states have addressed this inequity, the resulting laws are "infrequently enforced and are used primarily to induce the man to assist in prosecuting the prostitute by his testimony against her" (Mann 1984, 122). Typically, agents of the state continue to identify only the female as the criminal. The man who purchases the prostitute's services is ignored, like those who organize and exploit the prostitute, as well as those who own the property where the prostitution takes place. In the majority of cases, these are all males. An example of this is spelled out below.

> It is common practice for plainclothes police to stand in front of massage parlors (which frequently serve as houses of prostitution) pretending to be potential customers. When a male customer leaves the premises, he is asked whom he would recommend and what she did. When informed, the police make a bust, ignoring the role that the male customer played in the transaction [Balkan et al. 1980, 259]

Because of the way the laws on prostitution are written and enforced, inevitably the majority of those arrested and, therefore, processed through the criminal justice system for prostitution will be women. Indeed, women comprised approximately 70 percent of all those arrested for prostitution and commercialized vice in 1984 (FBI 1985, 179). Approximately one-third of the women in jails and prisons are there for prostitution, and, in the larger cities, over 50 percent of the female jail population are convicted prostitutes (Mann 1984, 121–122).

In addition to the bias against women, class bias and racism in the criminal justice system operates to put mostly minority and poor women behind bars (Sheldon 1982, 136). Simultaneously, the criminal justice system ignores the customers, mostly middle class, married, white suburban professionals or businessmen (James 1982, 293). I am not arguing that men should simply be arrested along with the women. My point is that the criminal justice system operates from an ideology that opresses women while appeasing the powerful. First, since the criminal justice system concentrates on repressing the prostitute and not the customer, women's involvement in the crime is exaggerated. The public learns that prostitution is solely a female crime, and, therefore, "those women" should be dealt with. This ideology effectively hides the criminality of the powerful (in this case men). Second, it publicizes (by reason of racism and class bias) that prostitutes are primarily minority women—indeed the least powerful individuals in this society—therefore exaggerating their involvement in prostitution while simultaneously maintaining "call girls" invisibility. As a result, men are allowed illegally to purchase the sexual services of women with what amounts to an exemption from punishment, while women, especially poor and minority women, are criminalized by the process. Once again, the powerless (marginalized minority women) are portrayed as criminals while the crimes of the powerful (middle and upper class men) are hidden away.

The manner in which the state regulates prostitution also reproduces the "double standard." By criminalizing the prostitute and ignoring the customer, the state is simply reinforcing the belief, and the accompanying ideology, that men should have sexual freedom while women should not. Prostitutes call into question the ideology stating that women are to be the sexual partner of only one man. Thus, the social control of prostitution, like prostitution itself, rests upon and reinforces masculine control of female sexuality.

The state and its legal system attempt to control female sexuality in other areas as well. The juvenile justice system, for example, attempts to "teach" women early on that their sexuality is not their own. From the juvenile court's beginning, the "child savers" were much concerned about the normative behavior of youth, particularly young women. As a result, young women were "prosecuted almost exclusively for 'immoral conduct,' a very broad category that defined all sexual exploration as fundamentally perverse and predictive of future promiscuity"(Schlossman and Wallach 1978, 68). Young women were rarely accused of violating criminal statutes, yet they received stiffer legal penalties for their "immoral conduct" than young men did for their criminal conduct (ibid.). By incarcerating young females, the state effectively "removed them from the unregulated sexual marketplace of ghetto streets and forced them to save their sexual favors, moral reputations, and health until they were of marriageable age" (ibid. 76).

The state and its juvenile justice system does not operate much differently today, as it continues to process primarily young women for specific violations of normative conduct and to sanction them severely. Young women today are far more likely to be arrested for "status offenses" (behaviors, that, if engaged in by an adult, would not be considered criminal), such as "promiscuity," running away, and "incorrigibility." Approximately 75 percent of girls, compared to 25 percent of boys, are processed for status offenses (Chesney-Lind 1978, 182). And, even though the overwhelming majority of females are charged with status offenses, females are much more likely both to be detained by the state and to be held for longer periods than males (Sarri 1976, 76). In short, the state continues to provide a mechanism for reproducing the "double standard" and therefore masculine control of female sexuality.

5
Powerful Men and Corporate Crime

F_{ew} people in the United States are aware of the extent and seriousness of corporate crime and the way the state maintains conditions favorable to its commission. When individuals are asked which harms to society are the most serious, they usually list violent street crimes first, while "white-collar crimes" such as corporate crimes "are not regarded as particularly serious offenses" (Rossi et al. 1974, 227). This chapter shows, however, that the perception of corporate crime as less serious than street crime does *not* result from an absence of criminality by corporations. Rather, the public's perception of what is criminal is deeply affected by the way the state defines and handles corporate crimes. Before I go on, however, it is important to understand what I mean by corporate crime. Corporate crime is defined here as illegal and/or socially injurious acts of neglect or intent that (l) are committed for the purpose of furthering the goals of a corporation, and that (2) physically and/or economically abuse individuals in the United States as well as abroad. Corporate crime victimizes large numbers of people worldwide and is substantially more devastating, injurious, and serious than the crimes committed by the powerless, yet is effectively hidden from our view. Let us begin by looking at the extent and seriousness of corporate crime.

The Extent and Seriousness of Corporate Crime

This section shows how corporations perpetrate violence on workers, consumers, and citizens; how they steal from all of us; and finally, how the criminality of transnationals affects peoples of other countries.

Corporate Crime Kills and Injures Workers

Every year approximately 14,000 U.S. workers are killed in job-related accidents. Somewhere between 120,000 to 200,000 additional people in the United States die each year from work-related illnesses.

This means that an individual dies from her/his work *every three minutes* (Institute for Labor Education and Research 1982, 178). By comparison, a one-on-one homicide occurs in the United States once every twenty-eight minutes (FBI 1985).

In addition to dying on the job, millions of workers in this society are injured and/or become ill while working. In 1977 for example, 5.3 million workers suffered injuries on the job, while approximately 162,000 workers became ill (Institute for Labor Education and Research, 1982; 178). Moreover, somewhere in the vicinity of 400,000 to one million workers contract new cases of job-related diseases each year (Ashford 1976, 93). Consequently, about thirty-six workers are injured or become ill at the workplace *every minute of the working day* (Institute for Labor Education and Research 1982, 178), as compared to fewer than two one-on-one aggravated assaults every minute (FBI 1985).

Reiman (1979, 68) notes that to "say that some of these workers died from accidents due to their own carelessness is about as helpful as saying that some of those who died at the hands of murderers asked for it." He points to the conditions under which workers must labor—the imposition of production quotas—affecting possible worker negligence and carelessness. Moreover, studies indicate that a good proportion of industrial accidents involve unsafe working conditions. For example, in a New York study, 57 percent of the accidents investigated involved a code violation, and a Wisconsin study found that 35 of 90 lethal accidents occurred because of safety violations (Bacow 1980, 38-39). Beyond this, the vast majority of occupational deaths result not from accidents but disease, the causes of which are in most cases outside a worker's control (Reiman 1979, 68).

Consequently, even though these figures indicate that very large numbers of workers are becoming ill and being injured and killed on the job, they most likely understate the seriousness of corporate violence directed toward workers, primarily because we have to rely on company reports. As a recent Department of Labor report points out,

> employer records understate the occupational disease problem because affected workers may no longer be employed by the firm where exposure occurred. In addition, some employers are reluctant to report occupational diseases when they are diagnosed because of their potential financial liability. [cited in Reiman 1984, 53]

A company's insurance rating and costs are connected to the frequency of injuries, illnesses, and deaths. By hiding accidents a company can lower its insurance costs. Moreover, company physicians, who are the first to see a worker who has contracted an occupational disease, are *encouraged* to diagnose the complaint as non-job-related. As one company's medical manual for its medical personnel states, "It should be noted that all claims cases are adversary cases . . . and the comments of company physicians to employees must be guarded as to causation and as to liability for costs" (cited in Berman 1978, 108). Indeed, a study conducted by the Occupational Safety and Health Administration (OSHA) found that at least in small plants, more than 40 percent of the injuries go unreported (ibid., 44). The amount of corporate violence in the workplace is most likely staggering.

While corporate violence affects all workers, racial minorities, because of racism, are the most severely affected. Historically blacks, Chicanos, and Native Americans have been excluded from education and trade union membership which might improve their status. As a result, they end up in the dirtiest, hardest and most hazardous jobs. As Morris Davis (1980, 724) states with regards to blacks,

> We enter the 1980's with the following statistics. Fifteen percent of the black work force (one to one and one-half million) are unable to work due to permanent or partial job related disabilities. Black workers have a 37 percent greater chance than whites of suffering an occupational injury or illness. Black workers are one and one-half times more likely than whites to be severely disabled from job injuries and illnesses and face a 20 percent greater chance than whites of dying from job related injuries and illnesses.

The vast majority of all these injuries and deaths occur because employers either neglect or intentionally violate safety standards (Reiman 1984, 56-57). For example, on February 10, 1983, Stefan Golab, a sixty-one-year-old Polish immigrant on a work visa, collapsed and died at his workplace. It was determined later that he had high levels of cyanide in his blood. Three top executives of the company were eventually charged and convicted of murder (Moberg 1985, 2). During the trial, witnesses revealed how insensitive the company was to worker health and safety:

> —one worker said that despite wearing five paper face masks at a time, he got headaches and vomited from the noxious cyanide fumes released from the company's treatment vat;
> —a saleswoman who reported an "overpowering smell" that "burned the back of your throat" when she visited the plant, tried unsuccessfully three times to sell the company safety equipment;
> —at his bosses' direction, another worker painted over the skull-and-crossbones on the steel containers of cyanide-tainted sludge and hid them from inspectors after Golab's death;
> —a former bookkeeper testified that illegal aliens were selected to work with the dangerous chemicals;
> —other workers testified about recurrent nausea and illness but said they were never warned of dangers. [ibid.]

Although the prosecution and conviction of the executives is unique, the case, unfortunately, is not. In 1978 at Willow Island, West Virginia, fifty-one workers died when, as a result of safety violations, a cooling tower collapsed. After investigating the tragedy, the Occupational Safety and Health Administration concluded that "the disaster was a direct result of illegal corner-cutting on the part of Research-Cottrell, Inc., a New Jersey firm that was building the tower," and that "the firm had faked test results on its concrete for nearly a year" (Sheils and Walcott 1978, 59-60). In 1981, fifteen miners were killed by an explosion in a mine that had received 1,133 citations and fifty-seven orders to correct known dangers from federal inspectors since 1978 (Eitzen and Timmer 1985, 293). And corporations today continue to expose workers to such "silent killers" as nuclear radiation, chemical compounds, asbestos fibers, and cotton dust. Asbestos, for example, was suspected as a "silent killer" as early as 1918, when many life insurance companies began denying policies to asbestos workers because of their high mortality rate (Institute for Labor Education and Research 1982, 181). Between 1933 and 1978 "high ranking executives in the asbestos industry suppressed scientific data and medical records that would have warned asbestos workers of the danger of contracting lung cancer and other crippling diseases" (Balkan et al. 1980, 171). Yet many companies today still fail to protect their workers from asbestos poisoning. Again, since the 1960's medical studies have confirmed that "byssinosis" (or brownlung disease) is a severe health problem for textile workers who work around cotton dust (Institute for Labor Education and Research 1982, 181). The textile industry however, continues to disregard its effect on worker health. Today, some 85,000 textile workers suffer impaired breathing because of acute byssinosis and another 35,000 former mill workers are totally disabled with chronic byssinosis (Reiman 1984, 56).

While men and women are *both* being killed and injured working on the job, women suffer additional harms from corporate violence because they are *women*. First, women workers are subjected to corporate violence as *childbearers*. As noted in earlier chapters, women are faced with a unique dilemma within patriarchal capitalism: on the one hand, women's existence, because women tend to be socialized into motherhood, revolves around family and childbearing/rearing; on the other hand, there are also social forces within patriarchal capitalism preventing women from exercising their right to become mothers. For example, the economic realities of many women's lives, as well as the lack of childcare facilities, are not conducive to childbearing/rearing (Jagger 1983, 292). Moreover, historically, as well as today, women of color and poor women have been denied control over their reproductive lives by being forced to undergo sterilization by the medical profession (Andersen 1983, 159–60).

In business today many working class women, to survive economically, are also being forced into sterilization. Unlike men who never (or seldom) are forced to make this choice, women are being required to surrender their right to produce children in order to work. For instance, five women who worked for the American Cynamid Corporation were recently forced to undergo sterilization under threat of losing their jobs (Balkan et al. 1980, 251). Arguing that women of childbearing years should not work in places contaminated by lead, the company gave these women the "choice" of sterilization or a lower-paid dead-end janitorial position. Lead poisoning does affect pregnant woman and fetuses (Hunt 1979), but it also affects the reproductive health of men by damaging male sperm (Wright 1979); however, this is not a workplace issue. The justification for requiring only women who work in these plants to be sterilized is that it protects the reproductive health of the population—clearly a sexist pretext. Nor is the "choice" that confronted the women at American Cynamid unique, for a number of corporations such as General Motors, B. F. Goodrich, St. Joe's Minerals, Allied Chemical, and Olin, have policies that ban women, but not men, from certain jobs unless they can prove they are sterile (Scott 1984, 80).

As we have seen, the sexual division of labor segregates women into certain occupations simply because they are women. Evidence indicates that women who work in the "pink-collar ghetto" (low paying, menial jobs) are also subjected to dangerous working conditions (Stellman 1977). Certain industries, such as electronic assembly, which rely primarily on female labor power, provide clear examples of how corporate violence affects women workers, who, by reason of their sex, are disproportionately subjected to particular hazards. The electronics industry, for example, prides itself on being "the clean industry." In California's "Silicon Valley," the home of the silicon chip manufacturing industry, women fill most of the assembly jobs. In approximately 500 electronics companies, more than 75 percent of the production workers are women, and at least 40 percent of these are minority women (Baker and Woodrow 1984, 22). In the late 1970s, it became clear that electronics was not as clean as male executives claimed. In fact, the industry uses hundreds of potentially dangerous substances to produce its "miracle chips" (ibid., 24). Organic solvents, such as xylene, chloroform, trichloroethylene, freons, methyl ethyl ketone, and others, are constantly used by production workers throughout the industry, mainly for cleaning, stripping, and degreasing. As Baker and Woodrow (ibid., 24) write, these chemicals "are known to cause a range of health problems, including dermatitis; central nervous system effects such as nausea, dizziness and headaches; liver and kidney damage; and even cancer". Moreover, the National Institute for Occupational Safety and Health concluded in a

1977 report that the scientific instruments industry and electrical manufacturers rank first and third as the *most hazardous among industries exposing workers to carcinogens* (ibid., 25). Other occupations—which to a large extent are filled by women—that maintain dangerous working conditions are nursing (Coleman and Dickinson 1984), office work of all kinds (Fleishman 1984; Henifin 1984; Chavkin 1984) and farm work (Jasso and Mazorra 1984). Consequently, women as powerless individuals, are many times subjected to hazardous working conditions in this society.

Workers have, of course, not always sat passively by and allowed employers to kill and injure them. They have organized into unions to gain some control over their working lives. However, capital has resisted this organizing effort every inch of the way. As others have pointed out (McIntosh 1973; Pearce 1976; Balkan et al. 1980; Simon and Eitzen 1982; Eitzen and Timmer 1985), employers have historically used violence and called in organized crime figures to halt unionization. Thus, workers who have rebelled against the workplace violence have been subjected to further violence.

Corporate Crime Kills and Injures Consumers/Citizens

Corporations perpetrate violence not only on workers, but also consumers and citizens. Corporate injuries of childbearers as consumers is a good example. Approximately 8,000 pregnant women who had taken the prescription drug thalidomide ended up giving birth to terribly deformed babies. The corporation that developed and distributed the drug deliberately falsified the test data and concealed the truth about the drug's serious side effects (Box 1983, 24).

The case of the Dalkon Shield, an IUD, is another example of corporate violence toward women as consumers and childbearers. The doctor who invented it, along with several other businessmen and a drug company, A. H. Robins, all agreed to manufacture, promote, and market it even though the company's files contained 400 "unfavorable reports" from physicians and others about the Dalkon Shield. None of these "unfavorable reports" were made public—even though they included substantial evidence linking the Dalkon Shield with seventy five instances of uterine perforation, ectopic pregnancies, and at least seventeen deaths (Balkan et al. 1980, 169; Braithwaite 1984, 258). A. H. Robins Company distributed approximately 2.86 million shields in the United States and nearly all of the women who used it "suffered life-threatening forms of infections known as pelvic inflammatory disease" (Mintz 1985, 20).

While childbearers are specifically subjected to certain types of corporate violence, many other products, ranging from flammable children's clothing and dangerous toys to tires and automobiles, are dangerous to men, women, and children (Simon and Eitzen 1982, 97–114). The production of a defective automobile, the Ford Pinto, stands out as a prime example. In the 1970s, Ford Motor Company, driven to produce a subcompact capable of competing with the Volkswagen bug, decided to produce the Pinto. Ford marketed the Pinto, even though high officials in the company knew it had a faulty gas tank design that was very likely to lead to fire fatalities. The company, after putting together a "cost-benefit analysis" which placed *a dollar value on human life at $200,000*, figured that the $11 per car it would take to remedy the gas tank problem would be more costly than paying off the families of burn death victims (Dowie 1977). As Dowie (ibid., 20) has shown, possibly as many as 900 burn deaths resulted from the exploding Pintos.

Corporate pollution provides a prime example of violence toward citizens. Between 1942 and 1953 for example, Hooker Chemical Company dumped over 20,000 tons of toxic waste into the Love Canal, near Niagara Falls, New York (Simon and Eitzen 1982, 4). After Hooker Chemical sold the dump site to the Board of Education for one dollar, an elementary school, playground, and housing development were built on the toxic waste dump site. However, as Simon and Eitzen (1982, 4) point out,

> For at least twenty years prior to 1977 the toxic chemicals had been seeping through to the land surface. It was in 1977, however, that highly toxic black sludge began seeping into the cellars of the school and nearby residences. Tests showed the existence of eighty-two chemicals in the air, water, and soil of Love Canal, among them twelve known carcinogens including dioxin, one of the deadliest substances ever synthesized. There is evidence that Hooker Chemical knew of the problem as far back as 1958 but chose not to warn local health officials of any potential problems because cleanup costs would have increased from four to fifty million dollars.

As a result, people living in the area experienced a disproportionately high rate of birth defects, miscarriages, chromosomal abnormalities, liver disorders, respiratory and urinary diseases, epilepsy, and suicide (ibid.). Despite all this evidence, Hooker Chemical continues to deny any liability for the violence perpetrated on the people in the Love Canal area.

Love Canal is not unique. The residents of Woburn, Massachusetts, have had a cluster of child leukemia deaths that have been tied to chemical contamination of drinking water; in Williamstown, Vermont, the toxic chemicals trichloroethylene, benzene, and napthalene from an industrial dry-cleaning facility contaminated a local elementary school; and in Riverside, California, contaminants from a waste dump threatened to contaminate the drinking water of 500,000 people (Asinoff 1985, 3).

As Steven Box (1983, 27) notes, corporate violence even enters the home, as

> consumers may be poisoned in their beds by improperly tested medical drugs, they may be killed over their dinner tables by unhygienically prepared food, they may be blown up to God knows where by the neighborhood chemical complex exploding, and they may become totally diseased in their living rooms by industrial pollution.

The victims of this type of corporate violence are disproportionately women, since they spend most of their time in the household. The sexual division of labor within the family particularly contributes to significant health and safety hazards for women who work in the home (Rosenburg 1984). Indeed, the National Commission on Product Safety (1971, 1) estimates that every year, while using ordinary household products, 20 million people are seriously injured, 585,000 are hospitalized, 110,000 are permanently disabled, and some 30,000 are killed. Moreover, approximately 140,000 deaths per year (or 9 percent of all deaths) may be traced to pollutants in the United States (Box 1983, 27).

All of this evidence (which represents only *some* of the cases that have come to public attention) argues that in this society corporate violence victimizes more people and causes greater suffering than does street violence. The powerful are clearly the major violent criminals, victimizing the powerless. Another and equally pervasive form of victimization arises from domestic corporate theft.

Corporate Crime Steals from Us

Sweatshops and *homework* in the United States are prime examples of corporate theft directed against women as workers and women as women. Annette Fuentes and Barbara Ehrenreich (1983) found sweatshops proliferating today, particularly in the garment industry. Garment sweatshops employ primarily women to sew clothes at substandard wages, under poor working conditions and labor abuse. It is difficult to estimate the exact number of garment sweatshops in the United States, as they seem to be "springing up by the hundreds" (ibid., 48). These shops operate illegally and usually as secretly as possible to avoid unemployment insurance, minimum wage rates, child labor laws, and overtime pay regulations. In many instances women work sixteen to eighteen hours a day, seven days a week, for $50 a week. The connection between the sweatshops and the clothing manufacturers is described by Fuentes and Ehrenreich (1983, 48–49):

> Garment sweatshops come and go frequently in the melee of intense competition. Anyone with a few thousand dollars can start a shop with a dozen sewing machines, a neighborhood workforce and a low rent building. The owners (or contractors) vie for orders from the middlemen to whom the large clothing manufacturers farm out bundles of pre-cut fabric for stitching. Neither the contractors nor the women they hire share in the huge profits collected by the jobbers and the big manufacturers.

As Fuentes and Ehrenreich (ibid., 50) go on to point out, however, the women "clearly make out the worst in the sweatshop scenario." Approximately 90 percent of sweatshop workers are women, mostly from the Third World and largely "undocumented workers," who, since they are unable to work in a licensed business, are particularly vulnerable to exploitation in sweatshops. What's worse, contractors "frequently use the threat of deportation to maintain abusive work conditions, and keep the women away from unions" (ibid.). As the *New York Times* makes clear, these women work under appalling conditions, appropriate to the late 1800s:

> While sweatshop conditions vary, there is a grim sameness to the basic appearance: rows of women bent over sewing machines, separated by narrow isles often made impassable by dress racks and piles of piece goods. Fire exits and windows, too, are often blocked or even padlocked, reducing emergency escapes to a rickety freight elevator and unlit stairs. [Salmans 1981, A1]

Indeed, sweatshops are the logical outcome of the position of women in patriarchal capitalism. Women who work in sweatshops are usually women with few options, such as single mothers, undocumented workers, or simply women who are unable to find better-paying jobs (Fuentes and Ehrenreich 1983, 50). Big manufacturers reap large profits from superexploiting women in sweatshops and illegally violating minimum wage laws and overtime pay regulations—clearly, a prime example of corporate theft.

Though earlier chapters discussed masculine control of female sexuality, masculine control of women's bodies occurs in the non-sexual aspects of women's lives as well. Sweatshops are just one example. Women are imprisoned not only in the home, but also in dangerous work environments (see above) and sweatshops (Jagger 1983, 292).

Sweatshops are complemented by exploiting women who work at home. Jobbers give women bundles of fabric to sew at home, paying them less than shop wages (usually piece-work rates), and the home-workers must provide their own sewing machines, electricity, and rent. Furthermore, to meet deadlines, many homeworkers must also "hire" their own children (Fuentes and Ehrenreich, 1983, 52). Homeworking, according to Fuentes and Ehrenreich (ibid.) is

> so widespread and popular with contractors that even Nancy Reagan's high-fashion dresses may be "homemade." Her favorite designer, Adolpho, farms out his garment work to Ruth Fashions located in Queens. Ruth Fashions in turn farms it out to homeworkers. In 1982 the New York State Attorney General cited the company as a chronic violator of laws prohibiting homework.

While some extoll the virtues of homework for mothers and children and the Reagan administration deliberately promotes it (Chavkin 1984, 9), the realities of this type of labor are quietly ignored. The following is a good example of the conditions facing most homeworkers.

> In a single room, an Ecuadorian woman named Rosa, who is in this country illegally, lives with her two children, one of whom is brain damaged. She . . . works 12 or more hours a day making skirts at 20 cents each. By working seven days a week at her sewing machine, she can make $120 a week or even a little more. But sometimes, too, the contractors cheat her out of her wages, knowing there's nothing she can do about it. [cited in Chavkin 1984, 9]

Clearly, sweatshops and homework are forms of corporate theft invisible to the majority of the U. S. population and that cost this group of women thousands of dollars yearly.

In addition, corporate theft costs all of us *billions* of dollars every year. The annual cost of corporate theft is between $114 and $331 billion a year (Barlow 1984, 280). Consumer fraud and deceptive practices alone cost $21 billion a year, and securities theft and fraud cost approximately $4 billion yearly (ibid., 281). Just one fraud—such as the Equity Funding fraud, which cost policyholders, stockholders, and other insurance firms almost $3 billion (Blundell 1976)—costs the public more than all the street thefts in the United States for one year (Douglas and Johnson 1978, 151). Pricefixing, costing approximately $45 billion a year, however, is the most damaging form of corporate theft (McCaghy 1976, 205).

Antitrust laws are supposed to hinder corporations from colluding to fix prices by ensuring that competition keeps prices as low as possible. Profits over and above those that would be made in an efficient competitive industry are illegal. Nevertheless, the volume of *illegal* profits is, as the figure above indicates, staggering, as is the number of firms involved in pricefixing. For example, between 1963 and 1972, companies producing the following commodities were found guilty of securing illegal excessive profits through pricefixing:

steel wheels, pipe flanges and rings, bed springs, metal shelving, steel castings, self-locking nuts, liquified petroleum gas delivery, refuse collection, linoleum installation, swimsuits, structural steel, carbon steel, baking flour, fertilizer, welding electrodes, ceiling materials, hydraulic hose, beer, gasoline, asphalt, milk, matches, drill bushings, linen supplies, school construction, plumbing fixtures, dairy products, fuel oil, gasoline, plumbing contracting, bread, auto repair, athletic equipment, maple floors, ready-mix concrete, industrial chemicals, vending machines, snack foods, autobody repair, shoes, overhead garage doors, automobile glass replacement parts, and meat (Hay and Kelly 1974). A "conspiracy among competitors" is most likely to occur and thrive when few companies are involved, particularly when fewer than four companies control 50 percent of the market, and when the product is homogeneous (ibid., 26-27). A prime example, which fulfills all of these conditions, is the Heavy Electrical Equipment case, where twenty-nine major companies (such as General Electric and Westinghouse) conspired to fix prices primarily on government contracts, thereby avoiding competition and acquiring large illegal profits. General Electric, for example, made at least $50 million excess, by charging as high as 446 percent on some contracts (Pearce 1976, 78). Westinghouse overcharged the Navy 500 percent on another contract (Green et al. 1972, 155). Overall, the cost to city, state, federal, and private purchasers of electrical equipment was $1.75 billion a year for seven years (Hills 1971, 162). To bring this one price-fixing case into perspective, Gilbert Geis (1978, 281) argues that this "conspiracy alone involved theft from the American people of more money than was stolen in all the country's robberies, burglaries, and larcenies during the years in which the price fixing occurred."

Corporate Crime Kills, Injures, and Steals Worldwide

Not all corporations are equally guilty of this vast corporate violence and theft. In fact, the largest corporations (transnationals) are the worst offenders, as Marshall Clinard and Peter Yeager (1980) found in the most comprehensive study to date on corporate crime. They analyzed administrative, civil, and criminal actions either initiated or completed by twenty-five federal agencies

> against the 447 largest publicly owned manufacturing (Fortune 500) corporations in the United States during 1975 and 1976. In addition, a more limited study was made of the 105 largest wholesale, retail, and service corporations, for a total sample of 582 corporations. [ibid., 110]

Since Clinard and Yeager restricted themselves to *actions initiated* against corporations for violations (roughly equivalent to arrests or prosecutions) and *actions completed* (equivalent to convictions), they were able to uncover only "the tip of the iceberg of total violations" (ibid., 111). Even so, their study does provide "an index of illegal behavior by the large corporations" (ibid.). What did they find?

> Manufacturing corporations were divided on the basis of annual sales into 30.5 percent small ($300-499 million), 27.2 percent medium ($500-999 million), and 42.3 percent large ($1 billion or more). Small corporations accounted for only one-tenth of the violations, medium-sized for one-fifth, but large corporations for almost three-fourths of all violations, nearly twice their expected percentage. Large corporations, moreover, accounted for 72.1 percent of the serious and 62.8 percent of the moderately serious violations [ibid., 119]

Violations were concentrated in certain industries; "the oil, pharmaceutical, and motor vehicle industries were the most likely to violate the law" (ibid.). As Box (1983, 76) points out, this means that some of those corporations dominating the world capitalist system are the worst offenders; "of the fifteen largest corporations in the world in 1978, three were car manufacturers, eight were oil companies, and one was chemicals." As would be expected, victims of the most serious criminality are not merely the domestic powerless, but the powerless worldwide. In short, corporate crime is transnational.

Corporations began to spread their operations outside the United States on a large scale in the 1950s, 1960s and 1970s. Concentrated primarily in the Third World countries of Asia, Africa and Latin America, transnational corporate investments increased from $5.7 billion in 1950 to $28.5 billion in 1974 (Edwards et al. 1978, 478). By 1978 transnationals exported capital worth $50 billion and imported income up to $132 billion, while reinvesting $171 billion abroad (U.S. Foreign Policy 1980, 7).

The transnational character of U.S. business has resulted in serious corporate crime—from bribery and corruption to exporting hazardous products and working conditions to the Third World, thus devastating the powerless in these countries. From 1969 to 1975, for example, Lockheed Corporation, to secure sales contracts, spent $202 million to bribe government officials in nine different countries: Indonesia, the Philippines, Japan, Turkey, Saudi Arabia, France, Germany, Italy and the Netherlands (Simon and Eitzen 1982, 152). In Indonesia, Lockheed, aided by the CIA, bribed several officials; in Saudi Arabia, $106 million went to one individual, the head of the Arab world's first transnational conglomerate, Adnan N. Khashoggi; and in Japan, Lockheed provided about $7 million to Yoshio Kodama, a known right-wing extremist and convicted war criminal (ibid., 152–153). Most of the payments to government officials in Indonesia, Saudi Arabia, and the Philippines were made to secure the purchase of Lockheed military aircraft (Jacoby et al. 1977, 116). Other examples abound. In 1976, Boeing disclosed that since 1970 it had paid nearly $70 million in "commissions" to foreign representatives to help sell its aircraft and that "in four of five instances" those commissions went to government employees (ibid., 117). In fact, in that same year, bribery scandals involving U. S.-based transnationals, such as United Brands, Northrop Aviation, Phillips Petroleum, Exxon, Gulf Oil, and Mobil Oil, indicated that bribery was most likely commonplace (Simon and Eitzen 1982, 154).

The case of United Brands provides a good example of how transnational corporate crime works. In 1974 Honduras, Costa Rica, and Panama imposed a $1 tax on every forty-pound box of bananas. Since these three countries supplied United Brands with more than half of their bananas, United Brands stood to lose close to $20 million in extra taxes. A meeting was arranged between Abraham Bennaton Ramos, the Honduras economics minister, and Harvey Johnson, vice-president of United Brands. In the meeting Ramos intimated that the banana tax might be reduced if he were paid $5 million. This was considered too much, so in a later meeting the two agreed to $2.5 million. United Brand's founder, Eli Black, approved the payoff, and $1,250,000 was transfered to a numbered Swiss bank account opened by Ramos. This case became known only when Black jumped forty-four floors from the Pan Am building in New York, and the Securities and Exchange Commission decided to investigate (Braithwaite 1979b, 129).

While bribery and corruption are profitable for transnationals and the political elites in Third World countries, they devastate the powerless in these countries. As Braithwaite (ibid., 126) argues, transnational bribery is one of the most pernicious crimes today because of its inegalitarian consequences.

> When a government official in a Third World country recommends (under the influence of a bribe) that his country purchase the more expensive but less adequate of two types of aircraft, then the extra millions of dollars will be found from the taxes sweated out of the country's impoverished citizens. For a mass consumer product, the million dollar bribe to the civil servant will be passed on in higher prices to the consuming public. While it is conceivable that bribes can be used to secure the sale of a better and cheaper product, the more general effect is to shift the balance of business away from the most efficient producer and in favour of the most corrupt producer. The whole purpose of business-government bribes is, after all, the inegalitarian purpose of

enticing governments to act against the public interest and in the interests of the transnational.

In addition, political corruption in a Third World country tends to
intensify itself. In other words, corruption in politics tends to select
out for public office those most skilled at corruption. Transnational
corruption/bribery is one of the most destructive crimes of our times
because "it involves robbing the poor to feed the rich, and brings into
political power rulers and administrators who in general will put self-
interest ahead of the public interest, and transnational corporation
interest ahead of national interest" (ibid.)

Transnational corporate crime, however, involves far more than
simply bribery and corruption. Transnationals are also involved in
"dumping" on the peoples of the Third World hazardous products
banned or not approved for sale in the United States. Businessmen in
U.S.-based transnationals sell to Third World nations "shiploads of
defective medical devices, lethal drugs, known carcinogens, toxic
pesticides, contaminated foods and other products found unfit for
American consumption" (Dowie 1979, 23). The racism and sexism
inherent in this dumping is clearly evident in the case of contracep-
tives. Depo-Provera, an injectable contraceptive that "works" for three
to six months, was banned for sale and testing in the United States
because of its very severe side effects. The Upjohn Company, its
producer, eventually sold Depo-Provera in seventy countries, particularly in the Third World, where it was widely used in U. S.-sponsored
population control programs (ibid.). Braithwaite (1984, 258) wrote
that throughout "Central America one can walk into a pharmacy and
purchase Depo-Provera without a prescription."

Above I discussed the effects of the Dalkon Shield domestically. A.
H. Robins eventually dumped approximately 1.71 million Dalkon
Shields in forty Third World countries, possibily killing thousands of
women (Mintz 1985, 21). Moreover, the U. S. government assisted
Robins' assault on Third World women, as the Agency for Interna-
tional Development bought more than 697,000 shields for use in the
Third World (Mintz 1986, 2).

> The staggering thing about this has been the involvement of the U. S.
> government's Office of Population with AID (Agency for International
> Development). AID purchased the contraceptive device at discount rates
> for "assistance" to developing countries after the product was banned in
> the U. S. Double standards for Third World consumers were even more
> remarkable when Robins sold AID *unsterilized* shields in bulk packages at
> 48 percent discount. AID justifies the discount Dalkon dump on the
> grounds of getting more contraception for the AID dollar (Braithwaite
> 1984, 258).

The shields went to countries in Africa, Asia, the Middle East, the Caribbean, and Central and South America where poor medical conditions make lethal complications even more likely (Mintz 1986, 2).

Various drugs, many lethal, are being dumped on the Third World. Lomotil, an effective antidiarrhea medicine, is sold in the United States only by prescription because just a slight overdose is fatal; however, Third World pharmacies sell it in packages proclaiming that it was used by astronauts and recommending it for children as young as twelve months old (Dowie 1979, 28). Winstol, a synthetic male hormone found to stunt growth in children, "is freely available in Brazil, where it is recommended as an appetite stimulant for children" (ibid.). Chloramphenicol, an antibiotic, which has been found to cause serious anemia that is 40 percent fatal, has, because of pressure applied to the Food and Drug Administration, been limited in the United States to use only in a few very serious cases. In Indonesia, Malaysia, Singapore, the Philippines, and Central America, however, the drug is recommended for minor infections and many times without any mention of anemia as a side effect (Silverman et al. 1982, ch. 2).

Examples of other products dumped on foreign markets are:

—An organic mercury fungicide prohibited in the U. S. market killed 400 Iraquis and put 5,000 others in the hospital (Michalowski 1985, 339).

—A chemical pesticide—leptophos, never accepted for use in the United States by the Environmental Protection Agency, was distributed to over thirty other countries where it has killed both farmers and stock (ibid., 340).

—Several million units of children's sleepwear treated with the cancer-causing fire retardant, Tris, were distributed to foreign markets after being banned from sale in the United States by the Consumer Product Safety Commission (ibid.).

—Nearly a half million baby pacifiers removed from the U. S. market by CPSC after a number of choking deaths were linked to their design have now been dumped worldwide (ibid.).

—DDT, a pesticide banned in the United States, is being sold particularly in Central and South America, only to come back home on imported food like bananas and coffee (Asinoff 1985, 3).

In addition to bribery, coruption, and dumping, transnationals have relocated dangerous working conditions to other countries. A prime example is the Bhopal, India disaster at Union Carbide. In Bhopal, Union Carbide produced a very dangerous chemical—

methyl isocyanate (used in manufacturing other chemicals that have been found seriously to contaminate groundwater)—that, after leaking from an underground storage tank, killed over 2,500 people and left thousands blind and disabled (ibid., 3). Transnationals seek out areas of the world where pollution controls and worker safety restrictions are minimal.

—Pesticide poisoning has reached epidemic proportions in developing countries—an estimated 22,000 people die each year, according to the Oxford Committee on Famine Relief.
—In India, workers at an asbestos-cement plant designed by the Manville Corporation were exposed daily to hazardous asbestos material and protected by only the most rudimentary safeguards. Outside the factory, children played in discarded piles of asbestos.
—In Indonesia, at a Union Carbide battery plant outside Jakarta, health and safety provisions were reportedly so poor that at one point more than half the workforce of 750 were diagnosed as having kidney disease linked to mercury exposure.
—In Brazil, in the factory town of Vila Parisi, known as "the valley of death," residents have a life expectancy of only thirty years—half the national average—because of the smothering air pollution (ibid.).

Undeniably, *both domestically and internationally*, the transnationals are the worst of all criminals and worldwide their victims are primarily the powerless.

Toward a Socialist Feminist Explanation

To explain why corporate crime occurs we need to understand the interaction of capitalism and patriarchy, specifically, the obstacles to profit-making and the patriarchal nature of the corporation.

The Obstacles to Profit-Making

First, corporations in a capitalist economy exist to make a profit, specifically through expanding capital. This is not a matter of greed on the part of individual capitalists, but on the other hand, the pressure to make profits is both *created* and *enforced* by the competitive structure of the capitalist mode of production. Consequently, if a corporation does not continually reinvest its capital and, therefore, expand and grow, it will be "eaten up" by those who do. This *pressure for profits* compels many corporate executives to engage in both domestic and transnational corporate crime.

In the pursuit of profits (also referred to as the process of capital accumulation) the corporation must overcome obstacles to succeed at profit-making. It is the existence of these obstacles (which are inherent in the accumulation process) and the way corporations attempt to overcome them that lead to much of corporate crime today. While these obstacles are numerous, three are of prime importance—minimizing costs, creating demand, and minimizing competition—will be analyzed to show the inherent relationship of corporate crime to the capitalist mode of production.

The bottom line in profit-making is the production of surplus value. Surplus value is the extra amount workers spend in production after they have produced enough output to cover their wage. For example, suppose a worker works an eight-hour day; however, in only five hours he or she produces enough output so that when it is sold, it equals in value his/her wage. The value of the output produced during the remaining three hours is surplus value and goes to the corporation. Profits, therefore, come from free labor performed by workers.

Since profits are based on surplus value, corporations potentially can increase profits by keeping costs down. The lower the cost of the factors of production—human labor power, tools, machinery and so on—the higher the potential profits. The effort of the corporation to minimize costs runs into obstacles that pave the way for corporate crime. For example, workers placed together in a work environment may recognize their common problems and organize into unions. Organizing puts them in a much better position to demand higher wages, an obvious obstacle to profit-making. Historically, corporations have responded to this obstacle (as noted above) by suborning violence and hiring organized crime figures to harass labor leaders. In addition, many corporations protect their profits by minimizing the costs of worker, consumer, and environmental safety. Maintaining safe working conditions, producing safe products, and controlling pollution cost money, eat into profits, and therefore hinder investment. The inherent need to minimize costs is not only essential for profit-making, but it also helps to create the conditions for the sort of corporate crimes discussed earlier: unsafe working conditions, unsafe products, environmental pollution, subminimum wages, and such transnational corporate crimes as dumping unsafe products and moving unsafe working conditions to a more "favorable" environment.

The second obstacle conducive to corporate crime, also related to profit-making, is creating demand. A corporation cannot make a profit unless it sells what it produces. Corporations push products onto the market and attempt to sell them as fast as possible. The need to create demand is conducive to corporate deception in marketing, particularly when demand for the product is "elastic and consequently fickle" (Box 1983, 36). Under such conditions, many corporations may overcome this obstacle by engaging in consumer fraud, false advertising, and other deceptive practices.

Finally, competitors may interfere with a corporation's ability to make profits and therefore invest by creating a threat to new and expanding markets (ibid.). New and expanding opportunities for investments are highly important to corporations, for that is where future, and higher profits, will be found. Profits depend upon the continuing pursuit of capital. Consequently, some corporations engage in bribery and corruption, for example, to obtain all or a share of those markets. Moreover, corporations must always be aware of more efficient competitors who threaten profits. Some corporations may, therefore, engage in such acts as price-fixing to "squeeze out" threatening competitors (ibid.).

In sum, the inherent aspects of the accumulation process, and the obstacles a corporation must overcome to achieve its desired goal—profit-making and continued investment—makes a corporation inherently criminogenic.

The Patriarchal Corporation

There is more to the picture than profit-making, however. It would be wrong to so depersonalize corporations as to hide the fact that they are created and maintained by real people who are active, conscious human beings. It is *individuals* pursuing profits who act for the corporation. Therefore, it is important to understand both who it is that has decision-making power in corporations and how they get it. The fact that *males* control the activities of management is important for understanding corporate crime.

As more and more women enter the paid labor market, including the corporation, they find that it is organized not only for the benefit of the capitalist mode of production, and, therefore, the capitalist class, but for men as well. In other words, patriarchy continues to operate within the labor market, especially in the corporate structure. Thus, the corporation is organized not only to make profits, but also to guarantee that men receive the largest share of material benefits, by exploiting women's labor power, and these related facts are directly connected to corporate crime.

First, women are very unlikely to become managers and executives in corporations. In 1981, for example, women made up only 2 percent of all corporate directors and 6 percent of all managers (Stallard et al. 1983, 18).

Second, those women who do become managers are segregated

into lower status managerial positions. In corporations, women are concentrated in staff areas such as personnel, research, affirmative action, and equal employment that do not lead to decision-making positions within the corporation. Also, these staff positions are often merely recommending bodies, where "*women do the work* to find out what is needed—make recommendations, and then *men decide* what is to be done with regard to these recommendations" (Sokoloff 1980, 243). This sex segregation of managerial positions within a corporation maintains patriarchy, since women work not only for capital but also for men. Moreover, women work for capital and men

> at lower wages, with fewer resources, and with less power than male managers, thus allowing men the benefits of money, status, power, resources, and specialization in decision-making control and order— without directly competing with other male managers for their privileged positions. [ibid.]

In short, the sexual division of labor, reproduced within the corporation today, places men in the positions of *power* where corporate crimes originate.

An important mechanism both for maintaining the sexual division of labor and understanding corporate crime is the *old boy network*. This mechanism is basically a sponsorship system that recruits junior male executives into the upper echelons of the managerial sectors of a corporation. Males recruit those who share norms, attitudes, values, and standards of behavior. Those junior male executives who make decisions in the interest of the organization are guaranteed career promotion. The patriarchal relations of senior executives over junior ones establishes "the allegiance of the former to the latter" (ibid., 240). In other words, if they do what they are supposed to do, they will be rewarded with wealth, power, and dominance over junior male workers and all women (ibid.). By keeping the business running as usual— that is, making profits—they will eventually be rewarded not only with money, but also power over other males and women.

The junior male executive, hoping to make it to the top, must learn what is right and what is wrong from his sponsor. Part of what he learns is to compromise personal principles to move up the ladder. In fact, junior male executives learn that they must, in many instances, sacrifice their personal ethics simply for the company to remain in business. As one study completed by the American Management Association concluded, "about 70 percent of the businessmen . . . admit they have been expected, frequently or on occasion, to compromise personal principles in order to conform either to organizational standards or to standards established by their corporate superiors" (cited in Simon 1981, 352). A study by Edward Gross (1978) sheds some light on this conclusion. He analyzed a large body of research on corporate mobility to discern what qualities corporate positions demand and what sort of young executives are most likely to be promoted. He found that those men who get promoted to the top of the corporation are ambitious, shrewd, and nearly amoral. Their ambition, however, is not merely personal, as they discover that their own goals are best pursued by assisting the corporation attain its goal—namely, profit-making. As Gross (ibid., 71) states, these men "believe in the organization, they want it to attain its goals, they profit personally from such goal attainment. So they will try hard to help the organization attain those goals." However, the patriarchal promotion system within the corporation promotes not merely men who strongly identify with the goals of the corporation, but also, as Gross found, those men who have the personal characteristics necessary to commit corporate crime if needed. If the corporation

> must engage in illegal activities to attain its goals, men with a nondemanding moral code will have the least compunctions about engaging in such behavior. Not only that, as men of power, pillars of the community, they are most likely to believe that they can get away with it without getting caught. [ibid.]

Those males with a nondemanding moral code are more likely to be promoted and reach the top, for this characteristic frees the individual to engage in corporate crime, and his code is reinforced by success itself. Corporate crime then is the result of the interaction of capitalism and patriarchy. Corporate executives face the problem of both the obstacles to profit-making and, therefore, the "pressure for profits," as well as promotion in the patriarchal system. Obviously these problems are many times solved by legal means, but when legal means will not work, both forms of "pressure" push these individuals toward illegal options. Male executives learn certain qualities to help guarantee not only their own, but the corporation's, success. Corporate crime assists the organization, as well as upwardly mobile male executives, reach their goal. As the corporate executives in the heavy electrical equipment case (discussed above) made clear, their criminal behavior was the result of both the pressure for profits and the pressure to get ahead in the patriarchal corporate system.

> We did feel that this was the only way to reach part of our goal, as managers . . . We couldn't accomplish a greater percent of net profit without getting together with competitors. Part of the pressure was the desire to get ahead and the desire to have the good will of the man above you. He had only to get the approval of the man above *him* to replace you, and if you wouldn't cooperate he could find lots of faults to use to get you out. [cited in Simon 1981, 352]

Corporate crime may become an integral part of the job, an "established way of life" (Geis and Meier 1977, 123). Once it becomes a "duty" to the corporation, refusal to engage in it, can result in sanctions from superiors (ibid., 124). As a report to the Securities and Exchange Commission concerning Lockheed's involvement in bribery noted, "employees who questioned foreign marketing practices damaged their claims for career advancement" (Clinard and Yeager 1980, 65). Corporate crime becomes a way for men to gain *power* within the corporation by maintaining profit margins.

Furthermore, the patriarchal character of middle-class masculinity helps us clarify this relationship between promotion, power, and corporate crime. In patriarchal capitalism, most men have an overwhelming commitment to work—it provides their masculine identity. However, within this common cultural context, masculinity differs across the class structure. As Tolson (1977, 81) points out,

> middle-class masculinity has a distinctive character which is alien to the working-class. There is a middle-class ideological world—the dominant, institutionalized code of behavior and belief. This code supports an image of masculinity which the working-class man sees all around him— in the mass media, the courts of law, the educational system, etc.—from which he cannot escape, and which in some respects (for it carries social status) he finds attractive. But it is an image which is, fundamentally, incongruent with his experience of the world. It is built around a notion of "professionalism"—untenable, by definition, by the wage laborer.

As Tolson (ibid., 81–82) goes on to argue, the "professional" differs from the "worker" in two important ways. First, the wage-laborer usually seeks work among a variety of jobs, while the professional seeks promotion. Highly committed to the future, the professional cultivates a particular expertise, and maintains an inner struggle to achieve. "The personal office, the telephone, the name-plate on the door, signify how far a man has come, and how far there is still to go" (ibid., 82). Second, the "professional ideal" carries with it a sense of moral justification clearly absent from the world of wage labor. The "career" is a long-term commitment and, therefore, requires a man's undivided identification and a sense of "duty." "The discipline of middle-class work is not the impersonal discipline of factory production, but *self*-discipline, an internalized desire to work" (ibid., 82). This desire is sustained by a man's faith in a higher authority, "the corporation."

A corporate executive's masculinity, then, is centered around a struggle for success, reward, and recognition in the corporation and community. The corporate executive sees working life as "a series of stages, leading finally to recognition by the community of individual achievement" (ibid., 83). This image of work, rooted materially in the corporate executive's gender/class position and rarely open to working class men, helps to create the conditions for corporate crime. Devotion to achievement and success, as measured by promotion, brings about the "need" to engage in such crime.

Consequently, the patriarchal system within the corporation creates a "masculine ethic" among the *men* at the top that reflects their patriarchal power. The masculine ethic specifies the traits men must assume to "make it" in the capitalist and patriarchal world of the corporation. These traits include not only the "nondemanding moral code" identified by Gross and the struggle for success, reward, and recognition identified by Tolson, but also "a tough-minded approach to problems" and "a capacity to set aside personal, emotional considerations in the interests of task accomplishments" (Kanter 1977, 22). Moreover, the gender role socialization of males reflects simultaneously the dominant values of capital and the masculine ethic in the corporate board room. Men are taught to be competitive, rationalistic, decisive, and aggressive—all traits that make it easier for male executives to commit corporate crimes. By setting aside "emotional considerations in the interest of task accomplishment," corporate executives are not only better prepared to handle the problems of profit-making, but also less inclined to question the theft and violence perpetrated on workers, women, consumers, and the powerless in other societies. "Tough decisions," as we have seen, often involve making people suffer. Not everyone can make "necessary" decisions that simultaneously inflict pain upon others. The patriarchal process in the corporation ensures that those who reach the top will be unemotional enough to make those "tough decisions." As Pleck and Sawyer (1974, 125) make clear, "Business executives succeed on their ability to make decisions that promote the interest of the corporation. Their masculine need to get ahead is validated by such measures as profits, prestige, and power."

The "old boy network" and the "masculine ethic" create the conditions for patriarchal control in the corporation while also, in interaction with "pressure for profits," setting the stage for corporate crime. Male executives who reach the top of the corporation are in a position of non-accountable and unconstrained power and also "in a high state of preparedness to commit corporate crime should they perceive it as being necessary 'for the good of the company' " (Box 1983, 41). Choosing corporate profit over people is made easier by a patriarchal system that demands emotional insensitivity in men. A male's socialized drive for interpersonal dominance, the "psychic engine" for patriarchal capitalism, facilitates corporate crime. In short, economically powerful males commit the most serious forms of criminality. Patriarchal capitalism makes crime necessary for corporate executives and determines that those executives will be male. Due to their position in patriarchal capitalism, their "field of possibilities" is narrowed to those behaviors that facilitate capital accumulation and patriarchal dominance in the corporation. The necessity to "get to the top" and maintain profit margins often entails illegal and socially harmful behavior. Their age and class isolate them from street forms of criminality; their gender reduces the likelihood that their crimes will be nonviolent; their position in the corporate board room insures that their deviance will be collective rather than individual and isolated. In short, it is the corporate executive's class, gender and age, in combination with the "pressure" for profits and patriarchal control, that leads to corporate crime. Corporate crime is simply a mechanism by which male executives maintain *dominance and control* over not only the working class (continued capital accumulation) but also women (patriarchy).

Keeping It All Hidden

The state, through a variety of mechanisms, effectively hides corporate crime from public view. Since the vast majority of these crimes fall under administrative or regulatory law and "enforced" by regulatory agencies such as the Occupational Safety and Health Administration (OSHA), the Food and Drug Administration (FDA), the Securities and Exchange Commission (SEC), the Consumer Product Safety Commission (CPSC), and the Environmental Protection Agency (EPA), most members of this society are unaware of the extent and seriousness of corporate crime. How is it, that this "regulatory agency system" effectively keeps corporate crime out of sight?

First, corporations enjoy the special advantage of being able to help determine which of their harmful acts will be criminalized and, therefore, regulated by the state. The Comprehensive Drug Abuse, Prevention, and Control Act of 1970 is a case in point. As Graham (1972) points out in his analysis, this act, intended to control the distribution and use of "dangerous" drugs, ended up, after considerable lobbying by the pharmaceutical industry, concentrating exclusively on drugs imported and/or produced easily by individuals (heroin, marijuana, and LSD). The dangerous drugs produced by pharmaceutical manufacturers (amphetamines and tranquilizers like Valium and Librium) were left untouched, even though testimony at congressional hearings indicated their use was more widespread, incapacitating, dangerous, and socially disrupting than narcotic use. Billions of amphetamines and tranquilizers are produced by the pharmaceutical industry every year, and usually consumed by housewives, businessmen, students, physicians, truck drivers, and athletes. These groups form a large and profitable market for the pharmaceutical industry. For example, Hoffman-LaRoche, the producers and distributors of Valium and Librium, reaped, in the 1960s, $40 million in profit just from those drugs alone (ibid., 22). Federal control of the distribution and use of these drugs may therefore represent a threat to profit-making. Not surprisingly, Hoffman-LaRoche "paid a Washington law firm three times the annual budget of the Senate sub-committee staff to assure that their drugs would remain uncontrolled" (ibid.). The end result was a bill that declared an all-out war on those drugs that are *not* a source of corporate profit and ignored all testimony and facts contrary to the drug industry's view. As Senator Eagleton stated: "when the chips were down, the power of the drug companies was simply more compelling than any appeal to the public welfare" (ibid., 53).

Others (see in particular Chambliss 1981; Chambliss and Seidman 1982; Box 1983) have provided numerous contemporary examples of how corporations are able significantly to influence the "criminalization of conduct." However, the ability of the powerful to secure their own laws is not new. Kolko (1965), for example, has shown that, far from opposing legislation to regulate the railroads, the railroad companies were, in the late 1800s and early 1900s, among its strongest supporters. Federal regulation helped the railroads solve problems they could not solve on their own, and the railroads determined basically what the controls would be. Similarly, when workmen's compensation laws emerged in the United States, big business initially opposed them but could not stop their passage. However, as Currie (1971, 140) notes, business eventually "discovered that direct compensation to injured employees was less cumbersome and not significantly more costly than having to litigate over and over again individual cases." Business therefore came to support workmen's compensation, not only because of its interest in rationalization and predictability, but also because of profitability. Business, in fact, was able to help write the kind of legislation they wanted.

> It was imperative that the new system be in fact as actuarially predictable as business demanded; it was important that the costs of the program be fair and equal in their impact upon particular industries, so that no competitive advantage or disadvantage flowed from the scheme . . . In exchange for certainty of recovery by the worker, the companies were prepared to demand certainty and predictability of loss—that is, limitation of recovery. The jury's caprice had to be dispensed with. In short, when workmen's compensation became law, or a solution to the industrial accident problem, it did so on terms acceptable to industry. [Friedman and Ladinsky 1967, 69].

As a final example, the Sherman Antitrust Act of 1890 originated at a time when farmers, faced with falling prices, rising costs, increased indebtness, and massive foreclosures, began to organize against rising monopolies, which they blamed for their problems. The anti-monopolistic populist movement of the time appeared to this rising business class as a threat to its political and economic dominance. By failing to respond to the demands of the agrarian movement, the powerful would have jeopardized their political-economic control. Consequently, the powerful supported the anti-monopoly, anti-big business Sherman Antitrust Act. However, as McCormick (1979, 410) has shown, "the Sherman Antitrust Act was deliberately constructed to *protect*, rather than interfere with, elite interests." The Sherman Act was the weakest of all the antitrust bills offered in Congress; a weak, remedial measure, it was "quite impotent as a regulatory instrument," and it existed solely "to serve as a token declaration of antimonopolism" (ibid.). As a result, the act turned out to be more suitable for regulating labor organizations and small businesses, than big business, while it simultaneously deflected the potentially disruptive power of the populist movement, thereby protecting and preserving patriarchal capitalism (ibid., 411).

The powerful, as has been shown, enjoy the opportunity to determine which of their acts will be defined as criminal in the first place. This does not mean, however, that the "criminalization of conduct" totally reflects the powerful's interests. Rather, the law reflects basic contradictions in the social structure and the attempts by state managers to deal with conflicts engendered by those contradictions. Yet, since the powerful hold an upper hand in the legislative process (for example, through lobbying) the shape and content of the law reflect their interests (Chambliss 1981).

While corporations have the capability of influencing significantly which of their behaviors will be defined as corporate crime in the first place, they also enjoy a special relationship with those who are supposed to police their activities. As Michael Parenti (1983, 296) points out, it is often difficult to tell the regulators from the regulated.

> More than half the appointees to regulatory jobs are persons who previously were employed by the "regulated" industry . . . Administrators who have supervised such things as water-development, labor, nuclear-energy, consumer-protection, and food and drug relations have had a history of previously serving as lobbyists, lawyers, and managers for the business firms they were to regulate.

For example, many of the top appointees of Ann Gorsuch (former administrator of the EPA) were former lobbyists or spokespersons for the corporations regulated by the EPA (Smith 1982, 233). Rita Lavelle, the EPA assistant administrator for solid wastes, came to the EPA from a public relations job with a company cited by EPA for violating its hazardous waste rules (ibid.). Moreover, many of the officials in regulatory agencies use their positions subsequently to obtain a high-paying position in a corporation they were charged with "regulating." A medical doctor, while employed by the FDA, prevented the recall of a synthetic antibiotic, despite evidence that it caused blood toxicity and even death. Soon after that, he resigned from the FDA and became vice president of the pharmaceutical firm that produced the drug (Parenti 1983, 294).

When workers demand investigations of their workplaces, regulatory agencies and industry often work together to curb the pressure. For example, the California OSHA office, pressured by electronics workers to investigate hazards in that industry, produced a "joint government-industry effort to quell the fears and outrage of industry at the prospect of having its hazards researched" (Baker and Woodrow 1984, 34). The study, by investigating only certain companies and obtaining no worker input, found only a few hazards and gave the industry a clean bill of health. After the study was over, its author "was promptly hired by a major electronics company in the Silicon Valley" (ibid.).

This close relationship between the "regulators and the regulated" provides ample opportunities for corruption. Parenti (1983, 296) states that officials in various agencies have received "illegal favors and gratuities from companies or have owned stock in firms under their jurisdiction, in violation of federal rules." A GAO study in fact found over *seventy-seven thousand* cases of fraud in federal agencies over a two-and-one-half-year period (ibid.).

Corporations, because of their close ties with agency officials, secured themselves immunity from criminal proceedings and, when "neccessary," have had officials unsympathetic to business practices replaced (Balkan et al. 1980, 177–78; Hills 1971, 176). As Fellmeth (1970, 247) found in his investigation of "The Regulatory-Industrial Complex," the existence "of permanent representatives of industry in Washington, a political advantage the general public does not possess, has helped cause the corporate acculturation of Washington agencies by the industries they supposedly regulate." Regulatory agencies many times refrain from formal proceedings against corporate crime because: (1) industry "entertains" agency personnel; (2) formal advisory groups, which are arranged by the agency but consist mainly of corporate representatives, advise against it; (3) lobbying efforts are successful; (4) personnel interchanges occur between corporations and agencies; and (5) corporations make political contributions to legislators able to influence agency appropriations or appointments (ibid., 247–52). Regarding the replacement of unsympathetic agency personnel, a Review Panel on New Drug Regulation found in 1977 that lower-level officers of the FDA who made things difficult for industry were often shifted to less sensitive positions. As the Review Panel concluded;

FDA has been managed, during the period in question, by individuals who have made a conscious determination that the agency shall be cooperative with, rather than adversarial towards, the pharmaceutical industry. With that decision firmly made, management asserted control over a group of medical officers whose approach to industry was more adversarial in a manner which could aptly be described as "political hardball." The dissenters were effectively suppressed, primarily by resorting to involuntary transfers. Moreover, management's execution of this policy was often untruthful, usually unkind, sometimes unlawful, and consistently unprofessional. [cited in Braithwaite 1984, 301]

In addition to exerting tremendous influence on the criminalization process, corporations also enjoy a close, warm relationship with their regulators, and therefore, in many instances, are immune from criminal proceedings. This, then, is the second mechanism that helps to keep corporate crime concealed.

Third, each regulatory agency has policing divisions known as "divisions of enforcement" that are supposed to investigate all violations that fall within the jurisdiction of their agency. However, mechanisms involved in this process result in corporations *not* being subject to high levels of surveillance and thus keep their crimes well hidden. First, in many instances, the divisions of enforcement *announce* their inspections months before they enter, for example, a factory. Second, many corporations can deny regulatory agencies like OSHA entrance to their property for inspection. Third, regulatory agencies are highly understaffed and underfunded, even compared to the law enforcement apparatus of the criminal justice system. For example, the SEC and the CPSC have total enforcement budgets of less than $20 million (Clinard and Yeager 1980, 96). The 1,581 compliance safety and health officers employed by OSHA can only inspect roughly 2 percent of the 2.5 million businesses covered by OSHA every year (Reiman 1984, 57). The Department of Labor's *Interim Report to Congress on Occupational Diseases* stated that in 1980, "one in every four workers in the U.S. is potentially exposed to an OSHA-regulated health hazard— approximately 25 million workers. Only 500,000 workers are in worksites inspected by OSHA health inspectors each year" (cited in ibid., 57). Fourth, corporations can further reduce the likelihood of surveillance "by simply shifting resources, records, money, and personnel between national boundaries thus rendering their behavior virtually disentangleable even to the most persistent regulatory agency" (Box 1983, 58).

For all these reasons, it is difficult for enforcement divisions to uncover corporate violations of the law, and this also helps to keep corporate crime well hidden. This does not mean that violations of the law are never found, but even when they are, very few corporations are held accountable for their violations, in part because of the adjudication process within regulatory agencies. This aspect of the regulatory agency system constitutes the fourth mechanism for keeping corporate crime invisible. When an agency receives notice of a violation from its enforcement division, a hearing *may be* held within the agency. If this hearing finds a violation, then a "warning"—the agency's first step to bring about compliance—*may be* issued. This warning *may* include "orders" to correct an injury (make refunds, replacements, or reimbursements, clean up pollution, reinstate discharged employee, and so forth). Also, certain agencies such as the Traffic Safety Administration, the Consumer Product Safety Commission, and the Food and Drug Administration, may implement "recalls." However, as Ralph Nader's report on disease and injury on the job found, giving corporations the opportunity to voluntarily comply with a warning is not much of a deterrent.

> Employers have little incentive to take any initiative to root out unsafe work conditions and practices. Instead, they can subject their employees to all kinds of hazards, to be corrected only if discovered by inspectors— if and when the plant is visited. [Page and O'Brien 1973, 74]

If the corporation continues to violate the law, an "injunction to cease and desist" *may be* issued. If this path is followed, the corporation must then sign a "consent agreement," agreeing to stop violating the law, even without admitting guilt. Since the chance of inspection is so low, there is not much incentive for compliance; hence, approximately 80 percent of corporate violations are "settled" by these consent agreements (Clinard and Yeager 1980, 87).

Some regulatory agencies, however, very seldom involve themselves in adjudicatory proceedings of any kind. For example, it was found that the FTC "rarely conducted hearings, was reluctant to use its tools of enforcement, and created long delays while offenders reaped profits of billions of dollars from illegal practices" (Balkan et al. 1980, 87). It took the FTC twelve years to get the producers of Geritol to stop claiming that their product fights something called "tired blood" (Parenti 1983, 295). Some companies have been able to delay action for more than twenty years (ibid., Balkan et al., 1980, 178). In 1976, three employees of the EPA resigned because that agency continued to avoid regulating possible cancer-causing chemicals, and other dangerous substances, in the air, food supply, drinking water, and waterways (Reiman 1984, 65). That same year, the Senate Subcommittee on Administrative Practices and Procedures issued a report very critical of EPA's regulation of chemical pesticides. As the chair of that subcommittee stated,

> I find it incredible that a regulatory agency charged with safeguarding the public health and the environment would be so sluggish to recognize

and react to so many warnings over the past 5 years. The EPA was warned and certainly should have known that listing data, submitted by industry as long as 25 years ago, should not be accepted at face value in the re-registration of thousands of pesticide products presently being used on our farms and in our homes. But EPA by and large ignored these warnings. [cited in ibid., 65].

The FDA has been severely indicted by Ralph Nader for being involved in a conspiracy with the food industry not only to defraud consumers, but also, to endanger their health (Balkan et al., 1980, 178). The FDA was also denounced for concentrating its investigations on "small-time quacks" while ignoring powerful food corporations (ibid.). For instance, although the FDA is authorized to stop transnationals from exporting an unapproved or disapproved product (drug dumping), it seldom does so (Silverman 1982, 110).

If a corporation continues to violate the law, the case *may be* referred to the Justice Department for criminal prosecution. The Justice Department then reviews the case and decides whether or not to prosecute, or to hold the corporation in civil contempt for violating the consent agreement. Criminal prosecution is very rare, since it is difficult to prove "criminal intent." Corporate criminals can very easily plead that they did not intend to defraud consumers or kill workers, but unfortunately, due to unpredictable circumstances, "matters went sour" (Box 1983, 59). Even if prosecuted, corporations and their employees are allowed to plead *nolo contendere*, which means that the corporation, while not disputing the charges, does not directly admit guilt. Of the convictions in antitrust cases from 1890 to 1969, 73 percent were by pleas of *nolo contendere* (McCormick 1977, 34). This is very important because this plea cannot be used as evidence in a civil suit for damages, and civil damages are potentially more severe than criminal penalties for corporate crimes (Coleman 1985, 167–68). Moreover, defendants using this plea receive lighter sentences because they help the court avoid costly litigation (McCormick 1977, 35).

The history of antitrust "enforcement" reveals how regulatory behavior maintains the invisibility of corporate crimes. Between 1890 and 1969 the government instituted 1,551 antitrust cases; the majority were handled as civil matters and only 46 percent were prosecuted as criminal cases, even though the type of antitrust behavior did not differ substantially among corporations (ibid.). Moreover, not until the 1961 Heavy Electrical conspiracy case (discussed above) were any businessmen actually imprisoned for violating the Sherman Antitrust Act of 1890; before that case, *all* of those sentenced to prison were *union and labor* defendants. As McCormick (ibid., 34) commented, "In view of the enforcement pattern outlined here, it is no wonder that the convicted defendants in the Electrical Conspiracy case expressed surprise and anger over their sentences, in spite of knowing the patent illegality of their behavior." Of the twenty-eight executives found guilty in the 1961 conspiracy trial, only seven went to prison, and none for more than thirty days (Geis 1967, 142). Things have improved very little since then. Between 1961 and 1975, for instance, over 700 corporate executives were convicted of violating the Anti-trust Act, yet only thirty-seven went to prison (Clinard and Yeager 1980, 278). In the Folding Carton conspiracy of 1976, the next most famous case after Heavy Electrical Equipment, only a little more than one-third of those convicted were sentenced to prison and the longest sentence was fifteen days (ibid., 281).

Overall, very few corporate executives go to prison. The most frequent sanction imposed for corporate crimes is a fine. However, these fines are ridiculous as a penalty. The Heavy Electrical Equipment case of 1961 and the 1976 Folding Carton case provide excellent examples, since both involved numerous corporate defendants and resulted in criminal fines. In the former, the two biggest losers, General Electric and Westinghouse, paid fines of $437,500 and $372,500 respectively. Each of the Folding Carton defendants was fined $50,000 (Ermann and Lundman 1982, 148). These figures seem large until they are calculated against the gross revenues of the individual corporations. Adjusting them as though they were fines imposed on an individual earning $15,000 annually shows how insignificant they are: so calculated, General Electric's fine becomes the equivalent of $1.45, while the fine imposed on Westinghouse is equivalent to $2.85, and the heaviest fine of all the Folding Carton conspirators is $1.80 (ibid.).

Moreover, this pattern applies to other types of corporate violations.

— Federal officials cited the Beryllium Corporation for safety violations and five "serious violations" for excess beryllium concentration in work place areas." Fine: $928. The corporation's net sales for 1970 were $61,400,000.
— On request from the Oil, Chemical and Automatic Workers Union, OSHA officials inspected the Mobil Oil plant at Paulsboro, New Jersey. Result: citations for 354 violations of the Occupational Health and Safety Act of 1970. Fine: $7,350 (about $20 a violation).
— In 1972, a fire and explosion at the same Mobil plant killed a worker. Fine: $1,215.
— In 1968, there were 24,845 violations recorded in Massachusetts, 28 prosecutions, and 12 fines. Average fine: $88.
— In 1980, OSHA found 128,760 violations, for which penalties

totaling $24,369,700 were proposed. Average penalty per violation: $189.26. (Reiman 1984, 58–59)

In short, the regulatory agency system operates so as to avoid stigmatizing and punishing corporate executives as criminals. Marginalized males and women find they face a terrifying criminal justice system determined to stigmatize them as criminals. Powerful males, on the other hand, enjoy a "justice system" which, while it may not be at their command, is clearly on their side. The state, with its "enforcement apparatus," accomplishes *two* objectives: (1) it effectively makes the least serious criminality and the least powerful people *visible as criminals*, while exaggerating their contribution to serious criminality, and (2) it keeps the most serious criminality and the most powerful criminals *invisible*.

6
Men, Power, and
Sexual Violence Against Women

Although public awareness of the criminal victimization of females by males has been growing over the last few years, it is still "the best kept secret." The majority of the U. S. population is unaware of the amount of sexual violence and exploitation that is directed toward females in this society. While stories of rape, wife-beating, the sexual abuse of children, and sexual harrassment are beginning to be commonplace in newspapers and the television evening news, the extent of these crimes is well hidden. This chapter explores the dimensions of one type of sexual violence, rape, considers why it occurs, and how the criminal justice system effectively keeps it largely concealed from public view.

The Prevalence and Fear of Rape

"Illegal" rape, or rape as defined by the state, is "unlawful sexual intercourse with a female person without her consent" (Perkins 1969, 152). By concentrating on consent, the state makes it imperative that the threat or actual use of physical violence by the offender be present to constitute proof that the victim did not consent. Consequently, the state definition of rape actually means, in practice, sexual intercourse obtained by the threat or actual use of physical violence. According to victimization surveys, this type of rape comprises less than one percent of the personal and household crimes and approximately 2.9 percent of all violent crimes (Schwendinger and Schwendinger 1981, 20). However, while it may be true that "illegal" rape occurs less often than other forms of interpersonal violence, and, therefore, clearly *most* men in the U. S. are not rapists, this does not mean that the number of rapes is small in this society. Allan Griswold Johnson (1980) recently analyzed victimization surveys to determine the overall probability that a female who was twelve years old in 1980 would be a victim of "illegal" rape sometime during her lifetime. Johnson (ibid., 145), excluding rape in marriage and assuming equal risk to all women, concluded that "20–30 percent of girls now twelve years old will suffer a violent sexual attack during the remainder of their lives." Moreover, Diana E. H. Russell's (1984, 51) random sample of 930 women in San Francisco revealed that there was a 26 percent probability that a woman in that city would be victimized by a completed rape sometime in her lifetime, and a 46 percent probability that she would become a victim of rape or attempted rape.

It must be kept in mind that the victimization surveys and Russell's sample only measured "illegal" rape. Yet even if we look only at "illegal" rape we can see that it victimizes many women every year. However, the "illegal" definition of rape is clearly inadequate, for it recognizes only *one* type of rape—sexual intercourse obtained through the threat or actual use of physical violence. It leaves out what I call "legal" rapes, or those that result from some intimidation or pressure other than the threat or actual use of *physical* force. One way "legal" rape occurs is when a female is coerced economically ("if you don't 'put out' you'll be fired") and her overt genuine consent is absent (see Box 1983, 122–27). This definition is both similar to and different from the "illegal" definition. It is similar in that absence of consent must exist; its difference lies in the concentration on economic, rather than physical, coercion. Moreover, the state definition of rape does not include *all* rapes that occur through the threat or actual use of physical violence. As I discuss further below, there are "tolerated illegal" rapes, such as violent wife-rapes, which many times are not included in the state definition of rape. In many states today the *violent* forcible rape of a wife is simply not considered rape (see the last section of this chapter). Consequently, while it is true that *most* men do not commit rape, if we add these "legal" and "tolerated illegal" rapes to the "illegal" ones, we see that rape occurs much more frequently in U. S. society than most people recognize.

As a result of the high incidence of even "illegal" rape in this society, women show a realistic fear of rape. Recently Mark Warr (1985) examined the fear of rape among urban women and found that women 35 years and younger fear rape more than any other offense, including murder, assault, and robbery. In addition, 42 percent of the women in his sample indicated that they have "avoided going out alone," while only 8 percent of the men indicated such a precaution; and whereas 9 percent of the men "avoided going out at night," 40 percent of women have done so (ibid., 248). Warr (1985, 242) concluded that "it is beyond question that rape is currently a central fear in the lives of a large proportion of women." And this fear helps to maintain women's dependence on men and, therefore, masculine control. As Dorie Klein (1982b, 211) argues, "All women are obliged to avoid public places at night, isolated areas, and conspicuous states of singlehood. Essentially women are under house arrest, their activities constrained by what is dismissed as a brutal fact of life." And as Weis and Borges (1973, 94) point out:

> The woman is constantly taught that she is both defenseless and responsible for the prevention of her victimization. She is encouraged to stay at home after dark. To avoid molestation, she is instructed not to spell out her first name on door bells and in telephone directories, but to use an initial to hide behind her father's or husband's last name. In so doing, she forfeits a symbol of her femininity and personhood. Rape operates as a social control mechanism to keep women in their "place" or put them there. The fear of rape, common to most women, socially controls them as it limits their ability to move about freely. As such, it establishes and maintains the woman in a position of subordination.

By establishing and maintaining women in a subordinate position, rape contributes to maintaining capitalism by reproducing a cheap reserve army of labor and to continuing patriarchy by insuring masculine dominance.

Patriarchal Capitalism and Rape

Certain aspects of patriarchal capitalism contribute to the prevalence of rape in U. S. society. As argued earlier in this book, patriarchal capitalism creates normative styles of feminine and masculine behavior that reproduce masculine dominance. The gender roles emerging from the position of men and women in the home and labor market give rise to the dichotomy of nurturance/nonviolence (feminine) and aggression/violence (masculine). Those socialized into these gender roles, both male and female, affirm masculine power, prestige, and dominance. Some have suggested that violence toward women can be traced to these socialized traits (Griffin 1971); rape, then, becomes an overconforming act rather than a deviant one (Russell 1975, 260). The rapist acts out, in extreme form, those qualities regarded as masculine; superiority, control, and conquest. Rape becomes simply an exaggeration of those traditional gender roles that encourage violence toward women as an act of aggression, dominance, and control.

Moreover, when these gender roles are combined with a culture that emphasizes violence in men, then we have the ingredients of a "rape-prone society." In chapter 3 we saw that the United States has the highest levels of violent crime in the industrialized world and that males overwhelmingly are the perpetrators. Peggy Sanday (1981), a social anthropologist, found that high rape rates have historically occurred in societies dominated by males and featuring male violence.

Looking at 186 tribal societies, she concluded that "rape-prone" societies were those where males dominated politically, economically, and ideologically and which glorified male violence (ibid.). "Rape free" societies, on the other hand, were characterized by relative sexual equality, the notion that the sexes are complementary, and a low level of interpersonal violence. Sanday's work helps us explain why the United States is a rape-prone society.

The degree of support in this society for *rape myths* suggests that this society condones rape. Martha Burt (1980) looked at rape myths (defined as prejudicial, stereotyped, or false beliefs about rape, rape victims, and rapists) and ascertained the amount of support they receive in U. S. society. Examples of rape myths Burt (1980, 223) included are:

> "Any healthy woman can successfully resist a rapist is she really wants to."
> "In the majority of rapes, the victim is promiscuous or has a bad reputation."
> "If a girl engages in necking or petting and she lets things get out of hand, it is her own fault."
> "Women who get raped while hitchhiking get what they deserve."

Burt (1980, 229) found in her research that over 50 percent of her sample (598 residents of Minnesota) agreed with these and/or other rape myths, and that the same number thought that 50 percent or more of reported rapes were reported as rape "because the woman was trying to get back at the man she was angry with or was trying to cover up an illegitimate pregnancy." Moreover, for those who believed in these rape myths, their rape attitudes were strongly connected to other deeply held and pervasive attitudes such as "sex role stereotyping, distrust of the opposite sex (adversarial sexual beliefs), and acceptance of interpersonal violence" (ibid.). In other words, masculine dominance, violence, and support for rape go hand in hand. The implications of Burt's research then is that the United States effectively maintains attitudes supportive of rape. Consequently, to understand rape in patriarchal capitalism we must first understand the patriarchal expectations of males and how this contributes to masculine dominance, violence, and a rape-supportive culture.

Additional aspects of patriarchal capitalism important for understanding rape are connected to masculine control over female sexuality and normative heterosexuality. Although support for rape myths is pervasive, Alison Jaggar (1983, 260–61) argues that rape is overtly condemned while covertly legitimized in patriarchal capitalism. It is condemned because it violates a woman's "honor," meaning either her virginity or her current or future sexual fidelity to a husband. At the same time that it condemns rape, however, patriarchal capitalism legitimizes it. Earlier chapters pointed out how women in this society, by reason of masculine control over female sexuality, are defined as sexual objects and through much of their lives evaluated in sexual terms. Only when she becomes older, and "male standards define her as no longer desirable does sexual interest in her fade" and she simply "sinks into invisibility" (ibid., 260). Accompanying the view that women are sex objects is the presumption that men have a special and overwhelming "urge" or "drive" toward heterosexual intercourse (ibid.). Males in patriarchal capitalism are expected not only to be sexual but to exhibit to other males their sexual prowess. A man who views women as sex objects rather than full human beings associates his masculinity with "how much he gets." Women come to be, to these men, justifiable objects of sexual exploitation. Thus, violence toward women often does not simply result in physical assaults. Men many times express their presumed right to use violence against women in sexual ways. The definition of women as sexual objects, and the perception of men as having a special "drive," are the necessary components for turning a violent situation into a *violent sexual situation*. Studies show that most rapists do not believe they have done anything wrong (Clark and Lewis 1977). Thus, some men see violent sexual situations as legitimate behavior—the culture of patriarchal capitalism tends to legitimize rape.

The exploitative conditions within patriarchal capitalist social formations specifically exacerbate these conditions. When people are encouraged to "objectify and exploit people as things," they may adopt an "amoral individualism," and some men in particular adopt "stereotypes of probable victims" *of violence*, such as "punk," "chump," "bitch," and "cunt" (Schwendinger and Schwendinger 1983, 204–5). This type of terminology clearly signifies the males' "amoral attitudes toward victims." In patriarchal capitalism this amoral exploitative individualism helps to intensify violence toward women. Stereotyping certain people as legitimate victims is a form of categorical devaluation in which people are treated as objects. They are accorded little value as human beings and are in many instances treated in exploitative ways (Schur 1984, 30–34).

In patriarchal capitalism, some men, in devaluing and objectifying women, deprive them of their personal autonomy. Rape represents the most extreme example of the exploitation of women as a devalued and dehumanized object. Although respect for women's "honor" is supposed to keep in check the male's special heterosexual "drive," stereotyping certain women as legitimate victims provides the excuse to disregard their "honor." Single and/or divorced women, prostitutes, women who frequent singles bars, hitchhikers, and black women are often viewed in this society as "common sexual property." Consequently, their "honor" may be violated. In fact the state, through the criminal justice system, condones this view by treating many of these women as "bad girls" and therefore not legitimate rape victims (see the last section in this chapter).

In addition, then, to the perception of women as sexual objects and the notion that men have a special "drive," an additional component necessary for turning a violent situation into a violent sexual situation is the patriarchal ideology of "honor." Rape, in patriarchal capitalism, is an act of violent sexual domination intended, in its social meaning, to devalue women. Thus, the choice of sexual assault is not accidental. The fact that a man frequently chooses to assault a woman by penetrating her with his penis rather than simply assaulting her with his fists, indicates that he is interested in inflicting a certain specific type of violence on her (Tong 1984, 117). The rapist is attacking a woman's pride and respect, her "honor." The rapist seeks to destroy those aspects of a woman's person that is her source of self-worth in patriarchal capitalism. Simply assaulting her would not accomplish what violating her "honor" does.

The evidence suggests that the rape is successful in producing the above result. A female rape victim is often considered to be "damaged goods" (Balkan et al. 1980, 236), one who has "allowed herself" to become not only "devalued," but also one who has now lost her "honor." Daniel Silverman and Sharon L. McCombie (1980, 175) report that lovers and husbands of rape victims, because they often cannot escape the thought that their lover or wife was "tainted" by the rapist, feel physical disgust when they approach their "unclean" wife or lover sexually.

And finally, the rapist uses sex as a violent attack on the integrity of the woman as a person. In a rape, what is normally understood as an act of affection becomes an act of hate. This act destroys the woman's integrity by denying the victim her own will to engage, or not to engage, in sexuality as she pleases. By prohibiting this freedom, the rapist creates conditions of dominance and subordination. The following account by a rapist illustrates this point.

> I tried to talk to this girl and she gave me some off-the-wall story. I chased her into a bathroom, and grabbed her and told her that if she screamed, I'd kill her. I had sex with her that lasted about five minutes. When I first attacked her I wasn't even turned on; I wanted to dominate her. When I saw her get scared and hurt, then I got turned on. I wanted her to feel like she's been drug through mud. I wanted her to feel a lot of pain and not enjoy none of it. The more pain she felt, the higher I felt. [cited in Beneke 1982, 74]

And as another rapist stated,

> Rape gave me the power to do what I wanted to do without feeling I had to please a partner or respond to a partner. I felt in control, dominant.

Rape was the ability to have sex without caring about the woman's response. I was totally dominant. [cited in Scully and Marolla 1985, 259]

Once again, however, it is important to point out that most men do not become rapists. On the contrary, *most* men in U. S. patriarchal capitalist society do *not* live out the scenario described here and many actively reject it. What I am pointing to is how patriarchal capitalism creates the conditions for rape to occur.

The patriarchal expectations of women in this society are also highly important for understanding rape. Many women learn in this culture to be passive, submissive, and dependent—all traits that contribute to the incidence of rape. Women are not taught to be assertive with men and *men know this*. They know that women are not taught how to fight, since physical violence is considered unladylike (Russell 1975, 269). Consequently, it is easy for men to use violence against women since they know that women will usually act passively. The social psychological processes at the victim's level then, and the assailant's interpretation of this, are both highly important for understanding rape. As one victim raped in a car by a man who offered her a ride stated,

I hated myself for not being able to take a stand in the situation. He wielded his power with such confidence, and there I was feeling absolutely helpless. I shouldn't have to feel small and less muscular and all that . . . But it's like once you're there, you become paralyzed with this feeling that he's a man, he's got muscles, and he knows about things like guns. [cited in Russell 1975, 268–69]

In a rape, men simply exploit what Germaine Greer (1975, 387) calls the "pathology of oppression." Many women are socialized not to fight back. Silence is *not* consent. Failure to resist is *not* consent. Rather, they are the direct result of the oppressed status of women, and the rape situation tends to intensify the pathology of oppression. Victims of rape often internalize their own victimization and develop a deep sense of guilt for the rape, viewing the whole thing as their own fault (Schwendinger and Schwendinger 1976). It is this internalization of the injury that makes rape doubly harmful to women, because what "men have done is to exploit and so intensify the pathology of oppression" (Greer 1975, 388).

In short, patriarchal capitalism maintains a culture supportive of rape. Thus, the existence of rape is structural at root. Very simply, males are in positions of power, while women are powerless. And as Lorenne Clark and Debra Lewis (1977, 176) state in their book *Rape: The Price of Coercive Sexuality*, "All unequal power relationships must, in the end, rely on the threat or reality of violence to maintain themselves." Rape is just one example of all the violence existing to help maintain the unequal power relations in patriarchal capitalist society. Moreover, by reason of the fear of rape, women do not have freedom of movement—only men do. Rape, by keeping women "in their place," serves the interests of both patriarchy (men) and capitalism (reproducing the labor force).

While the above helps us to comprehend why rape in general occurs in patriarchal capitalism, understanding the different types of rape in this society requires more thought. I turn now to an analysis of three common forms of rape, and how they are related to the position of men and women in the gender/class hierarchy.

"Illegal" Rape

Again, "illegal" rape constitutes that act the state defines as rape—namely, sexual intercourse (penal-vaginal penetration) under the threat or actual use of physical force. Who are the victims of this type of rape?

Victimization studies over the last several years clearly indicate that a woman's chance of being raped under the threat or actual use of physical violence is closely tied to her economic condition. The most recent study (McDermott 1979), found nationwide an overwhelming correlation between "illegal" rape victims and family income. These findings are shown in figure 6.1.

This relationship is neither accidental nor idiosyncratic. After analyzing the victimization studies done in the 1970s, Julia and Herman Schwendinger (1983, 213) concluded that study after study "has found that the *overwhelming* majority of women who experienced ["illegal"] rape or attempted rape have had annual incomes of less than $10,000." Moreover, with regard to age, teenage females experience the highest rate of rape (McDermott 1979, 11). Consequently, the majority of women who experience "illegal" rape are teenage females living in marginalized communities. In a society where men rule the economy, all women, but marginalized teenage women in particular, have their humanity stripped from them daily. Forcible rape is the most graphic instance.

Black women have one of the highest rates of "illegal" rape victimization (McDermott 1979, 6–7), which is not explained solely by their disproportionate economic marginalization (see chapter 4). Because black women in this society, owing to racism and sexism, have historically been devalued as a group, some men have taken this as an excuse to disregard their "honor" and deny them their own will and desire.

The devaluation of black womanhood and the rape of black women began when they were first brought to this country, as slaves.

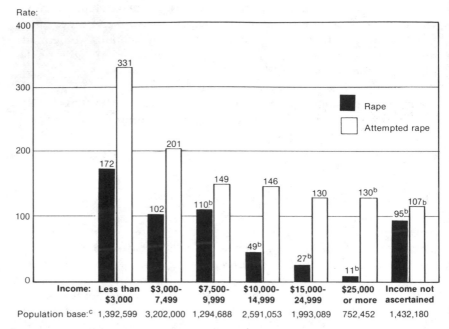

[a] Excludes rape and attempted rape victimization by nonstrangers and victimization of males.
[b] Estimate, based on about 50 or fewer sample cases, may be statistically unreliable.
[c] Estimated number of females 12 years of age or older in the population in given income categories.

Fig. 6.1. Estimated rates (per 100,000 females 12 years of age or older) of rape and attempted rape victimization, by family income of victim, 26 cities aggregate.[a] (M. Joan McDermott, *Rape Victimization in 26 American Cities* [Washington, D.C. U.S. Government Printing Office, 1980], 10).

On the boats coming from Africa, slavers commonly used violent rape to subdue recalcitrant black women (Hooks 1981, 18). On the plantation, the black male slave was exploited as a laborer in the fields, but the exploitation of the black female included making her serve as "a worker in the domestic household, a breeder, and as an object of white male sexual assault" (ibid.). As Bell Hooks (1981) and Angela Davis (1983) have clearly shown, the mass sexual exploitation of enslaved black women resulted directly from the interlocking institutions of an exploitative, racist, colonial patriarchal society, which were designed specifically to enrich whites through the super-exploitation of black people but also led to the demoralization and devaluation of black women. While an exploitative slave economy determined that a certain group of people would be enslaved, racism decreed those people would be black, and patriarchy confirmed that the black female slave's experience would—because of sexual exploitation—be more brutal than the male's. Slavery and racism provided the white plantation class the property rights over all black people, but it was patriarchy that legitimated the sexual exploitation of black women, which has had the lasting efffect of a continued devaluation of black womanhood. Part of this devaluation came from stereotyping black women as "sexual savages"—they were "labled jezebels and sexual temptresses and accused of leading white men away from spiritual purity into sin" (Hooks 1981, 33). The image of black women as chronically promiscuous helped to legitimate continued sexual assault upon them.

> White women and men justified the sexual exploitation of enslaved black women by arguing that they were the initiators of sexual relationships with white men. From such thinking emerged the stereotype of black women as sexual savages, and in sexist terms a sexual savage, a non-human, an animal cannot be raped (ibid., 52).

Thus the image of black women as whores and the devaluation of their womanhood, as well as their economic condition, all help to explain their relatively high frequency as victims of "illegal" rape. In a racist and sexist society, black women, because they are viewed as less worthy of respect than other women, become rape victims in very high numbers.

Who are the perpetrators of "illegal" rape? Rape, like other violent street crime, is primarily intraclass. That is, just as marginalized men are more likely to be robbed by other marginalized men, so marginalized women are more likely to be raped by marginalized men (Platt 1978, 30). Consequently, the socioeconomic status of the offenders in this type of rape is similar to that of the victims.

"Illegal" rape, like homicide, assault, and robbery, is largely the work of adolescent marginalized males, who experience the highest rates of unemployment (see chapter 3). Thus, the analysis already suggested for homicide, assault, and robbery is applicable in an important respect to "illegal" rape: economic status is significantly associated with "illegal" rape, as both the victims and their attackers come disproportionately from marginalized communities.

"Illegal" rape is encouraged by capitalist economic conditions in interaction with patriarchal social relations. In all social classes men learn to see themselves as privileged, yet society prohibits marginalized men a privileged economic position. Marginalized male youth experience disproportionately severe economic problems arising from the inherent mechanisms of capitalism. Given these conditions, for some males, "the importance of manipulating and controlling women, by violence, if necessary, is elevated" (Schwendinger and Schwendinger 1981, 19). The "cultural portrayal of the 'superstuds' and 'superflies' " emerge under conditions of marginalization, and "the control of women, no matter how precarious it is, is one of the many substitutes that these men use for uncontrollable labor market conditions" (ibid.).

The "superstud" ideology that Julia and Herman Schwendinger identify is especially prevalent in the macho street culture. As chapter 3 pointed out, communities with marginalized populations show "a greater proportion of peer groups that subscribe to violent macho ideals" (ibid.), and violent forcible rape thus becomes a more severe problem in such settings. According to a victimization study of twenty-six cities, group rapes (two or more male offenders) expands the victimization of this type of rape by sixty-one percent (McDermott 1979, 13–14). Group rapes also involve disproportionately youthful offenders and victims. As the victimization study reports:

> Almost one-half (47 percent) of the victims of multiple offenders were in this range (12–19 years old). Similarly, in rapes and attempted rapes committed by more than one offender, the attackers were also younger. Forty-three percent of the total rape and attempted rape victimization committed by multiple offenders involved offenders perceived to be under 21 years old. [ibid., 13]

Moreover, the study by Amir (1971, 218) found "that violence, especially in its extreme forms, is *significantly* associated with GR (group rape)." As argued in chapter 3, for marginalized adolescent males, male bonding occurs primarily in the street gang and the macho street culture, where they find assurance of their masculinity through ritualized ways of rejecting femininity. Group rape is one of those ways, for it not only maintains and reinforces an alliance among men, but also humiliates and devalues women and therefore strengthens the notion of masculine power. In group rape the individual proves himself a man among men. An account by one gang rapist illustrates this point: "We felt powerful, we were in control. I wanted sex and there was peer pressure. She wasn't like a person, no personality, just domination on my part. Just to show I could do it— you know, macho" (cited in Scully and Marolla 1985, 260). By participating in gang violence (whether between gangs or in group rape), marginalized adolescent males prove their masculinity to each other.

While *most* marginalized males do not commit "illegal" rape, nor is this type of rape limited to the economic marginal, still economic marginalization combined with patriarchal power increases the *likelihood* of this *type* of rape taking place, for physical violence is many times the only resource marginalized men control. As Dorie Klein (1982, 212) argues,

> Male physical power over women, or the illusion of power, is none the less a minimal compensation for the lack of power over the rest of one's

life. Some men resort to rape and other personal violence against the only target accessible, the only ones with even less autonomy. Thus sexual warfare often becomes a stand-in for class and racial conflict by transforming these resentments into misogyny.

This helps us understand why some men adopt a particular means, physical violence, as opposed to another means, economic coercion, to assault women sexually. Due to their class and gender position, marginalized males are more likely to be involved in "illegal" rape.

However, "illegal" rape is quite possibly the least frequent of all rapes. The next two sections discuss rape as related to the power of the male in the family and the workplace—the two areas where most rapes may occur today.

"Tolerated Illegal" Rape and "Legal" Wife Rape

Those few individuals who have written about wife rape tend to agree that this type of rape is more frequent than rape by strangers, acquaintances, or others (Gelles 1977; Hunt 1979; Dobash and Dobash 1979; Russell 1982). For example, Dobash and Dobash (1979, 75) state, "It is within marriage that a woman is most likely to be slapped and shoved about, severely assaulted, killed or raped." And as Morton Hunt (1979, 24) argues, "incredible as it may seem *more women are raped by their husbands each year than by strangers, acquaintances, or other persons.*" The best study to date of wife rape tends to support these conclusions. Diana E. H. Russell (1982, 65–68), in her book, *Rape in Marriage*, after interviewing a large random sample of women residing in San Francisco, analyzed the frequency of attacks of men who raped a woman (in "illegal" terms) on more than one occasion. Russell organized her data so as to tell whether the attacks occurred from 2 to 5 times, from 6 to 10 times, from 11 to 20 times or more than 20 times. These ranges were then converted into midpoints, so that if a woman reported, for example, being raped by the same individual 6 to 10 times, it was counted as 8.0 incidents of rape. Using this methodology, Russell obtained startling results. As table 6.1 shows, rape by husbands and ex-husbands is by far the most prevalent, followed by lovers or ex-lovers, aquaintances, relatives other than husbands, dates, authority figures, boyfriends, strangers, friends of the respondent, and friends of the family. Although Russell (1982, 67–68) was quick to point out that "questions regarding prevalence depends greatly on how one chooses to approach the question," she concluded that "wife rape is clearly one of the most prevalent types of rape, and by some measures, it is the most prevalent form."

Russell's survey defined wife rape as violent *forcible* rape by hus-

Table 6.1.   The Prevalence of Rape and Attempted Rape by Type
of Assailant

Type of assailant	Total number of incidents	Percent	Number of women for whom data on frequency available
Husband or ex-husband	979	38	74
Lover or ex-lover	344	13	61
Acquaintance	237	9	178
Other relative	209	8	32
Date	196	8	128
Authority figure	180	7	64
Boyfriend	165	6	29
Stranger	156	6	122
Friend of respondent	100	4	63
Friend of family	22	1	17
Total	2,588	100	

Source: Reprinted with permission of Macmillan Publishing Company from
Rape in Marriage by D. E. H. Russell. Copyright © 1982 by Diana E. H.
Russell.

bands or ex-husbands, or what I have referred to above as "tolerated
illegal" rape; if to that we add rape by husbands or ex-husbands
without the threat or actual use of physical violence, wife rape clearly is
one of the most prevalent forms of rape in U. S. society. "Legal" wife
rape, or rape without the threat or actual use of physical violence,
may occur because the husband can gain sexual access to his wife—
without her genuine consent—because she depends upon him economically. As pointed out earlier, patriarchal capitalism creates conditions under which the husband has economic power, while the wife is
dependent, often even if she works outside the home. A husband may
threaten "his wife" with divorce if she does not "put out" when he
wants her to, and the wife may conclude that unwanted sexual
intercourse is not as harmful as the alternative, economic poverty and
distress. This situation is exacerbated for women with children and/or
without skills. In "legal" wife rape then, "the female *appears* to be
consenting because she does not overtly resist" (Box 1983, 124), yet
her "consent" is not genuine since it is given—under the threat of
sanction—to the more powerful husband by the economically vulnerable wife. This clearly does not imply that economically dependent
wives can never consent, nor that all sexual intercourse between

husbands and wives is rape. What it does point out is how the sexual division of labor in the patriarchal capitalist family reflects and perpetuates the husband's power over the wife, and therefore can create the conditions for "legal" wife rape. Wife rape, whether "tolerated illegal" or "legal," is an act of domination by which some husbands maintain that power imbalance.

Beyond their economic dependency and powerlessness, women's isolation in the home is also important. By the late nineteenth century, the family wage system (discussed in chapter 2) isolated women in the home to work for both men and capital. The family became very hierarchically structured around the power of the male, as "motherhood" and "nurturance" were isolated in the home. This isolation gave rise to the "cult of domesticity" (Cott 1977), which although somewhat tempered today compared to the nineteenth century, still isolates women who do not work outside the home. Furthermore, the family prides itself on the ethic of family privacy, another phenomenon contributing to wife rape. Privacy suits the needs of the "rapist" husband, since it isolates the wife from the public and other forms of protection. In short, the structure of the patriarchal capitalist family facilitates the wife's victimization. The "rapist" husband does *not* have to worry about catching her in an exploitable position (such as "a dark alley") because the structure of the family insures that she will usually be in such a position. This is one reason why wife rape is probably committed much more frequently than "illegal" rape.

Moreover, the structure of the family encourages the powerful (husband) to view the powerless (his wife and children) as being under his control. In early patriarchal capitalism, marriage laws recognized the family as the husband's domain and subordinated women to the dictates of the husband (Dobash and Dobash 1979). To be a wife meant to come under the control of the husband (ibid., 33). As Dobash and Dobash (ibid., 60) point out in their extensive history of the family, under patriarchal capitalism

> The wife came under the control of her husband and he had the legal right to use force against her in order to insure that she fulfilled her wifely obligations, which included the consummation of the marriage, cohabitation, maintenance of conjugal rights, sexual fidelity, and general obedience and respect for his wishes.

Rape has always been one method some husbands used to control their wives. Historically, husbands have had the freedom, without state interference, to rape their wives, whether in the "illegal" or "legal" sense. As Susan Brownmiller (1975, 380) writes,

> The exemption from rape prosecutions granted to husbands who force their wives into acts of sexual union by physical means is as ancient as the

original definition of criminal rape, which was synonymous with that quaint phrase of Biblical origin, "unlawful carnal knowledge." To our Biblical forefathers, any carnal knowlege outside the marriage contract was "unlawful." And any carnal knowledge within the marriage contract was "lawful." Thus, as the law evolved, the idea that a husband could be prosecuted for raping his wife was unthinkable, for the law was conceived to protect *his* interests, not those of his wife.

The transformation of the family to its nuclear form strengthened the husband's power over his wife, and today this power, while changing, continues as a widely accepted fact of life. Since many men continue to view their relationship with their wives as one of control, they believe they should have free sexual access whenever they please. This is clearly evident in those rapes by *ex-husbands*, as separation or divorce does not, for some men, seem to alter this ideology of maintaining dominance, control, and sexual access. In the Russell (1982, 237) study, approximately *one in every seven* victims of wife rape *volunteered* to the interviewer that she had been raped by her ex-husband. The following is an example of what happened to a woman separated from her husband.

> He came over to my house in a jealous rage. He accused me of seeing other men and he wanted me to say what I was doing with them. Then he proceeded to beat me up for a long time. He started at 10:00 P.M. that night. By 6:00 A.M. the next day it was over. After all the beating, kicking, and throwing finally concluded, I ended up in the hospital with a broken jaw, broken fingers, concussion, and bruises all over. Then before he left, he made me lie down and have sex with him on threat of doing me more bodily harm if I didn't. [cited in ibid., 228]

Not only does this illustrate the close relationship between wife rape and the ideology of control, but also the close relationship between wife beating and wife rape as ways of controlling the wife. Research today indicates that in those households where traditional gender roles are the strongest (woman the nurturer, man the breadwinner and head of the family), wife beating is most frequent (Walker 1977– 78). Apparently, the structure of the traditional patriarchal nuclear family creates conditions which *facilitate* violence against women in the home. It is estimated that some form of violence occurs in approximately 50 percent of all intimate relationships, with women by far the most abused (Klein 1979, 20). In those homes where beatings occur, the "nurturer" becomes the scapegoat when things go wrong: when "life" is not just right for the head of the household, he takes it out on the "nurturer" (Klein 1982b, 213). As the home became more privatized and appeared to lose its productive function, women were locked into a devalued position, making them easy targets for male rage (Schecter 1982, 225). The "nurturer" is punished and "taught lessons" because some men feel they have the right to dominate and control their wives, and wife beating serves to insure continued compliance with their commands.

However, the importance of wife beating for our discussion is that many times it occurs along with wife rape. Lenore Walker (1978, 112), for instance, found in her study of wife beating that most women who were battered by their husbands were also raped by them. Another study indicated that approximately one-third of all wife beating involves some form of sexual abuse. (Prescott and Letko 1977, 18). The Russell (1982, 91) study found that 36 percent of the women interviewed experienced some combination of beating and rape: 9 percent were primarily the victim of wife rape, but were beaten also; for 22 percent of the women, wife rape and wife beating were approximately equal; 5 percent were primarily the victim of wife beating, but were also raped. In some instances, rape occurs after the beating. Indeed, one study found that a number of husbands seem "to experience sexual arousal from the violence—since the demand for sexual intercourse immediately followed the assault" (Davidson 1978, 31). In many families across the United States, women are working desperately to make sure everything runs smoothly so that their husbands will not become angry and consequently beat and rape them.

While *most* wives do not experience direct violence, the power, dominance, ideology of control, and the isolation of the "nurturer" in the house all help us understand why rape occurs in marriage and why it tends to remain concealed. Women who are the victims of wife rape "suffer in shameful silence, convinced that no one else is experiencing the horror and that no one wants to know about it. As a result, male domination is restored in the family and in the community" (Schecter 1982, 225). Wife rape, like other forms of sexual violence against females, results from an historically created gender hierarchy and sexual division of labor in the home, by which men dominate and control women. And it is a mechanism used to maintain that domination and control.

Sexual Harassment and "Legal" Rape at Work

While "illegal" rape definitely crosses class lines, upper- and middle-class men are in the unique position in which violence is unnecessary to gain sexual compliance from women. By reason of their position in patriarchal capitalism, they can resort to "legal" rape in the workplace.

As shown in chapter 4, the sexual division of labor leaves women in a tremendously subordinate position. In all locations in the labor market, the average status of women is lower than that of men, and most women workers are segregated into the "pink collar ghetto." The upshot is that "women at work are vulnerable to the whim and fancy of male employers or organizational male superiors, who are in a position to reward or punish their female subordinate economically" (Box 1983, 152). In other words, middle- and upper-class men, economically able to exploit a woman, can gain access to her sexually without her *genuine* consent. This constitutes not only a type of sexual harassment, but also another form of "legal" rape, or what may be called "rape at work."

Sexual harassment includes not only sexist jokes, "accidental" collisions, and constant ogling and pinches, but also "legal" rape at work (MacKinnon 1979, 2). However, while "legal" rape at work is a form of sexual harassment, other types of sexual harassment are not "legal" rape. Jokes, collisions, and ogling and pinches are quite different from unwanted coitus. "Legal" rape at work involves economic threats by male supervisors, that if the female employee or possible employee does not engage in sexual intercourse with him she will, on the one hand, not be hired, retained, or promoted, or on the other hand, will be fired, demoted, or transferred to a more unpleasant position. Assuming that the female employee or possible employee does not secretly desire sexual intercourse with the male supervisor, these threats can be just as coercive as physical violence. Given the economic conditions of women, termination, demotion, or not obtaining a job can be economically devastating. Like "legal" wife rape, which arises from a woman's financial dependence, so "economic deprivation is a serious and expensive cost even when set beside unwelcome and undesired coitus" (Box 1983, 143). In such a situation, where there is no equality between the male employer who is threatening the female employee, her genuine consent is doubtful. Because the female *depends* upon the male for economic well-being, some males take advantage of her economic vulnerability. As Steven Box (1983, 129) writes,

> given her relatively weak position, the female often makes a rational choice that the alternatives to coitus are even more personally harmful; her consent though is not an expression of her desire, either for sexual pleasure or to please and physically comfort her male partner, nor is it genuine because the conditions under which it is given—conditions of economic or social vulnerability created by relative inequality—are not those under which consent can be said to exist.

Consequently, "legal" rape at work becomes possible in a social system that puts some men in positions of economic power, enabling them to exploit women, and the structural situation of middle- and upper-class men insures that this exploitation will more likely be manipulative than violent.

While the imbalance of power can be coercive by creating the conditions for "legal" rape at work, such rape by no means automatically occurs. Women often enter into genuine and humane relationships with men at work, even if those men are in supervisory positions vis-à-vis the woman. What is important to understand is that this power imbalance can create the condition for the male supervisor to use economic coercion to gain sexual access without the female employee's genuine overt consent. Clearly, most supervisors do not engage in either "illegal" or "legal" rape at work.

Although much work needs to be done in this area, and it is very difficult to quantify the amount of "legal" rape at work, it is possible that this type of rape occurs much more often than most believe. Studies of sexual harassment, while not providing direct evidence of "legal" rape at work, do indicate the prevalence of nonconsenting sexual agression in the workplace, while also demonstrating that many women are in a position where they can be exploited by male superiors (ibid., 144). One study, by the women's section of the Human Affairs program at Cornell University, although not based on a random sample, found significant results: 92 percent of the respondents said sexual harassment was a serious problem, 70 percent personally experienced some form of sexual harassment, and 56 percent reported some form of *physical sexual harassment* (Farley 1978, 39–40). More recently, the Merit Systems Protection Board conducted a study of sexual harassment among federal employees for the Subcommittee on Investigations of the House Committee on Post Office and Civil Service (Russell 1984, 269–70). Basing its conclusions on completed questionnaires of over 20,000 federal employees (and constituting a random sample), the board found that 42 percent of all female employees reported being sexually harassed at work within a two-year period prior to the survey. Obviously, if the study had questioned employees about sexual harassment over their entire careers, the figure would have been substantially higher (ibid., 270). Nevertheless, these studies clearly indicate that sexual harassment at the workplace is common.

The perpetrators of this harassment are overwhelmingly male superiors, the victims are women who work at low paid "white-collar" jobs, and a good proportion of this sexual harassment is connected with issues like promotion (MacKinnon 1979, 28–40).

In "legal" rape at work, the female subordinate is coerced economically. Two women who experienced this rape talked about it in one sentence:

"If I wasn't going to sleep with him, I wasn't going to get my promotion."
"I was fired because I refused to give at the office." [cited in ibid., 32]

If women refuse to "give at the office," some men retaliate by using their power over the woman's career. In one case, a supervisor,

> following rejection of his elaborate sexual advances, barraged the woman with unwarranted reprimands about her job performance, refused routine supervision or task direction, which made it impossible for her to do her job, and then fired her for poor work performance. [ibid., 35]

All types of sexual harassment, including "legal" rape at work, assert male power and undermine the autonomy and personhood of female workers. It is a form of aggression that contributes to the ultimate patriarchal capitalist goal of keeping women in subordinate positions at work. As noted in chapter 2, patriarchal capitalism, and the resulting job segregation by sex, has been the primary factor in keeping women subordinated in the workplace. "Legal" rape at work, and other forms of sexual harassment, simply perpetuate job segregation. Sexual exploitation at the workplace ensures that female wages stay low, undermines promotion possibilities, and keeps women divided so they are unable to organize for change. As Lin Farley (1978, 208) writes,

> working women, by and large, have succumbed to this male extortion by escaping sexual aggression at the expense of their jobs or by keeping their jobs at the expense of their self-respect. They have forfeited their independence and equality at work either way.

Similarly, Mary Bularzik (1978, 26) states that sexual exploitation

> is used to control women's access to certain jobs; to limit job success and mobility; and to compensate men for powerlessness in their own lives. It functions on two levels: the group control of women by men, and personal control of individual workers by bosses and co-workers . . . To offer such a model is to suggest that it is not simply an individual interaction but a social one; not an act of deviance but a socially condoned mode of behavior that functions to preserve male dominance in the world of work.

Because males control female labor power in the workplace, female subordinates are required to nurture their male supervisors. For example, a secretary is often expected to boost the boss's ego as well as make his coffee, clean up, and make sure he is presentable to the public (Sokoloff 1980, 220). Rosabeth Moss Kanter (1977, 88) notes that a "tone of emotional intensity" pervades the relationship between secretary and boss. The secretary comes to "feel for" the boss, "to care deeply about what happens to him and to do his feeling for him." In fact, according to Kanter (ibid., 88), secretaries are rewarded for their willingness "to take care of bosses' personal needs." In other words female subordinates perform an extensive nurturing service for their male supervisors. They do in the workplace what women traditionally have done in the home. Some men come to expect nurturance from their female subordinates, just as they do their wives. Patriarchy structures relationships in the workplace just as capitalism structures relationships in the family: "the capitalist is often the father or the sexual predator and the worker is often the mother or the sexual prey" (Balbus 1982, 78). Some male supervisors expect an extension of this personal attention by women to include sexual nurturing. Women are forced to exchange sexual services for material survival. "Legal" rape at work becomes another mechanism for controlling the sexuality of women. As MacKinnon (1979, 174) concludes, two forces of patriarchal capitalism coverage in "legal" rape at work and other forms of sexual harassment, "men's control over women's sexuality and capital's control over employees' work lives."

Keeping It All Hidden

A major argument throughout this book has been that the state and thus the criminal justice system serve the interests of the powerful—the capitalist class *and* men. The legal order is both patriarchal and capitalist. This section looks at how the legal order serves the interests of men by keeping the vast amount of rape hidden from public view, thereby implying that male criminality toward women is minimal and of minor concern.

The Law on Rape

The state defines rape as the unlawful sexual intercourse with a female person without her consent. While there are minor variations in this definition from state to state, this is, broadly defined, the U. S. definition of rape. However, this definition clearly serves the interests of men in general, and, as I will show, powerful men in particular. In short, the state definition of rape is class and gender specific.

As Steven Box (1983, 121–26) has shown, the state definition of rape maintains a spousal exception clause, concentrates on only forcible vaginal penetration with a penis, and focuses on the consent of the victim. Each of these components serve the interests of men.

The above definition of rape excludes what has been argued here as possibly constituting the most frequent *type* of rape, namely "tolerated illegal" wife rape. Married women who are raped by their husbands are not "protected" by the law in forty-one states (Sokoloff and Price 1982, 24). In nine states the husband cannot be charged with "illegal" rape even if the couple is legally separated (ibid.). Consequently, the law on rape provides husbands with the opportunity to impose themselves sexually upon their wives whenever they so choose, regardless of the wife's feelings (Box 1983, 122). Largely due to the feminist movement, some states have begun to abolish this spousal exception. However, the law on rape continues effectively to conceal much of the rape occurring today and thus serves the interests of many men.

The second aspect of the state definition of rape discussed by Box also serves the interests of men by concentrating on sexual intercourse. This exclusive focus on sexual intercourse ignores the violation of women by other means than forcible vaginal penetration by a penis. The forcible insertion "of objects and instruments into the vagina, such as curling tongs and broomhandles, is considered not nearly so heinous" by the law and is processed usually as "indecent assault" or "grievous bodily harm" (Edwards 1981, 17). Moreover, although some states have ruled that rape can be oral, anal, or vaginal and that penetration need not be by a penis (Battelle Law and Justice Study Center 1978, 5–20), anal and/or oral penetration by either a penis or another instrument is often not defined as rape and therefore treated much more leniently. Is anal penetration or the insertion into the vagina of an object other than a penis any less of a violation? Is there a lesser injury psychologically? Brownmiller (1975, 378) answers, "All acts of sex forced on unwilling victims deserve to be treated in concept as equally grave offenses in the eyes of the law, for the avenue of penetration (and the type of instrument used) is less significant than the intent to degrade." In fact one could argue that a woman suffers more *harm* when violated by instruments other than a penis. Articles such as sticks, bottles, or entrenching tools (used by U.S. soldiers in Vietnam), are clearly more physically, and probably more psychologically damaging, than a penis. Yet such offenses are treated more leniently. Susan Brownmiller (1975, 422) argues that this preoccupation with vaginal penetration by a penis reflects a man's need to protect himslf as the "sole physical instrument governing impregnation, progeny, and inheritance." Whatever one thinks of Brownmiller's argument, it is difficult to dispute the fact that the law on rape does not serve women's interests. The law operates to hide a large number of acts from the U.S. citizenry that otherwise would be considered rape.

Finally, the law's concentration on consent by the victim clearly exhibits its class and gender bias. The concentration on consent means that unless the offender uses or threatens physical violence, the victim is assumed to have consented. However, as Steven Box (1983, 123) points out, the law misses an important point,

> it is not so much the absence of consent, although that has to exist, but the presence of coercion which makes rape fundamentally different from normal acts of sexual intercourse. In a situation where the female's choice is severely restricted by the male being able to impose sanctions for refusal, the question of her consent should become secondary to his ability to coerce. In other words, by focusing on consent under direct physical coercion, the law misses submission under threats of all types.

Examples of female submission under coercion where the actual or threatened use of physical violence is absent are found in "legal" rape at work and "legal" wife rape. Here physical violence is not necessary (although there clearly does exist "illegal" rape at work and "tolerated illegal" wife rape), since employees and wives can be coerced economically and, therefore, forced to submit. A coercive act is "one where the person coerced is made to feel compelled to do something he or she would not normally do," and the compulsion is accomplished by the "coercer's adversely changing the options available for the victim's choosing" (Hughes and May 1980, 252). By threatening a woman with a demotion if she does not go to bed with him, and assuming she does not secretly desire sexual intercourse with him, her "boss" has created the condition in which she is compelled to do something she would not normally do. As a result, the legal definition of rape, with its concentration on the consent of the victim, effectively weeds out many rapes and, therefore, conceals them from our view and our consciousness.

In addition, since the state definition of rape *only* concentrates on one type of rape, namely forcible physical rape, it makes marginalized males the "illegal" rapists in U.S. society. The legal definition of rape consequently has not only a masculine bias but also a class bias. The law operates ideologically, by picturing marginalized males as the only rapists, thereby exaggerating their involvement in rape generally. Rape by powerful men is effectively hidden from our view, even though it is quite possibly more common.

The Enforcement of Rape Laws

While the law restricts its definition of rape to only one kind, the enforcement process of the legal system guarantees that even most offenders of this type will escape unscathed. By reason of the trauma a victim experiences from not only the rape but the additional ordeal she must go through to secure a conviction, a large number of victims do not report rape. Victimization surveys indicate that the actual

incidence of "illegal" rape is close to four times the number reported
to the police (Robin 1982, 242). The FBI estimates that for each rape
reported, ten are not (ibid.). A large number of "illegal" rapes are
kept hidden, since many women are reluctant to face the ordeal
and/or they believe it will not result in bringing the criminal to justice.

The legal system does not stop there in keeping the bulk of even
"illegal" rape hidden. Of the rapes reported to the police, a large
percent are classed as "unfounded." According to the FBI, "unfounded" means "the police establish that no forcible rape offense
occurred" (cited in Russell 1984, 49). The police simply dismiss the
case as a false report. The FBI stopped publishing the "unfounded"
rate in 1977, but in the year prior to that, the FBI reported that the
police classed as unfounded *19 percent* of all reported rape cases
nation-wide (ibid., 30). Of course, there must be cases where women
have falsely accused men of rape. However, it is also safe to assume
that many rape cases are dismissed as unfounded because of the
sexism of male-dominated police departments. Consider the following questions rape victims have been asked by male police officers:

> "How many orgasms did you have?"
> "Didn't I pick you up last week for prostitution?"
> "How big was he?"
> "What were you thinking about while he was doing it?" [cited in Wood
> 1973, 209–10]

Many victims in tattered clothes, crying and shaking with fear, and
showing visible signs of having been beaten, have been exposed to
such interrogations immediately after reporting the rape (Robin
1982, 245). Is it safe to conclude that rape cases are only unfounded
because of a false accusation, and that sexism plays no role? Brownmiller (1975, 435) reports that when police*women* take rape reports,
the unfounded rape rate tends to drop to 2 or 3 percent, about the
rate of all other violent crimes. Moreover, many police officers, as well
as sociologists (Amir 1971), believe that the victim causes her own
rape. For example, if the woman allows a man to come into her house,
if she goes into his, or if she frequents a singles bar, she is, according
to the thinking of many police officers, indicating her willingness to
have sexual intercourse or at least risking attack—thus police officers
often simply blame the victim and "unfound" the case (Wood 1973,
200–201).

Racism is also an important influence. One study found that the
police disbelieved black rape victims more often than white victims
and therefore dismissed more such cases as unfounded (Robin 1982,
277). In addition, black rape victims have sometimes suffered a
second rape, at the hands of the police. For instance, in December
1974 a seventeen-year old black woman reported that she was gang-

raped by ten Chicago police officers. The whole thing seems to have been swept under the rug (Davis 1983, 173).

When, however, the police decide to consider rape cases, the evidence suggests that they are not very effective in achieving arrests. Only 53.6 percent of all reported rapes in 1984 were followed by an arrest (FBI 1985, 152).

Even after his arrest, the rapist has a number of ways to remain invisible. First, the criminal justice system maintains a conception of the "legitimate" and "illegitimate" rape victim. Certain characteristics of a rape *victim* are likely to make her case seem unsubstantiated to the male-dominated criminal justice system. If she is single and/or divorced, has delayed reporting the crime, was under the influence of drugs or alcohol, or if she is a prostitute, a black woman, a welfare recipient, a hitchhiker or frequents singles bars, the police and prosecution are less likely to believe her story and, therefore, more likely to dismiss the case (Andersen 1983, 199–200). These women are frequently considered "common sexual property" and therefore "illegitimate rape victims." If a married woman living in a traditional nuclear family setting—thus attached to one man—reports a rape, her complaint is taken more seriously. They are the legitimate victims of rape, according to the male-dominated criminal justice system. As Clark and Lewis (1977, 92) state, the selective prosecution of rape cases, in many instances, has "nothing to do with whether or not the complainant was actually raped." While poor women are disproportionately the victims of "illegal" rape, they have the least opportunity to obtain justice for their victimization. If a woman who exercises her right to bodily freedom, for example, by hitchhiking or frequenting a singles bar, is raped, the state sees it many times as justified (Petersen 1977, 363). The state operates to punish those women who do not stay in their place. As Susan Rae Petersen (1977, 364, 366–67) points out,

> It is legally permissible for women to exercise their freedom of bodily movement, but only so long as they accept the resulting constraint: that any act of rape committed against them cannot be prosecuted. . . . A woman cannot be free to go where she pleases if a rapist is free to rape her. What is wrong with rape, then, is that it is really not wrong at all.

Second, the iniquitous corroboration requirement helps keep many rapists invisible. In many states the victim's testimony in a rape case must still be corroborated by, for example, evidence of actual penetration by a penis, that force was present, and, therefore, that "consent" was absent. With most crimes, the victim's testimony is enough to guarantee a conviction—even *sexual offenses where the victim is a male.* However, in some states rape is treated differently, since many male criminal justice practitioners believe in feminine malice (the victim fabricating the charge) and feminine masochism (the victim wanting to be raped).

The victim must prove that she attempted, with all her will, to resist the attack. However, only in the case of rape does the victim have to show utmost resistance. For example, in auto theft, if the victim does not aggressively pursue the thieves, he or she is not assumed to have consented to the theft. The absence of resistance does not establish the presence of consent (Robin 1982, 250). Yet in rape cases, the victim must show resistance, and this criterion favors the rapist. As Clark and Lewis (1977, 49) state: "Rape is the only criminal offense in which the testimony of one witness, the victim, is considered to be inherently less trustworthy than that of others, notably the accused." Thus, even though some states have abandoned corroboration rules, in a judicial system that systematically favors rapists, juries will have difficulty with uncorroborated rape cases (Tong 1984, 105). In short, corroboration rules or not, the judicial system favors the rapist and helps to keep him hidden. Furthermore, because of the necessity for corroboration in rape cases, the victim spends much time preparing for her testimony at trial, and begins to "feel more like the criminal than the victim." Hence, many victims decide they cannot face any more ordeals, especially in open court, and end up dropping the charges.

Third, in most cases the offender has the opportunity to bargain the case with the prosecution and, by admitting guilt to a lesser charge, such as indecent assault, close the case without a trial. For these reasons, (the conception of "legitimate" and "illegitimate" rape victims, the corroboration requirement, and plea bargaining), many rapists never come to trial and, therefore, their crimes are effectively concealed.

If the offender is one of the few unlucky ones brought to trial, conditions in the proceedings favor him. In most areas the victim's character and reputation are admissible and can be used to question nonconsent. Defense attorneys destroy the character and reputation of the victim to persuade the jury that the victim is the "type of person" who would willingly have sex with the offender. Such a line of questioning, while possibly beneficial to the offender, can damage the victim horribly.

Cautionary instructions to the jury also help to keep many rapes hidden. These instructions, given by the judge, advise the jury to evaluate a rape victim's testimony carefully. While most states have abandoned these instructions, some still use them. A standard version of this cautionary instruction is as follows:

> A charge such as that made against the defendant in this case, is one which is easily made and, once made, difficult to defend against, even if

the person accused is innocent. Therefore, the law requires that you examine the testimony of the female person named in the information with caution. [cited in Battelle Law and Justice Study Center 1978, 30]

Moreover, given the judicial attitudes toward rape victims, one wonders how any rapists are ever convicted. One study found that judges tend to classify rape cases into three categories (Bohmer 1976): The first category includes what judges call "genuine victims"—for example, a woman attacked by a stranger in a dark alley. The second category involves "consensual intercourse," meaning that the woman in the case was "asking for it"—a woman meets a man in a bar, agrees to let him drive her home, "and then alleges he raped her." Judges have described these cases as "friendly rape," "felonious gallantry," "assault with failure to please," and "breach of contract." The final category is the "vindictive female"—a woman who is tired of her husband or lover, wants to get rid of him, and "convinces her daughter to allege the defendant raped her" (pp. 227–28).

This latter category was also, according to the study, connected specifically to black women, as judges "alluded to the chaotic lifestyles and attitudes of ghetto dwellers." As one judge stated: "With the Negro Community you really have to redefine the term rape. You never know about them" (ibid., 231). As stated earlier, black and other minority women, because of the racism and sexism embedded in the criminal justice system, receive far less "justice" than white women. The case of Inez Garcia is pertinent. Garcia was convicted of second-degree murder for killing her rapist. After the trial, one of the jurors in the case was interviewed and asked if a woman could ever be found not guilty, by reason of self-defense, if a woman killed her rapist during the attack. The male juror answered, "No; because the guy's not trying to kill her. He's just trying to give her a good time. To get off, the guy will have to do her bodily harm, and giving a girl a screw isn't doing her bodily harm" (Blithman and Green 1975, 86).

As a result of these enforcement, or nonenforcement processes, very few "illegal" rapists are ever labeled as criminals. In fact, for every 100 "illegal" rape cases, only 25 are ever reported, 13 suspects are arrested, 9 are eventually prosecuted, and 5 are convicted (Smithyman 1979, 101). Thus, the enforcement of the rape law operates in an ideological manner that serves the interests of men, but powerful men in particular. First, it publicizes to U.S. men that there are certain women (poor minority women in particular), who may legitimately be raped. Second, it effectively hides possibly the majority of all rapes—"legal" rape at work and both "legal" and "tolerated illegal" wife rape—while keeping a very large proportion of the rapes the state does define as criminal hidden from public view. Third, due to racism in the legal system, in cases involving a black offender and a white victim, the offender receives a far more severe sentence than any other offender-victim combination (Balkan et al. 1980, 124). The criminal justice system effectively hides the rapes by powerful white men (rape at work) and married men (wife rape) while creating the impression publicly that all rape is actually the type of rape engaged in by some marginalized minority men, thereby exaggerating their contribution to the total amount of rape. Marginalized minority men are viewed as *the* rapists, while the sexual exploitation and assault of women by other men is hidden from our sight. While the rape laws and thus mechanisms for enforcement serve the interests of men generally, powerful white men are the primary beneficiaries.

7
Curbing Crime

The previous chapters have shown that to understand crime we must comprehend its gender (patriarchal) and class (capitalist) dimensions. Crime of both the powerless (working class and women) and powerful (capitalist class and men) is created by the interaction of patriarchy and capitalism. Further, the *most serious* crimes are not found among the disadvantaged and powerless, but rather, among the *powerful*. Those with gender and class power in U.S. society commit the most serious forms and amounts of crime. First, the concentration of economic and patriarchal power in national and transnational corporations has created large numbers of powerless people *worldwide* who are victimized by powerful males. Second, since men as a group benefit from patriarchal power, some impose themselves on women and commit sexual violence against them. And third, many marginalized men, while economically powerless, simultaneously maintain patriarchal power within their class, which, in many powerless communities, results in high rates of interpersonal violence. In contrast to the harmful acts of the powerful, females, powerless in terms of class and gender, engage in substantially less serious forms and amounts of criminality. Crime then is clearly socially determined and rooted in power; furthermore, the state and its legal system serve powerful men by doing all it can to conceal their criminality while publicizing and thereby exaggerating the importance of the less serious criminality of powerless men and women.

In the face of these conditions, what can be done to curb criminality under patriarchal capitalism? I begin my answer with a critique of right-wing criminology and radical feminism, both of which propose law and order politics (repression) for curbing crime. I show that the state, which remains in the service of powerful men, currently takes repressive action that not only continues to keep the crimes of the powerless visible and the crimes of the powerful concealed, but also, is most likely increasing our victimization by both powerless and powerful criminality. From there, I turn to a socialist feminist alternative.

Right-Wing Criminology, Radical Feminism, and Law and Order Politics

In the 1960s, as corporate crime remained hidden in the suites of corporations and the files of regulatory agencies, and as sexual violence against women remained hidden in the home and workplace, the dominant ideology for curbing crime—that is, street crime—was liberalism, with its emphasis on rehabilitation and a more humane criminal justice system. However, by the 1970s, in spite of a host of liberal efforts, street crime continued to rise and became progressively more serious. By the early 1980s, the liberal answer to street crime was clearly in a shambles and so lost credibility drastically as the dominant ideology for solving the crime problem.

Liberal ideology collapsed, and the left, arguing simplistically that criminals were proto-revolutionaries and that the fear of street crime was a form of "false consciousness," failed to propose a viable alternative (Greenberg 1981, 12). The right wing entered the controversy with its "analysis" of crime and anticrime program.

According to right-wing criminologists, we have a lot of crime—that is street crime—because we do not sufficiently control those who are most prone to crime. For right-wing criminology, crime is a part of human nature and the source of the problem is the nature of the individual (his or her physiology, chemistry, genetic make-up, or abnormal psychology), not the nature of society. The leading theoretician on the right is James Q. Wilson, who in a book titled *Thinking About Crime* (1975, 209), argued that an "unflattering view of man" shows us that "wicked people exist" and that "nothing avails but to set them apart from innocent people." Wilson has now extended his perspective to a biological determinism bordering on neo-Lombrosianism.

In 1876 Cesare Lombroso published *Criminal Man* and in 1894 he and his son-in-law Enrico Ferrero completed *The Female Offender*. Grounded in the particular racist, sexist, and class-biased notions characteristic of nineteenth-century bourgeois thought, both of these works view crime as being biologically based in differences between whites and nonwhites, women and men, and the fit (upper classes) and the unfit (working classes). Crime, for Lombroso, resulted from the survival of primitive traits and physical stigmata. He used the theories of evolution (Social Darwinism) to support his belief that criminals were not only physically different from noncriminals but also inferior. In other words, he explained crime by arguing that women, nonwhites, and the poorer classes had evolved less than white upper-class men and, therefore, were more susceptible to primitive urges and crime. As Dorie Klein (1982a, 39–43) notes, Lombroso concluded that individuals develop differently "within sexual and racial limitations which differ hierarchically from the most highly developed, the white men, to the most primitive, the non-white women."

Lombroso's theory emerged at a time of rapid expansion of capitalist wealth derived from the exploitation of ethnic and racial minorities (Schwendinger and Schwendinger 1974). The dislocation of capitalist industrialization and increasing urbanization created a visible urban-poor population whose "deviant" activities required explanation. Social Darwinism and thus Lombroso's theory of crime both filled this void and served the interests of white male capitalists. As John D. Rockefeller asserted to a Sunday School class:

> The growth of a large business is merely survival of the fittest. . . . The American Beauty rose can be produced in the splendor and fragrance which bring cheer to its beholder only by sacrificing the early birds which grew up around it. This is not an evil tendency in business. It is merely the working out of a law of nature and a law of God. [cited in Andersen 1983, 39]

Lombroso's theory, which helped justify the rule of capitalist over worker, white over black, and men over women, has also, not surprisingly, been discounted as an explanation of crime.

With Richard Herrnstein in *Crime and Human Nature* (1985), James Q. Wilson argues that Lombroso was in fact on the right track. While, according to these right-wing criminologists, no one is born a criminal, many individuals are born with "constitutional factors" that predispose them to criminality. Wilson and Herrnstein contend that mounting evidence shows that, on the average, offenders differ from nonoffenders in physique, intelligence, and personality. Criminals, according to Wilson and Herrnstein, are mesomorphic (muscular) rather than ectomorphic (thin), have lower than average intelligence as measured by I.Q. tests, and are impulsive, with a "now"-oriented personality. There is a link, they argue, between body type, intelligence, temperament, and crime.

Opinion within certain segments of the radical feminist community reflects a similar biological determinism. For example, writing about rape, Susan Brownmiller (1975, 16) argues, "By anatomical fiat—the inescapable construction of their genital organs—the human male was a *natural* predator and the human female served as his *natural* prey" (emphasis added). For Brownmiller and some other radical feminists, sexual inequality is found in the anatomical and biological makeup of men and women. The anatomy and biology of the male allows him the possibility of raping women "but she cannot retaliate in kind" (ibid., 14). It is this biology that accounts for women's subordination and men's criminality, particularly male violence against females. As Brownmiller (1975, 13–14) goes on,

> Man's structural capacity to rape and women's corresponding vulnerability are as basic to the physiology of both our sexes as the primal act of sex itself. Had it not been for this accident of biology, an accommodation requiring the locking together of two separate parts, penis into vagina, there would be neither copulation nor rape as we know it.

This "single factor," human anatomy, was sufficient, according to Brownmiller, to create a male ideology of rape. "When men discovered that they could rape, they proceeded to do it" (ibid., 14). For some radical feminists then, rape, found in the nature of men, serves a universal social function, the subjugation of women. Men are natural predators, and rape and violence are biological acts.

The idea that men are natural predators seems to turn up in some radical feminists writings and public speeches on pornography as well. For example, Andrea Dworkin, the chief theoretician of the antipornography movement, has been accused by socialist feminists of not discussing masculine sexual behavior as *learned* sexual behavior, but rather, speaking of *male* sexual behavior as ascribed sexual behavior (Burstyn 1984). Dworkin is criticized for attacking the whole male sex in terms close to biological determinism, implying that "misogyny and brutality are biologically coded into men's sexual response" (ibid.). This clearly places the radical feminist antipornography movement hand-in-hand with the likes of Wilson and Herrnstein and other members of the New Right.

> Far from undermining the Right, this conception reinforces it, because it shares a philosophical approach to sexuality as something which is pregiven. In the case of the New Right the "natural" form of sex is heterosexual monogamy; in Dworkin's case, it's brutal "male sexuality" (as opposed to a gentle, caring "female sexuality"). In either case, sex emerges as something to be *controlled*. [ibid., 32.]

For the patriarchal right, pornography is propaganda for nonprocreational sex. For some radical feminists like Dworkin, pornography is propaganda for "male sexuality," which is by definition inherently aggressive and harmful to women. As a result, some radical feminists and the New Right "seek to exorcise pornography as if it were the devil incarnate" (ibid.).

The above brief discussion points to a similarity between right-wing criminology and some radical feminists, as well as an important difference between the two. Both right-wing criminology and some radical feminists are similar in the sense that they advance arguments close to biological determinism. From Lombroso to Wilson and Herrnstein to Brownmiller and Dworkin, the sources of crime and male aggression/violence are found biologically. However, right-wing criminology and radical feminists make their biological arguments differently. Right-wing criminology points to *wicked individuals* as being the problem; some radical feminists argue *all men are wicked*. Radical feminism therefore makes a gender distinction whereas right-wing criminology does not.* Yet those who ignore the social structure should also be able to explain corporate crime, political crime, organized crime, white-collar crime, and the increasing involvement of women in property crimes. Can we assume that corporate executives engage in corporate crimes because they are mesomorphic? Does a biological argument help us much in understanding why the United States has the highest level of violent street crime in the industrialized world? Do men rape because they are naturally predisposed to it? How would the !Kung respond to such an argument? And finally, are women increasingly involved in nonviolent property crimes because they are increasingly mesomorphic and biologically defective? In short, right-wing criminology and some radical feminists not only fail to explain the above problems, they even fail to recognize them.

Since right-wing criminologists locate the problem within the individual, and some radical feminists within the "male sex" (as opposed to what I have referred to as the "male gender"), both strongly support *a law-and-order agenda* to eradicate the problems of crime and male aggression/violence. Both support procedures that rely upon the patriarchal capitalist state, and so help extend its control, repression, and power to punish. For Dworkin, passing laws and ordinances that combine class action and civil rights legislation to eliminate pornography is an effective way to combat masculine dominance, power, and violence. For Brownmiller, not only pornographers, but

---

*I stress "some" radical feminists because the overall record of radical feminism contains very positive elements as well. The battered woman shelters, rape crisis centers, and child abuse programs now in place all over the continent are products, in the first instance, of the work of grass-root feminist activists, radical feminists in the lead. Not only have radical feminist activists given hundreds of thousands of women help, they have raised awareness of these issues in society and shown women they need not be eternally victimized. Charlotte Bunch's work reflects and articulates much of this work. For whatever reason, Dworkin and Brownmiller have eschewed the popular base of this kind of organizing and put forward strategies with what is, in effect, a law-and-order orientation. The so called Minneapolis ordinance, drafted by Dworkin and Catharine MacKinnon, is an example of right-wing legislation in feminist clothing (for a detailed critique of this proposed legislation and the larger censorship strategy see Burstyn 1985). A radical criminology needs to take much of its assessment of the depth and contours of women's oppression from insights developed by radical feminism—the analysis in this book, like that of all socialist feminism, is deeply indepted to them. But radical criminology needs to think about social policy and legal reform in ways that reject the dangerous biological determinism that haunts the writings of some of its leading thinkers.

criminals (street criminals) in general, must be harshly repressed. As she states,

> Parenthetically I want to note at this point that I am one of those people who view a prison sentence as a just and lawful societal solution to the problem of criminal activity, the best solution we have at this time, as civilized retribution and as a deterrent against the commission of future crimes. [1975, 379]

Neither Dworkin nor Brownmiller offer concrete suggestions for attacking the patriarchal and capitalist sources of crime in U.S. society. Their law-and-order politics supports and strengthen the position of right-wing criminologists and their political allies, by giving it the "stamp" of feminist approval.

For right-wing criminology, the answer to the crime problem is simply to increase the "costs" of crime—that is, provide more police surveillance, longer and more punitive prison sentences, and extended use of the death penalty. In short, greater state repression of the powerless.

The Reagan Administration: A Case Study

A good example of putting this right-wing ideology into practice, is the Reagan administration's so-called "crime control" program. This administration has taken it upon itself to answer the continuing problem of crime with increased state repression. However, this program has little to do with curbing criminality and much to do with more easily controlling the powerless, while leaving the powerful free to be as criminal as they like.

Increasing Powerless Crime and Keeping It Visible

The Reagan administration's plan for "solving" violent street crime (they have no proposals to curb crime by women or corporations) will not curb powerless crime. Instead, it will increase it, while at the same time severely limiting our overall civil rights.

First, let us look at some of the other Reagan programs and how they have affected those most vulnerable to street crime—women and youth. The Reagan administration's budget policies have cut billions of dollars from social programs. Tremendous cutbacks in low-income programs primarily affecting youth and women have taken place, as the figures in table 7.1 make clear.

Households headed by a woman account for approximately 83 percent of all recipients of Aid to Families with Dependent Children (AFDC) (Stallard et al. 1983). As a result of President Reagan's

Table 7.1 Budget Cutbacks in Low-income Programs, Fiscal Years
1981–1984 (in billions of dollars)

	1981 appropriations	1983 appropriations	1984 proposed appropriations
AFDC	8.5	7.8	7.1
Food stamps	11.3	12.8	11.7
Medicaid	17.4	19.3	20.8
SSI (Supplemental Security Insurance)	7.2	8.1	8.6
Subsidized housing	24.8	8.7	− 2.3
Employment and training	7.9	4.1	3.6
Legal services	0.3	0.2	0.0
Community services	0.5	0.4	0.0
WIC	0.9	1.1	1.1
Free and reduced-price meals	2.9	3.0	2.8
Maternal and child health	0.5	0.4	0.4
Primary care and migrant health	0.4	0.3	0.3
Low-income energy assistance	1.85	2.0	1.3
Compensatory education	3.5	3.2	3.0
Financial aid for needy students	3.8	3.6	3.6
Headstart	0.8	0.9	1.05
Child welfare services	0.5	0.6	0.6
Social services	3.0	2.45	2.5
Veterans' pensions	3.8	3.8	3.8
Earned income tax credit	1.3	1.2	1.2
Total	101.15	83.95	71.05

Note: After adjustment for inflation, proposed funding for the above programs represents a 40 percent reduction from FY 1981 levels and 19 percent
below FY 1983 levels.
Source: K. Stallard, B. Ehrenreich, and H. Sklar. *Poverty in the American Dream:
Women and Children First* (Boston: South End Press, 1983), 46.

policies, 365,000 such families lost all aid and another 260,000 families had their benefits reduced in 1982. In almost 50 percent of the states, AFDC recipients lose Medicaid coverage when they are dropped from AFDC. Before Reagan took office, more than one out of every four women on welfare held a paying job, a job so poorly paid that the woman was still eligible for AFDC (Ackerman 1982, 86). As these women face the loss of most or all of their benefits, some will most likely decide it is not worthwhile to keep working and many may even turn to crime, if they have not already done so.

By 1983 some 203 million people—between 400,000 to 600,000 families—had been eliminated from the food stamp program. Six out of every ten food stamp households are headed by a woman (Eisenstein 1984, 120). Despite inflation, the Reagan administration has postponed the cost-of-living increases in food stamp benefits, tightened eligibility rules, and actually *lowered* the eligibility ceiling for food stamps. Prior to the Reagan presidency, a family of four with an annual income of $14,000, was eligible for food stamps. Under Reagan, the limit has been lowered to $11,000 (Ackerman 1982, 84).

Around 66 percent of households in subsidized housing are headed by women and the rents have increased from twenty-five percent of annual income to thirty percent. Public service jobs funded by the Comprehensive Employment and Training Act (CETA) have been totally eliminated, sixty percent of these 300,000 former CETA employees were women. The following anecdote shows how the Reagan CETA layoffs affected one teenage marginalized male.

> Danny had been angry and frustrated in eighth grade. "I was flunking everything," he recalled. Then he got a part-time CETA. . . job at a dog pound, fell in love with animals, and decided to become a veterinarian. After a few weeks, a teacher noted, "Danny felt better about himself." His grades improved, and he used his money he earned on his job to help his mother buy groceries and to buy clothes for himself.
>
> In the Fall of 1981, as Danny Salb was beginning ninth grade, he and more than 300,000 other CETA employees were laid off by Ronald Reagan. "I was pretty upset," said Danny. His mother said he had counted on spending his income to buy the shoes he needed for the winter. [Ackerman 1982, 81–82]

The Reagan administration lays people off, and makes their conditions of unemployment much harsher. For example, the trade adjustment assistance (TAA) program was intended to provide a full year of unemployment benefits to those who lost their jobs to imports. When Reagan took office, half a million workers were receiving TAA. By 1982, Reagan cut TAA funds in half, leaving hundreds of thousands of the unemployed desperate (ibid., 82).

New regulations affecting unemployment benefits leave large

numbers of individuals without compensation. Ex-military personnel who become unemployed are denied benefits if they are eligible for reenlistment or if they received a bad conduct discharge. People out of work thirteen weeks or longer must take any job offering as much as half their former pay, or lose benefits. And finally, it is much more difficult under Reagan to receive an extension of compensation (ibid., 82–83).

Clearly, the government programs implemented by the Reagan administration have hit women, youth, and minorities the hardest. The losers in President Reagan's budget cuts are those who once had CETA jobs, unemployment benefits, food stamps, AFDC, Medicaid, and subsidized housing; they join the ranks of those for whom street crime is a real alternative for solving economic problems.

In addition to cutting social programs that primarily affect women and children, the Reagan administration is eliminating state jobs for women and racial minorities. Those who administer state welfare programs are disproportionately black men and white and black women (Eisenstein 1984, 117). Therefore, dismantling the welfare state decreases the jobs for these individuals and adds greatly to those marginalized from economic activity. As Augustus F. Hawkins has shown,

> Minority employees of the federal agencies have been laid off at a rate 50 percent greater than non-minority employees. Women administrators have been laid off at a rate 150 percent higher than male administrators. Minorities in administrative positions have been laid off at a rate about 220 percent higher than non-minority employees in similar positions. [cited in ibid., 117–18]

The Reagan administration's policies, an example of right-wing political ideology in action, are clearly racist and antifeminist in their results, if not their intent. Their effects are to dismantle the welfare state, remove women (especially married black women) from the labor market, and return them to the home. The argument put forth by the New Right—Viguerie, Falwell, Gilder, and others—is that welfare state capitalism raises taxes, and this diminution of real family income, combined with inflation, pulls married women into the labor market. Consequently, the fabric of U.S. society—the traditional patriarchal family—is destroyed, and along with it the moral fabric of society. Therefore, the New Right argues, welfare state capitalism must go, and women *must* "return" to the home.

"Pro-family" politics can be seen as a reaction to both the demographic changes taking place in the family and the crisis of international capitalism. As discussed in chapter 4, only around ten percent of all households are now traditional nuclear families: the father/husband as sole breadwinner and the mother/wife at home full-time with two or more children. As Rosalind Petchesky (1984, 247) argues, the new situation of the family has brought greater openness about sexuality and flexibility concerning living and childrearing arrangements, while unsettling some people's lives and expectations.

> For one whose belief has remained unshaken in his prerogative, as a man, to "have the authority and make the decision," or her privilege, as a woman, "to be happy with it," it must seem a very alien and treacherous world. For many more, the economic strains and social changes of the contemporary period are experienced as personal crises, as "family" crises: loss of job, loss of children, loss of a sense of security, or loss of mother (or wife) at home. Thus the construction of a "profamily" politics, with the embattled fetus as its motto, appeals, or is intended to appeal, to a level of longing and loss (homelessness) buried deep in the popular subconscious. [ibid.]

The New Right plays upon this sense of "homelessness" by constructing an "antifeminist backlash" aimed at all aspects of sexual freedom and alternatives to the traditional nuclear family. It has become a "preservatist" movement made up of individuals who feel their way of life (patriarchal capitalism) threatened (ibid., 244). Historically, right-wing movements have needed to invoke "some system of good and evil which transcends the political and social process and freezes it" (Lipset and Raab 1970, 117). In this way, dismantling the welfare state imposes discipline and social control on those who are "evil" (Petchesky 1984, 247–52).

Piven and Cloward (1982), in their important book, *The New Class War*, argue that dismantling the welfare state is a class-specific means of disciplining the working class. The global capitalist crisis provides a fertile context for right-wing policies (Ratner and McMullan 1983, 31-34), and as Piven and Cloward (1982, 39) point out, the welfare state and its programs, such as income-maintenance, "intrude upon the dynamics of the labor market, augmenting the power of workers. And that is why they have become the target of a concerted attack by the privileged and powerful." Petchesky (1984, 251), however, adds that while this argument is not wrong, it ignores the fact that most of those affected by the budget cuts are women and children. Thus, while dismantling the welfare state does discipline the working class in an increasingly crisis-ridden world capitalist system, it is also "undeniable that a major goal of the conservative state's effort to contract if not dismantle social welfare is to discipline and punish women who try to survive, and be sexual, outside the bounds of the traditional family" (ibid.).

In essence, the Reagan administration is attempting to restabilize patriarchy and capitalism simultaneously, by disciplining the working class, women, youth, and racial minorities. However, this "disciplining" can only *increase* crime by these groups, as "pro-family" policies escalate the number of marginalized individuals.

Along with these policies that result in increasing street crime, the Reagan administration has planned to limit civil rights under the guise of "solving" the violent crime problem. This plan, revealed in the administration's 1981 *Attorney General's Task Force Report on Violent Street Crime* (U.S. Department of Justice 1981), contains a long list of ways to limit the right to due process in the court system. For example, bail could be denied to those individuals found "by clear and convincing evidence" to present a danger to the community and those who had committed a "serious crime" while in a pretrial release status (ibid., 50). Ignoring the constitutionality of such a policy, the Task Force is recommending someone be punished prior to being proven guilty beyond a reasonable doubt. This recommendation would sabotage the "presumption of innocence" and therefore the due process clause of the Fourteenth Amendment. The proposal would have virtually no effect on violent street crime, since only a fraction of defendents are arrested for violent crimes while on bail (Gordon 1984, 18). An American Civil Liberties Union study found that "only 1.9 percent of those released before trial are later convicted of and imprisoned for serious crimes committed during the release period" (Gross 1982, 138). It will, however, most likely lead to more crime, since preventive detention may cause the individual to lose his or her job, forcing family members into crime and/or onto welfare rolls (Gordon 1984, 18). Moreover, it will make it easier to convict marginalized males, as research shows that those incarcerated (and, therefore, unable to meet with attorney as often and unable to obtain evidence and witnesses) are more likely to be found guilty and tend to receive harsher sentences than those who have been released prior to trial, regardless of the charge (ibid.). Thus, while preventive detention will not curb violent crime, it will serve the interests of powerful men by increasingly publicizing to the people in this society that it is marginalized males who are the *real* threats to our safety.

The Task Force also found the "exclusionary rule" a hindrance to curbing violent street crime. The exclusionary rule exists "to deter illegal police conduct and promote respect for the rule of law by preventing illegally obtained evidence from being used in a criminal trial" (U.S. Department of Justice 1981, 55). However, the Task Force proposed that evidence acquired during an unreasonable search and seizure "should not be excluded from a criminal proceeding if it has been obtained by an officer acting in the reasonable, good faith belief that it was in conformity" with Fourth Amendment standards for search and seizure (ibid.). Moreover, evidence obtained prior to a search warrant being issued "constitutes *prima facie* evidence of such a good faith belief" (ibid.). While such a proposal may give the state an advantage in drug-related prosecutions for example, its impact on our basic freedom is quite clear. As Diana Gordon (1984, 18) of the National Council on Crime and Delinquency states, this clearly shows us how far the Task Force is willing "to extend police power at the cost of the right of the people guaranteed in the Fourth Amendment 'to be secure in their persons, houses, papers, and effects. . .' " By repealing the exclusionary rule, the state may be able to arrest lower-level drug dealers, but not the rise of violent crime. Violent crime is a *structural* problem, not an individual one. As more and more power-less people are incarcerated at the expense of all of our civil liberties and pocket books, other powerless people will fill their spots in violence-ridden communities.

To "curb" violent crime the Task Force also wants to limit a defendant's right to an appeal, eliminate the federal parole commission, establish a "sentencing commission" to package sentences so individuals in a "given category of offender" would receive comparable punishments, and allow the federal system to prosecute youth gang members rather than leave them to state-run juvenile courts. Clearly, the Reagan administration has put together a repressive crime control program threatening our individual rights. What the Task Force tells us is that we need to sacrifice some personal liberties if we want to curb violent street crime. However, *none of these proposals will reduce violent street crime.*

Consider, as a last example, the principal recommendation by the Task Force, and the only one with a specific budget—$2 billion of federal money to be given to states to build and/or rebuild prisons. This recommendation was considered the "lynchpin" of all the other recommendations (ibid., 20). As one of the members of the Task Force stated in a press conference, the "bottom line" of their findings is that "we have to lock up more violent offenders and we have to keep them locked up" (cited in ibid., 20). They argue that increasing the "costs" of crime—that is, increasing imprisonment, will curb violent crime. The argument—one supported, as we have seen, by right-wing criminologists and some radical feminists—is that sending more people to prison for longer periods (while simultaneously limiting everyone's civil liberties) will reduce violent crime substantially. However, can violent crime be curbed by building more prisons and filling them up? First, the vast majority of street crimes are never reported, and, of those reported, only a small proportion result in an arrest. Second, prisons do very little to prevent or reduce crime. Prisons throughout the United States are well known for their incredibly high rates of recidivism (reinvolvement in criminality after release). The longer individuals remain in prison the greater their chances for recidivism and the more severe their crimes (Eitzen and Timer 1985, 571). Ironically, the United States has been locking people up faster than ever before—the "lock-up" rate increased one third between 1975 and 1981 alone (Currie 1982a, 29)—yet we still have the highest violent crime rate in the industrialized world. Not only are we locking people up at a relatively higher rate, but we lock up more people—in absolute numbers—than any other country except the Soviet Union and South Africa. As Elliot Currie (1982a, 30) explains:

> At the end of the 1970's our "incarceration rate" (*excluding* those people locked in local jails) was about 140 per 100,000 population. The Dutch rate, at the other end of the spectrum, was about 18 per 100,000. (The average *length* of prison sentences is dramatically longer here as well.) Many European countries, in fact, including Denmark, West Germany, Sweden, and Switzerland, moved during the 1970's to decrease their use of prisons even further. We have moved with great velocity in the other direction, to the point where our prisons, staffed to the rafters and overflowing into local jails, and exploding fairly regularly with terrifying violence, have long since passed the point of judicial tolerance.

The threat of incarceration is meaningless. Study after study reveals that neither the threat of punishment nor increased incarceration has any real impact on the crime rate (ibid., 31–33; Gordon 1984, 20–22). This should not surprise anyone who considers the fact that those most prone to violent street crime, marginalized males, often find life on the street no better than life inside prison. As one individual put it:

> "It is not a matter of a guy saying 'I want to go to jail (or) I am afraid of jail.' Jail is on the street just like it is on the inside. The same as, like when you are in jail, they tell you, 'Look, if you do something wrong you are going to be put in the hole.' You are still in jail, in the hole or out of the hole. You are in jail on the street or behind bars. It is the same thing. . ." [cited in Gordon 1971, 59]

The deterrent effect of incarceration is negligible. However, with the support of the Reagan administration, money is being poured into prison construction rather than being used to help make community life meaningful. In 1984 approximately $1 billion was spent on new state and federal prisons, and at least 20 states have allocated $1 billion for additional cell space, while 33 states debated whether to use another $1.5 billion for prison construction (Eitzen and Timmer 1985, 568). A bill recently introduced in Congress would provide "states with up to $6.5 billion in federal monies to improve their prison facilities, and the Reagan Administration asked Congress for $94 million to build new federal prisons—the largest one-year funding request for new prisons in U.S. history" (ibid.).

In short, the Reagan administration has declared war on the

powerless. The Reagan crime control program is being set up to criminalize the more powerless people and, therefore, create the public belief that powerless people threaten the attempt to, as Reagan put it, "reclaim this clearing we call civilization" (cited in Currie 1982a, 26). At the same time, the Reagan administration is doing all it can to increase and hide the crimes of the powerful. Indeed, crime control represents another manifestation of the dichotomization of social reality into "good" and "evil." As Michalowski (1981, 31) points out,

> By identifying "street criminals" as the *real* criminals, the Reagan Admin-
> istration has accelerated the policy of absolving corporate lawbreakers—
> the fixers, polluters, worker safety violators, labor oppressors and truth
> manipulators—from any stigma or punishment for the death, destruc-
> tion, despoilation, and billion dollar bilkings of American society. . . .
> Dichotomizations of social reality into the good and the evil are ideal
> weapons in the game of scapegoat politics. They enable substantial public
> hostility to be vented toward officially designated evil ones while leaving a
> clear field of action for others.

Increasing Powerful Crime and Keeping It Invisible

While the Reagan administration strengthens "law and order" against the powerless—the "evil ones"—it is drastically cutting enforcement of the law against the "good ones"—corporations. The Reagan administration is doing all it can to keep powerful crime invisible and allow corporations freedom to pursue their habitual criminal activity.

One of the first moves of the Reagan administration after taking office was to make the Office of Management and Budget (OMB) the clearance center for all regulatory decisions. Through Presidential Executive Order 12291, Reagan shifted authority over regulatory agencies to the OMB, which now reviews existing programs, postpones and eliminates regulations, and controls agency budgets (Claybrook et al. 1984, xix). OMB began to work quickly behind the scenes with regulated industries to eliminate government safety and environmental standards (ibid.). For example, on April 6, 1981, Vice-President Bush announced thirty-four "Actions to Help the U.S. Auto Industry." This list was adapted from a longer list prepared by Ford, General Motors, and Chrysler to relax safety, quality and emission standards (ibid.). Moreover, the first budget David Stockman (as head of OMB) sent to Congress cut conservation, solar energy, and environmental clean-up severely and eliminated many programs entirely.

The Environmental Protection Agency (EPA) was particularly hard hit. The four major programs of the EPA are water, air, hazardous waste, and pesticides. Programs dealing with air pollution, ground water protection, and pesticides were cut $9 million, while those concerned with cleaning up toxic waste dumps were cut $50 million (Regenstein 1982, 376). In both 1981 and 1982, the budget for these programs fell by 30 percent and an additional 19 percent reduction was sought in 1983 (Claybrook 1984, 122). In February 1981, Stockman prepared a target list of regulations, ranging from food and drug safety, to pollution control and disposable chemical waste control, that the Reagan administration was determined to "defer, revise, or rescind" (Behr 1981, A1). Moreover, President Reagan has decided to make it easier for corporations to ship their dangerous products to other—usually Third World—nations. In September 1981, the Reagan administration prepared to eliminate practically all the rules requiring that foreign governments be notified about the "dumping" of such dangerous products. According to *The Washington Post*, these rules were being dropped because the Reagan administration felt they "placed U.S. exports at a competitive disadvantage" (Mayer 1981, B4). Most hazardous-waste regulations were either suspended or weakened after President Reagan took office. The budget also decreased drastically. In 1981 the EPA spent $11.3 million for hazardous-waste enforcement, but in 1983 the EPA requested only $1.9 million (Claybrook et al. 1984, 129).

To help him carry out his plans for a pro-business EPA, President Reagan appointed Anne Gorsuch as head; as an attorney in Denver, she was known for her antiregulation background. In addition to Gorsuch, the EPA was filled with officials who had been lobbyists, lawyers, and consultants for some of the nation's biggest polluters:

— Dr. John Todhunter, who opposed pesticide regulation on behalf of industry clients, was named assistant administrator for pesticides and toxic substances;
— Nolan E. Clark, whose law firm was representing the Dow Chemical Company in its efforts to prevent the cancer-causing and fetus-damaging herbicide 2,4,5-T from being banned, was put in charge of policy and resource management;
— John E. Daniel, a lawyer and lobbyist for the Johns-Mansville Corporation, a leading manufacturer of the health-destroying and cancer-causing product asbestos, was named as Gorsuch's chief of staff;
— Robert M. Perry, a lawyer for Exxon Oil Company, was named EPA General Counsel;
— Kathleen Bennett, who, as a lobbyist for the American Paper Institute and the Crown Zellerback paper company, fought to weaken the Clean Air Act, was named assistant administrator for air pollution control programs;
— Rita M. Lavelle, a public relations executive for Aero-Jet-General

Table 7.2   Selected Workplace Hazards Whose Regulation the Reagan Administration Is Delaying

Agent	Health effects	Current OSHA standard	Recommended NIOSH standard
Benzene	Leukemia, respiratory irritation, pulmonary edema, dermatitis, CNS depression, aplastic anemia, chromosome abnormality	10 ppm TWA (8 hr.)	1 ppm TWA (8 hr.)
Ethylene dibromide	Potential stomach cancer, birth defects, lung, liver, and kidney damage	20 ppm TWA (8 hr.) 300 ppm ceiling peak of 50 ppm for 5 minutes	0.13 ppm ceiling average over a 15-minute period
Ethylene oxide	Dermatitis, burns, eye irritation, pulmonary edema, cancer: leukemia, possibly stomach cancer	50 ppm TWA (8 hr.)	10 ppm TWA (8 hr.)
Formaldehyde	Respiratory, eye irritation; possible nasal cavity cancer; pulmonary edema; hypersensitivity	3 ppm TWA (8 hr.)	1 ppm TWA

Occupations at risk	Estimated No. of workers affected	U.S. consumption/ production 1970–1979	Changes in consumption/ production over 20 years
Chemical workers Shoe makers Furniture makers Glue makers Chemists	1,495,706	93,203 million lbs. (production)	Increase + 43,840 million lbs.
Anti-knock compound workers Fumigant workers Pesticide formulators Truckers Warehouse workers Farmworkers	12,500 Anti-knock manufacturing; rough estimate up to 100,000 exposed packers, truckers, ware- housemen, farm and dock workers	340–360 million lbs. per annum	NA
Hospital workers Fumigant makers Textile/food fumigators Organic chemical synthesizers Detergent makers	144,152	43,484 million lbs. (production)	Increase + 22,125 million lbs.
Wood preservers Embalming fluid workers Textile printers/ workers Anatomists/biologists	1,400,000	7 billon lbs. (production)	NA

Note: TWA—time-weighted average.
Source: J. Grozuczak, *Poisons on the Job: The Reagan Administration and American Workers* (San Francisco: Sierra Club, 1982), report no. 4, 32–33.

Corporation, the third biggest polluter in California, which had been charged by the state with illegally dumping 20,000 gallons a day of toxic waste, was named assistant administrator in charge of the "Superfund" hazardous waste cleanup program;
— Frank A. Shepherd, a lawyer who had represented General Motors, a leading opponent of the Clean Air Act, was placed in charge of law enforcement;
— William A. Sullivan, Jr., an attorney who fought against environmental controls for steel mills, was appointed as Shepherd's deputy. Commenting on his appointment, Sullivan said, "If I were an environmental activist, I'd be scared to death." (Regenstein 1982, 378–79)

It is not surprising that these appointees have consistently supported business interests in areas ranging from hazardous waste, to clean air and water, to pesticides. Consider the "Superfund" legislation, which at EPA fell under the hands of Rita Lavelle. Superfund was intended to provide EPA with money and resources both to uncover abandoned hazardous-waste sites and to charge those responsible with partial reimbursement for their clean-up. However, Rita Lavelle used Superfund money to support polluters rather than the people.

> The first use of the Superfund authority came after a toxic site in Santa Fe Springs, California, caught fire in July 1981. Reagan had been in office only six months. But the EPA quickly negotiated an extraordinary settlement with one of the responsible parties. Rather than requiring it to finance complete removal of the hazard, the EPA limited the company's cleanup responsibility. The settlement also included a remarkable commitment. The EPA agreed to testify on behalf of the company in any subsequent lawsuit brought by injured citizens. This early settlement set a clear precedent for future administration negotiations with industry. [Claybrook et al. 1984, 138]

The same type of deregulation and perversion of purpose occurred for air and water pollution and dangerous pesticides. Under President Reagan's EPA, definitions of pollution have been so changed that only a fraction of pollutants are being controlled; standards have so relaxed that they no longer are acting to control these dangers to U.S. society (ibid., 114–64).

The policy of simultaneously increasing and hiding powerful criminality has extended to other areas. Under Reagan, the Occupational Safety and Health Administration (OSHA) has weakened critical health standards, refused to issue new regulations or improve old ones, failed to enforce safeguards, and drastically cut funds and staff (Grozuczak 1982). Chapter 5 pointed out the violence directed against workers through disease, injury, and death in the workplace. Yet upon taking office, President Reagan proposed to cut $50 million from the OSHA budget (ibid., 2). Since January 1981, OSHA has been asked repeatedly to set exposure standards on well-known carcinogens, like ethylene oxide, chromium, and formaldehyde, which threaten workers in the auto, chemical, and health industries. Yet even after numerous pleas and petitions,

> The Reagan Administration OSHA has not issued a single new standard on a carcinogenic substance in nearly 2 years; the agency is unlikely even to propose a single standard for many months. This inaction leaves, for example, more than 3,995,000 workers potentially exposed to uncertain levels of [ethylene, chromium, and formaldehyde]. [ibid.]

Under the Reagan administration, OSHA is delaying needed regulation of workplace hazards and cutting back on the enforcement of workplace hazard standards (see tables 7.2 and 7.3).

In addition, OSHA is no longer automatically inspecting a company accused of violating safety or health codes. Instead, OSHA will limit its inspections to companies that are accused of "violations which pose physical harm or imminent danger" to employees. The "minor" complaints are being resolved by registered mail (Earley 1982, A21). President Reagan's OSHA created this policy not only because of its pro-business mentality, but also because budget cuts have depleted its staff. In 1982, for example, one-third of all the agency's field offices were shut down, forcing hundreds of employees out of work (Claybrook 1984, 111). These budget and staff cuts have tremendously decreased OSHA's enforcement. Comparing the first eight months of fiscal 1982 to a similar period in fiscal 1980, table 7.4 shows how the enforcement of the occupational safety and health requirements has plunged in every relevant category.

Clearly, the Reagan administration cares less that the powerful continue to kill and injure workers and more that business increase its profit margins. Moreover, President Reagan's attack on OSHA can be seen as a means of "disciplining" the labor movement. As Frank Ackerman (1982, 114) notes, the "establishment of the legal right to a healthy and safe work environment, even if poorly enforced, is a gain for workers." When health and safety at the workplace were made a union issue, important organizing drives occurred in the textile, chemical, and automobile industries, and the issue was central, as well, to the movement to organize clerical workers. By stripping OSHA of its effective powers, the Reagan administration not only reduces OSHA's assistance to the labor movement, but at the same time only increases the victimization of workers by corporate crime.

The EPA and OSHA are not the only regulatory agencies being stripped of their limited power. While I argued in chapter 5 that regulatory agencies were, essentially and historically, pro-business,

Table 7.3   Selected Serious Workplace Hazards for Whose Standards the Reagan Administration Is Cutting Back Enforcement

Agent	Health effects	Current OSHA standard	Recommended NIOSH standard
Crylonitrile	Eye irritation, skin irritation, blistering (can be absorbed through shoes and clothing), nausea, vomiting, headache, asphyxia, possible lung and colon cancer	2 ppm TWA (45 mg/m³) 10 ppm ceiling (15 min.—skin)	4 ppm ceiling
Arsenic	Skin cancer, lung cancer, disturbance to bone marrow (blood-making), peripheral neuritis, lymphatic cancer	0.010 mg/m³ TWA	0.002 mg/m³ TWA
Asbestos	Asbestosis, lung cancer, GI cancer, mesothelioma	2,000,000 fibers/m³ TWA (8 hr.) 10,000,000 fibers/m³ ceiling	0.002 mg/m³ (over 5 microns)
Carbon tetrachloride	Dermatitis (defats skin), CNS depresant, nausea, vomiting, toxic hepatitis, renal failure, possible liver cancer	10 ppm TA (8 hr.) Ceiling of 25 ppm; maximum peak of 200 ppm for one 5 min. period in 4 hours	2 ppm Ceiling
Beryllium	Lung cancer, dermatitis, nasopharyngitis, chronic beryllium disease (respiratory)	.002 mg/m³ TWA	0.0005 mg/m³ TWA

Occupations at risk	Estimated no. of workers affected	U.S. consumption production 1970–1979	Changes in consumption/ production over 20 years
Plastic manufacturers Textile workers Pesticide formulators Rubber makers	374,345	14,047 million pounds (production)	Increase + 7,823 million lbs.
Agricultural workers Pesticide formulators Paint makers Leather/tannery workers Pharmaceutical workers Miners and smelter workers	255,277 432,017 (As_2O_3)	NA (confidential industry data)	NA
Auto mechanics Insulators Demolition/construction workers Paper manufacturers Miners/millers paint makers	1,280,202	6,987,000 short tons (consumption)	Decrease − 286 short tons
Solvent makers Insecticide makers Flourocarbon makers Rubber makers Refrigerant makers Grain fumigators	1,380,223	9,251 million lbs. (production)	Increase + 3,365 million lbs.
Nuclear reactor Workers Electrical equipment makers Cathode ray tube makers Missile technicians	855,189	33 million lbs. (consumption)	Decrease − 84 million lbs.

(Continued on next page)

Table 7.3 (continued)

Agent	Health effects	Current OSHA standard	Recommended NIOSH standard
Chromium (VI) (oxides)	Lung cancer, skin ulcers, lung irritation	0.100 mg/m^3 ceiling	0.001 mg/m^3
Nickel (oxide)	Skin sensitization, upper respiratory tract, irritant, lung cancer, nasal passage cancer	1 mg/m^3 8 hr. TWA	.015 mg/m^3 8 hr. TW
Cadmium	Respiratory tract, irritant, lung damage ("emphysema"), kidney damage, anemia, liver damage	0.1 mg/m^3 8 hr. TWA 0.3 mg/m^3 ceiling	.04 mg/m^3 TWA 0.2 mg/m^3 ceiling
Vinyl chloride	Liver cancer, chloracne, CNS depressant	1 ppm, 8 hr. TWA 5 ppm ceiling	Minimum detectable level 1 ppm Ceiling
Lead (inorganic)	Kidney, blood and CNS disease, peripheral nerve disease	0.5 mg/m^3 8 hr. TWA Blood lead less than .060 mg/100 g blood	Less than 0.100 mg/ TWA
Silica	Chronic lung disease (silicosis)	10 mg/m^3/% SiO$_2$ TWA respirable quartz	0.050 mg/m^3 TWA[a] respirable free sili
(Toluene) Diisocyanates	Hypersensitivity asthma pulmonary edema dermatitis	0.02 ppm ceiling	0.005 ppm TWA wit 0.02 ppm ceiling

Occupations at risk	Estimated No. of workers affected	U.S. consumption/ production 1970–1979	Changes in consumption/ production over 20 years
Metal workers Electroplaters Welders Glass workers	1,451,631	11,579 thousand short tons (consumption)	Decrease − 1,557 thousand tons
Battery makers Ceramic makers Varnish makers Dyers Chemists Ink makers	1,369,270	1,692 thousand short tons (consumption)	Increase + 200 thousands of short tons
Alloy makers Pesticide workers Engravers Textile printers Dental amalgram workers	1,376,871	53 million lbs. (production)	Decrease − 52 million lbs.
Rubber makers Organic chemical workers Polyvinyl resin makers	239,375	53,626 million lbs. (production)	Increase + 33,555 million lbs.
Smelter workers Battery makers Steel foundry workers Welders Metalizers	835,000	10 million tons	NA
Fiber glass insulation workers Foundry workers Miners Tunnel workers Granite workers	NA	NA	NA
Adhesive workers Insulation workers Print sprayers Polyurethane makers	130,000	10 million lbs.	

Source: J. Grozuczak *Poisons on the Job: The Reagan Administration and American Workers* (San Francisco: Sierra Club, report no. 4, 34–36).
Note: TWA—Time-weighted average

under President Reagan matters are getting profoundly worse. In all areas of corporate regulation—food and drugs, product safety, the health and safety of workers, environmental protection, transportation safety, and energy—the Reagan administration, by deregulating the powerful, not only increases their criminality but also further hides it (see Claybrook et al. 1984 for an extensive review of President Reagan's deregulation plans and actions).

The Right-Wing Plan: A Blueprint for Increasing Crime

The right-wing "answer" to the crime problem, as spelled out in the example of the Reagan administration, both publicizes the criminality of the powerless and increasingly conceals the criminality of the powerful. What's more, it is *not* a program that can curb any type of crime, but rather, *a program that encourages both types of criminality.* In other words, the right-wing plan greatly increases criminal victimization by both the powerful and powerless.

First, deregulation concentrates economic power. As fewer and fewer firms dominate a sector of the economy, those firms can more easily engage in corporate crime because there is less competition and, therefore, fewer checks on their behavior. As Harold Barnett (1981, 183) found in examining wealth and the generation of illegal income, those firms possessing market power "have the potential to illegally expand or segment markets, create barriers to entry, eliminate competitors, and control wages, other costs and prices."

Second, the concentration of capital and the resulting increases of corporate crime mean that the incomes of the wealthy, and therefore income inequality, increases (ibid.). As earlier chapters pointed out, when income inequality increases, so do property offenses and violent street crime. John Braithwaite (1979a), after reviewing the data, concluded that increased economic inequality is the most important factor for increases in street crime. Regardless of population or region, cities with the widest income gaps, Braithwaite found, have the highest rates of street crime. More recently, Elliott Currie's (1985, Chap. 5) review of a variety of studies confirms Braithwaite's conclusions, and several studies have shown that the level of income inequality correlates significantly with the level of violent crime (Carroll and Jackson 1983; Blau and Blau 1982).

And finally, the New Right's antifeminist, "pro-family" attempt to discipline women, youth, racial minorities, and the working class by dismantling the welfare state will increase street crime by pushing more and more individuals from these groups into crime.

In short, the right-wing plan will increase criminality at all levels of U.S. society. Under such a plan, we will more likely fall victim to

Table 7.4 Decline in Enforcement of Occupational Safety and Health Requirements, 1980–1982

Aspect of enforcement	Percent decline
Number of workers covered	
(1.5 million fewer)	41
Work inspections	17
Accident	10
Response to workers' complaints	54
Follow-up after violation	86
Violations recorded	
Serious	50
Willful	86
Repeated	65
Total penalties imposed	67
For failure to abate hazards	79
Average hours per inspection	
Safety	18
Health	13

Note: Figures based on first 8 months of fiscal years 1980 and 1982.
Source: J. Claybrook and the Staff at Public Citizen, *Retreat from Safety* (New York: Pantheon Books), 100.

crimes by both the powerless and powerful. An alternative is clearly necessary.

A Socialist Feminist Alternative

It is very important that an effective alternative to the Reagan plan be articulated. As Ian Taylor (1981) pointed out in his important book, *Law and Order: Arguments for Socialism,* the construction of an alternative plan for curbing crime is urgently necessary for two reasons: first, the law-and-order stance of the right justifies both a continued expansion of the coercive apparatus of the state and a diminution of funds for social programs; and second, in countries like Britain and the United States, crime will continue to increase and, therefore, be an even greater social problem. However, while radical, progressive, and Marxist criminologists have picked up on Taylor's ideas and begun to address this issue, none in the United States have thought to consider patriarchy and crimes against women as essential areas of attack for a crime control program. I want to contribute to the progressive crime control program by emphasizing the importance of patriarchy and power, in addition to class conditions.

Crime, as emphasized throughout this book, is rooted in power and therefore structured inequality, in both the patriarchal (gender) and capitalist (class) spheres. Moreover, the "social control" of crime in serving the interests of the powerful by ignoring most of their criminality—and simultaneously publicizing, yet not curbing, the criminality of the powerless—has been ineffective. It should be clear, then, that to curb crime we do not need to expand repressive state measures, but we do need to reduce power and, therefore, class *and* gender inequality. While I believe criminality in the United States will be dramatically reduced only through a thorough transformation to a *democratic socialist feminist society,* this type of social change cannot occur in an instant and nothing indicates the current existence, or early emergence, of a unified socialist feminist revolutionary movement. However, this does not mean that individuals cannot work together to "chip away" at patriarchal capitalism. Below, I have put together, while hardly exhaustive, a discussion of elements that are not only essential for curbing crime, but also will help delegitimize patriarchal capitalism and, therefore, contribute to the emergence of that revolutionary movement.

Full Employment and Workplace Democracy

Chapters 3 and 4 showed that marginalization, unemployment, and, therefore, poverty, are related to violent and nonviolent forms of street crime. Studies have shown how important it is to consider economic conditions to understand street crime. A crime control policy therefore must address those elements of patriarchal capitalism that lead to poverty. The inherent structure of a capitalist economic system is unable to provide jobs for all who need, want, and can work. However, there are ways of ameliorating this situation. First, we need an expanded program of social construction to serve human needs. There is a vast amount of work to be done—urgently needed to revitalize a decaying U.S. society—that would generate millions of jobs. Many people today lack accessible, good quality health care, acceptable, affordable housing, childcare services, and low-cost recreation facilities. A policy directed at serving these needs would provide substantial employment. The United States has one of the worst public transportation systems in the industrialized world. Constructing an effective mass transit system would provide thousands of jobs for people as well as save energy and curb air pollution. Moreover, millions of jobs could be created by cleaning up and protecting the environment, and switching to alternative forms of energy, such as sun, wind, and tidal power. Fossil fuels and nuclear power are not only costly but also environmentally destructive. Moving labor and capital into alternative energy production would provide jobs for people as well as a cleaner and safer society.

Second, as pointed out in chapters 3 and 4, people need not just jobs, but *meaningful* ones. We therefore need to direct economic policy toward designing jobs that increase the rewards of legitimate work in economic as well as social and psychological terms. Increasing the availability of socially constructive work that is safe and rewarding, for example, would help to ameliorate the psychological problems associated with so much alienating work in the secondary labor market. Additionally, we need to provide all working people with the opportunity to earn a living wage. A progressive program of crime control must support raising the minimum wage above the poverty level to guarantee those who work an adequate income. Both of these suggestions, meaningful work and an adequate wage, decrease property and violent crime. Currie (1982b, 21) found in his survey of job programs for ex-offenders that the "better employed" individuals committed not only fewer crimes, but less serious ones as well. Fagan, Hansen, and Jang (1983, 117) found in their study of juvenile dlinquency that "youth employment per se does not reduce delinquency," but rather, "the *quality* of work opportunity (i.e., status, skills, promotion, wages)" affects all types of delinquency, including interpersonal violence. As these researchers go on to point out, "where working youths perceive growth, benefits, and tangible rewards from their employment, they commit fewer of each type of offense" (ibid., 107). Moreover, in the 1970s the Department of Labor sponsored studies of the impact that stipends (equivalent to the amount of unemployment insurance) would have on ex-offenders. Despite the low level of economic support, these programs lowered rearrests for property crimes and violent crimes by as much as 30 percent. As Currie (1982b, 19) states, "What's striking about this is that clear-cut results were accomplished with so little." Providing everyone with a *wage above the poverty level as well as a meaningful job* is, in short, necessary for curbing crime.

And finally, we need to end racist and sexist discrimination in the labor market by providing equal pay for comparable work, systematic affirmative action, and effective job training and retraining programs for all who desire it. These would not only help to achieve equality in the labor market, but also publically state the social equality of men, women, and people of color. Moreover, we need similar reforms, possibly implemented by unions, to increase the power of women *within* the workplace itself and to eliminate sex segregation in the labor market. Such reforms would combat not only workplace crime like sexual harassment and "legal" rape at work, but also street crimes and masculine dominance in general. It is *essential to attack the sexual division of labor,* if we want to curb inequality, power, and thus crime. The sexual division of labor both reinforces patriarchy and creates the conditions for crime. The type of work women are segregated into—in the "pink-collar ghetto"—reinforces the ideology that women are naturally nurturant and subservient. Economic desperation also forces many women to depend on men and/or property crime (larceny, fraud, embezzlement) for survival. If women did not need to sell sex to survive, most would not, since many prostitutes, given a choice, would rather work at a nonalienating, quality, "straight" job (Mann 1985). Moreover, many women fail to leave relationships that involve "legal" and "tolerated illegal" wife rape, wife battering and other forms of domination because they do not have an alternative source of economic support for themselves or their children. To change this situation, the sexual division of labor must be eliminated through policies or other efforts aimed at empowering women both economically and politically.

Where will the money come from to support the necessary economic policies? First, we need a truly progressive income tax, stipulating that those who make the most money pay the highest percentages of their incomes in taxes. Second, we need to reduce the military budget substantially. As Frank Ackerman (1982, chap. 4) argues, the Reagan administration's military budget could drop by close to $100 billion a year without reducing our ability to defend ourselves from outside aggression. Third, we need to begin democratizing decisions about the allocation of labor power. Therefore, public organizations at the local level, with proportionate race and sex representation and funded out of the progressive income tax, as well as a substantially increased levy on employers for unemployment—a special "corporate unemployment tax" providing that those who create unemployment are taxed for it (Michalowski 1983, 17)—need to be established to create and administer jobs in their communities. As Michalowski (ibid., 17–18) points out, the corporate unemployment tax would serve several purposes.

> First, it would require that the segment of the society responsible for unemployment be required to pay for ameliorating its effects. Second, because the unemployment tax would be indexed to the rate of unemployment it would perhaps provide a greater incentive upon industry as a whole to minimize unemployment. Third, the corporations would provide the unemployed a dignified alternative to the present degrading "dole" of unemployment insurance payments. Fourth, by demonstrating that the majority of the unemployed will work when given the opportunity, such corporations would subsantially undercut the conservative ideological warfare against the unemployed as little more than victims of their own laziness or incompetence.

And probably most important, it would begin to "chip away" at the *power* corporations wield over all of us, and contribute to the socialist feminist ideology that *people* can manage their own affairs.

While a move toward full employment will definitely diminish street crime, we also need an economic policy aimed at curbing corporate crime. As shown in chapter 5, corporations, especially transnationals, are the major contributors to *serious* criminality worldwide. Since this criminality derives from their economic and patriarchal *power*, reducing corporate crime must begin by reducing the concentration of corporate power. Understanding that these corporations cannot be dismantled under current conditions, we must put forth a program that requires corporate decisions be made in the *public* interest (Simon and Eitzen 1982, 235). To do this we need to democratize corporations by placing on their boards of directors not only the managers or owners, but also workers and members of the community where the corporation operates. Simon and Eitzen (ibid., 235) explain why such an arrangement is important.

> Representatives of the workers are important to democratize the work-place and to improve the morale and the material conditions of the workers. The public also must be represented on the boards so that the decisions of the organizations will take into account the larger public issues of pollution, use of natural resources, plant location, prices, and product safety. These moves from economic oligarchy to industrial democracy represent a monumental shift from the present arrangements.

However, democratization of the workplace means more than just "workers and the public" on the boards of directors. In addition, these boards must be proportionate across *race* and *gender* lines. Democratization is important because it neutralizes the power of corporations in terms of gender, race, and class and makes corporations more responsive to the community.

How can this be achieved? A number of ways have been suggested by Simon and Eitzen (ibid., 235). First, as we have indicated, to do business a corporation could be required to have worker and public representation on its board of directors. Second, a corporation could be required to add worker and public representatives every year, depending upon its profits the previous year. This second option would mean "in effect, that after fifteen or twenty years the corporation would be controlled by the workers and public representatives" (ibid.). And finally, in return for subsidies, such as tax breaks and low interest loans, a corporation could be required to relinquish a portion of the company's stock to workers.

Emphasizing workers' rights and democratization will promote the organizing of groups addresing worker problems. In Sweden, for example, "labor-management safety committees" are required in every workplace with fifty or more employees (Engler 1986, 16). These union-dominated committees

— can veto, for safety and health reasons, new machines, work processes, or construction;
— must sign all blueprints for new processes or construction;
— select and direct the work of doctors, nurses, safety engineers and industrial hygienists;
— interview prospective safety and health personnel during hiring;
— receive medical records, monitoring results and all other information on hazards;
— examine proposed budgets to insure they include funding for health and safety;
— can shut down dangerous operations until they have been corrected;
— are entitled to extensive work environment safety training at employers' expense (ibid., 16–17).

In sum, what has been briefly discussed here—establishing full employment and workplace democracy—is the first part of what is required to reduce class and gender inequality and, therefore, crime. The second part entails democratizing the family.

Democratizing the Family

I have emphasized throughout this book the equal importance of patriarchy to both powerless and powerful criminality. It is clear that we need to develop policies to "chip away" at this ingrained and oppressive system of reproduction. A progressive program for curbing crime cannot stop at economic transformation, as men will continue to exercise patriarchal power and dominance. We need to challenge patriarchy directly by not only restructuring the sexual division of labor in the market, but also democratizing the family. A movement attacking power and inequality—the sexual division of labor—in the family can begin to challenge masculine dominance within, and outside, the home. The nuclear family reinforces women's dependence on men, normative heterosexuality, and patriarchal character structures, and provides a reserve army of labor for capital (women), while simultaneously providing a high level of demand for commodity production. Democratizing the family, and therefore changing living arrangements, can both challenge these functions and reduce crime. Moreover, as pointed out earlier, the traditional ideal of the nuclear family has become outmoded, as most people no longer live in a family where the father/husband is the sole breadwinner and the mother/wife stays at home with two or more children. Therefore, many need and, in fact, are searching for alternative household structures.

While extended families, singles, and communal arrangements are all models to be explored, the last seems to be the best way to democratize the family and possibly reduce not only violence in the home, but crime generally. Communal living arrangements create a situation entailing more diverse friendships and greater possibilities for shared responsibilities for housework (cleaning, cooking, and childcare) and, therefore, more equally shared free time. Moreover, communal living draws women out of isolation, thereby increasing the ability, of *both* men and women, to challenge patriarchal power. This challenge, of course, must be consciously *real* on the part of all members of the household, as communal living in itself does not "give rise" to a nonsexist environment. (In the hippie peace communes of the 1960s, for example, gender roles found in the broader society were often replicated.) The United States has a long tradition of communal living experiments, many of which worked to redefine "household" and "family" and break down the sexual division of labor (Hayden 1976). We should draw upon the successes of these attempts at nonsexist community life. One possibility is to organize what Ann Ferguson (1980; 15–17) calls "revolutionary socialist feminist family communities," which work toward (1) eliminating childrearing inequalities between men and women in order to help provide the structural base for men and women to be *equal nurturers* for children, and to each other, as well as *equally autonomous;* (2) challenging the sexual division of labor by reorganizing childrearing, other domestic tasks, and whatever aspects of public life the family community can control; (3) breaking down the possessive privacy of familial relationships such as the couple and parent/child; (4) equalizing power in terms of age—parents versus children, adults versus children; (5) eliminating the base for heterosexism by allowing gay men and lesbians into the revolutionary family community; (6) breaking down elitist attitudes concerning the superiority of mental work to manual work; (7) eliminating racism and class biases; and (8) instituting community economic sharing to help develop a sense of mutual commitment. These "revolutionary family-communities" would help organize new ways to structure childrearing, household labor, and sexuality, and therefore express in "embryo some new egalitarian values of loving and parenting," as well as providing the "material support needed to continue to challenge the combined domination system of capitalist patriarchy" (ibid., 13).

Dolores Hayden (1980, 181) notes however that since most people today are not interested in communal families, programs should be devised to provide community services for private households to reinforce economic independence for women. She suggests that groups of individuals could cooperatively own a number of private dwelling units near each other. They could then share childcare, laundry, food preparation, and other services necessary for daily maintenance. This would help to cut into the isolation of the nuclear family and facilitate the movement to alternative, and more communal, forms of living. Hayden (ibid., 181) suggests that this cooperative living arrangement, to succeed, must be governed by principles similar to those outlined by Ferguson.

Communal living may help break down the "macho" ideology and, therefore, curb crime. A large and growing body of research "has demonstrated the importance of communal networks of support in mitigating the impact of social and economic stress, with very significant consequences not only for crime but for physical and mental health as well" (Currie 1982b, 24).

While it is essential to encourage these communal forms of living as a first step in curbing masculine dominance and so crime within and outside the household, most people do, and will continue to, live in isolated nuclear family or single-parent settings. Although divorce rates are high, the majority of the divorced eventually remarry. Any progressive program directed at curbing crime must, therefore, seek to establish equality for women in more orthodox family arrangements. We need to redefine male-female relations, and an appropriate starting place is a strong emphasis on *shared parenting*.

Research suggests that gender differentiation and sex oppression will exist as long as women continue to be totally responsible for mothering (Chodorow 1978; Dinnerstein 1976). Shared parenting is likely to create new generations of men and women whose thinking challenges traditional gender-role socialization. Properly socialized, men are just as capable as women of nurturing children and maintaining the household. Shared parenting democratizes the household since it relieves a major burden placed on women and hinders the reproduction of patriarchal power, both of which help create criminality. Diane Ehrensaft (1980, 45) has shown, in her important article "When Women and Men Mother," the effects shared parenting can have. Shared parenting

(1) liberates women from full-time mothering; (2) affords opportunities for more equal relationships between women and men; (3) allows men more access to children; (4) allows children to be parented by two nurturing figures and frees them from the confines of an "overinvolved" parent who has no other outside identity; (5) provides new socialization experiences and possibly a breakdown in gender-differentiated character structures in children; (6) challenges the myth buttressed by sociobiology

that women *are* while men *do;* (7) puts pressure on political, economic, and social structures for changes such as paternity and maternity leaves, job sharing, and freely available childcare facilities.

In short, shared parenting is a very important way to challenge domination by the male and bring forth a more egalitarian situation. However, I am not suggesting that as a few progressives adopt lifestyles involving communal living and shared parenting, other people will simply see these alternatives as more attractive and follow in their footsteps. While it is important for progressives to set an example and work at consciously changing the sexual division of labor, we also need to organize for specific changes at the state level that will help make these alternatives possible—such as full-time parenting leave, with pay, for either the mother or father of a newborn. Moreover, we cannot forget the fact, emphasized through-out this book, that production and reproduction, rather than separate territories, "are really intimately related modes that reverberate upon one another and frequently occur in the same social, physical, and even psychic spaces" (Petchesky 1979, 376). Consequently, policies directed at shared parenting and communal forms of living must be interrelated with policies (discussed earlier) aimed at restructuring power in the economic and political spheres. It is extremely impor-tant to devise policies to reduce female dependency in *both* the home and the labor market, to undercut patriarchy by providing "individual women with the power to dictate the basic terms on which men must relate to them" (Schwendinger and Schwendinger 1983, 217).

To help democratize the family and curb criminality, social services must be provided. To allow both parents, or single parents, the right to work outside the home, expanded community-centered childcare is absolutely essential. All children have the right to healthy, educa-tional, and supportive childcare services. Moreover, reproductive freedom is essential for any program aimed at democratizing the family and empowering women. Young and adult women should have a full range of reproductive health services, from contraception and abortion to prenatal care. As Stallard, Ehrenreich, and Sklar (1983, 57) point out,

> a truly pro-life program would fund prenatal and child health and nutrition care for the millions of women and children who need it. The ability to plan wanted births and prevent unwanted births is fundamental to a woman's health and dignity as well as her economic survival and that of any children she may already have.

In addition to these programs, it is essential that adequate eco-nomic assistance be provided to the poor. A recent study of the impact economic assistance has on crime found that an increase of $10 a month in AFDC assistance per family member would cut the homicide rate by approximately 1 per 100,000, and the "illegal" rape rate by about 6 per 100,000 (DeFronzo 1983, 130).

The rape crisis centers and family violence centers the women's movement has created need expansion. Very few women report their sexual victimization to the police, primarily because of the way the police and other criminal justice personnel treat them. Many women, however, do report their victimization to rape crisis centers and shelters established and run by women, because here they receive significant attention and support (Taylor 1981, 189). Therefore, we need to support the establishment and expansion of rape crisis centers and shelters, as well as other support systems encouraging female bonding.

This does not mean, however, that the police should be totally abandoned. They are the only agency accessible to women that are, at the present time, "adequately equipped (and legally authorized) to impose the necessary level of restraint and isolation in any given circumstance" (Boehringer et al., 1983, 7). As discussed in chapter 6, domestic violence is widespread in this society. But in addition, approximately one in four victims of domestic violence suffers from *repeated* incidents involving the same offender, and those serious cases resulting in injury or death have usually been preceded by many previous calls to the police (Currie 1985, 230). Thus, women must still be able to turn to the police. Recent evidence suggests that victims of assaults by family members are almost twice as likely to be assaulted again if the police make no arrest. This is true even though very few assaulters are convicted after arrest (ibid., 231). Consequently, the police can help reduce the risk of repeated domestic violence. A progressive crime control program must, therefore, as Ian Taylor (1981, 190–91) points out, "be accompanied by new relationships with the police to ensure that women who are experiencing violence within a family, either directly or through the children, or within some other kind of relationship with men, *can* turn to the police for help when necessary." This "new relationship" will not be easily created. To be successful it must be accompanied by at least two efforts to democratize the police: maintain democratically organized community police review boards to monitor police activity and be available for citizen complaints; and demand the recruitment of more women and minorities into police work. The latter would entail pressuring police departments to aggressively adhere to affirmative action guidelines; place new female and racial minority recruits into all aspects of policing—not only in ghetto areas and only for complaints about "sexual crimes"—and begin training programs concerning racist and sexist oppression in U.S. society. The police review board should encourage public participation in controlling the police and help hold the police accountable to the community. Women not satisfied with the police response to their calls would be heard by these boards.

In addition to reforms in the police force, it is essential that the criminal justice system overall not "be surrendered to the Right and proponents of 'law and order' " (Platt 1984, 193). A progressive crime control program must also press for; better street lighting in high crime areas, escort services for the elderly, aid for victims, prison reform, a moratorium on prison construction, restoration of rehabilitative and work programs, abolition of mandatory sentences, bail reform, community corrections, and prisoners rights (ibid).

Expanded social services, from community eating halls and laundries to recreation facilities, are also desperately needed. These services could easily be funded out of public money, particularly if a truly progressive tax system was implemented and far less money devoted to the military. This democratization in political, economic, and gender spheres would have a tremendous impact on criminality.

Finally, we need to call for and work to end enforced or normative heterosexuality, which divides women, creates oppressive conditions for gay men and lesbians, reinforces the sexual division of labor, and helps to create "masculine" men and "feminine" women. Moreover, as has been emphasized throughout this book, normative heterosexuality contributes substantially to criminality in U.S. society. By supporting gay and lesbian struggles for equality, we can move toward abolishing the sexual stereotypes that support masculine dominance, power, and crime.

As stated earlier, the policies suggested here for reducing class and gender inequality (as well as the criminal justice reforms) are neither exhaustive nor comprehensive. The purpose of this alternative to the right wing-plan is to make it clear that there are effective alternatives to the law-and-order approach for curbing crime and that we must work toward them now. We live in a society in which patriarchal capitalism limits alternative ways of working, living, and developing consciousness. Challenging those limits is both *essential and possible,* if we truly care about curbing inequality and therefore crime.

In sum then, a progressive crime control program must work toward reducing gender and class inequality, as well as short term reforms. The New Right has proposed a "crime control policy" that will not only increase the amount of victimization, but also escalate repression of the powerless while concealing the crimes of those with power. In challenging the right, progressives must articulate the gender and class character of both crime and the social control mechanisms of the state. Rather than simply viewing criminality through a narrow class lens, we must develop strategies for curbing crime that serve working people, women, and racial minorities. Only then will we be able to expose the sexist, racist, and class-biased nature of this society.

References

Ackerman, F. 1982. *Reaganomics: Rhetoric vs. Reality.* Boston: South End Press.

Adler, F. 1975. *Sisters in Crime.* New York: McGraw-Hill.

Allen, J. 1978. *Assault with a Deadly Weapon.* New York: McGraw-Hill.

Althusser, L. 1971. *Lenin and Philosophy.* New York: Monthly Review Press.

Amir, M. 1971. *Patterns in Forcible Rape.* Chicago: University of Chicago Press.

Andersen, M. 1983. *Thinking About Women.* New York: MacMillan.

Ashford, N. 1976. *Crisis in the Workplace.* Cambridge: MIT Press.

Asinoff, R. 1985. "India Accident Raises Questions of Corporate Responsibility." *In These Times,* December 19–January 8.

Atkinson, D., A. Dallin, and G.W. Lapidus. 1977. *Women in Russia.* Stanford, Calif.: Stanford University Press.

Bacow, L. 1980. *Bargaining for Job Safety and Health.* Cambridge: MIT Press.

Baker, R., and S. Woodrow. 1984. "The Clean, Light Image of the Electronics Industry: Miracle or Mirage?" In *Double Exposure: Women's Health Hazards on the Job and at Home,* ed. W. Chavkin. New York: Monthly Review Press.

Balbus, I. 1982. *Marxism and Domination.* Princeton: Princeton University Press.

Balkan, S., R. Berger, and J. Schmidt. 1980. *Crime and Deviance in America: A Critical Approach.* Belmont, Calif.: Wadsworth.

Barlow, H. 1984. *Introduction to Criminology.* Boston: Little, Brown.

Barnett, H. 1981. "Wealth, Crime and Capital Accumulation." In *Crime and Capitalism,* ed. D. Greenberg. Palo Alto, Calif.: Mayfield.

Barry, K. 1979. *Female Sexual Slavery.* Englewood Cliffs, N.J.: Prentice Hall.

Bartky, S. 1982. "Narcissism, Femininity, and Alienation." *Social Theory and Practice* 8: 127–43.

Battelle Law and Justice Study Center. 1978. *Forcible Rape: An Analysis of Legal Issues.* Washington, D.C.: U.S. Government Printing Office.

Baxandall, R.F. 1979. "Who Shall Care for Our Children? The History and Development of Day Care in the United States." In *Women: A Feminist Perspective,* ed. J. Freeman. Palo Alto, Calif.: Mayfield.

Beasley, R.W., and G. Antunes. 1974. "The Etiology of Urban Crime: An Ecological Analysis." *Criminology* 11: 439–61.

Behr, P. 1981. "Regulation Target List Being Prepared." *The Washington Post,* February 21, A1.

Beneke, T. 1982. *Men on Rape.* New York: St. Martins Press.

Benjamin, H., and R. Masters. 1964. *Prostitution and Morality.* New York: Julien Press.

Benston, M. 1969. "The Political Economy of Women's Liberation." *Monthly Review* (September): 13–27.

Berch, B. 1982. *The Endless Day: The Political Economy of Women and Work.* New York: Harcourt Brace Jovanovich.

Berman, D. 1978. *Death on the Job*. New York: Monthly Review Press.

Bernard, J. 1975. *Women, Wives, Mothers: Values and Options*. Chicago: Aldine.

Bernstein, I.N., J. Cardascia, and C. Rose. 1979. "Defendants' Sex and Criminal Court Decisions." In *Discrimination in Organizations*, ed. R. Alvarez and K.G. Lutterman. San Francisco: Jossey-Bass.

Binder, A., and P. Scharf. 1982. "Deadly Force in Law Enforcement." *Crime and Delinquency* 28: 1–23.

Blau, J.R., and P.M. Blau. 1982. "The Cost of Inequality: Metropolitan Structure and Violent Crime." *American Sociological Review* 47: 114–29.

Blithman, N., and R. Green. 1975. "Inez Garcia on Trial." *Ms.* (May): 49–54, 84–86.

Blumberg, R.L. 1978. *Stratification: Socio-economic and Sexual Inequality*. Dubuque: William C. Brown.

Blundell, W.E. 1976. "Equity Funding: 'I did it for the jollies.' " In *Swindled?* ed. D. Moffit. Princeton, N.J.: Dow Jones Books.

Boehringer, G., D. Brown, B. Edgeworth, R. Hogg, and I. Ramsey. 1983. " 'Law and Order' for Progressives? An Australian Response." *Crime and Social Justice* 19: 2–12.

Bohmer, C. 1976. "Judicial Attitudes Toward Rape Victims." In *The Criminal Justice Process*, ed. W.B. Sanders and H. Dandistel. New York: Praeger.

Box, S. 1983. *Power, Crime and Mystification*. New York: Tavistock.

Box, S., and C. Hale. 1983. "Liberation and Female Criminality in England and Wales Revisited." *British Journal of Criminology* 22: 35–49.

Boxer, M., and J. Quataert. 1978. *Socialist Women*. New York: Elsevier.

Braithwaite, J. 1979a. *Inequality, Crime, and Public Policy*. London: Routledge & Kegan Paul.

———. 1979b. "Transnational Corporations and Corruption: Towards Some International Solutions." *International Journal of Sociology and Law* 7:125–42.

———. 1984. *Corporate Crime in the Pharmaceutical Industry*. Boston: Routledge & Kegan Paul.

Brake, M. 1980. *The Sociology of Youth Culture and Youth Subcultures*. Boston: Routledge & Kegan Paul.

Braverman, H. 1974. *Labor and Monopoly Capital*. New York: Monthly Review Press.

Brenner, H.M. 1976. "Estimating the Social Costs of National Economic Policy: Implications for Mental and Physical Health and Criminal Aggression." Prepared for the Joint Economic Committee, U.S. Congress. Paper no. 5. Washington, D.C.: U.S. Government Printing Office.

Brown, C. 1965. *Manchild in the Promised Land*. New York: Macmillan.

Brown, C. 1981. "Mothers, Fathers, and Children: From Private to Public Patriarchy." In *Women and Revolution*, ed. L. Sargent. Boston: South End Press.

Browning, F. 1981. "Life on the Margin: Atlanta Is Not the Only City Where Black Children Are Dying." *The Progressive* 45: 34–37.

———. 1982. "Nobody's Soft on Crime Anymore." *Mother Jones* (August): 25–31, 40–41.

Brownmiller, S. 1975. *Against Our Will: Men, Women, and Rape*. New York: Simon & Schuster.

Bryan, J.H. 1965. "Apprenticeships in Prostitution." *Social Problems* 12: 287–97.

Bularzik, M. 1978. "Sexual Harassment at the Workplace: Historical Notes." *Radical America* 12: 25–43.

Burstyn, V. 1983a. "Economy, Sexuality, and Politics: Engels and the Sexual Division of Labor." *Socialist Studies,* 19–39.

———. 1983b. "Masculine Dominance and the State." In *The Socialist Register,* ed. R. Miliband and J. Saville. London: Merlin Press, pp. 45–89.

———. 1984. "Anatomy of a Moral Panic." *FUSE* (Summer): 29–38.

———, ed. 1985. *Women Against Censorship.* Vancouver and Toronto: Douglas & McIntyre.

Burt, M. 1980. "Cultural Myths and Supports for Rape." *Journal of Personality and Social Psychology* 38: 217–30.

Calvin, A.D. 1981. "Unemployment Among Black Youths, Demographics, and Crime." *Crime and Delinquency* 27: 9–41.

Cameron, M. 1964. *The Booster and the Snitch.* Chicago: Free Press.

Campbell, A. 1984. *The Girls in the Gang.* New York: Basil Blackwell.

Carroll, L., and P.I. Jackson. 1983. "Inequality, Opportunity, and Crime Rates in Central Cities." *Criminology* 21: 178–94.

Chambliss, W. 1975. "Toward a Political Economy of Crime." *Theory and Society* (Summer): 167–80.

———. 1978. *On the Take: From Petty Crooks to Presidents.* Bloomington: Indiana University Press.

———. 1981. "The Criminalization of Conduct." In *Law and Deviance,* ed. H. Lawrence Ross. Beverly Hills, Calif.: Sage.

Chamblis, W., and R. Seidman. 1982. *Law, Order, and Power.* Reading, Mass.: Addison-Wesley.

Chavkin, W., ed. 1984. *Double Exposure: Women's Health Hazards on the Job and at Home.* New York: Monthly Review Press.

Chesney-Lind, M. 1978. "Chivalry Reexamined: Women and the Criminal Justice System." In *Women, Crime, and the Criminal Justice System,* ed. L. Bowker. Lexington, Mass.: D.C. Heath.

Chodorow, N. 1978. *The Reproduction of Mothering.* Berkeley: University of California Press.

Clark, L., and D. Lewis. 1977. *Rape: The Price of Coercive Sexuality.* Toronto: Women's Press.

Claybrook, J., and the Staff at Public Citizen. 1984. *Retreat from Safety.* New York: Pantheon Random House.

Clinard, M.B., and P.C. Yeager. 1980. *Corporate Crime.* New York: The Free Press.

Cloward, R., and F.F. Piven. 1979. "Hidden Protest: The Channeling of Female Innovation and Resistance." *Signs* 4: 651–69.

Coleman, L., and C. Dickinson. 1984. "The Risks of Healing: The Hazards of the Nursing Profession." In *Double Exposure: Women's Health Hazards on the Job and at Home,* ed. W. Chavkin. New York: Monthly Review Press.

Collier, J.F., and M. Rosaldo. 1981. "Politics and Gender in Simple Societies." In *Sexual Meanings: The Cultural Construction of Gender and Sexuality,* ed. S.B. Ortner and H. Whitehead. Cambridge: Cambridge University Press.

Cott, N. 1977. *The Bonds of Womanhood.* New Haven: Yale University Press.

Croce, E. 1978. *Feminism and Socialism in China,* New York: Schoken Books.

Currie, E. 1971. "Sociology of Law: Unasked Questions." *Yale Law Journal* 81: 134–47.

———. 1982a. "Crime and Ideology." *Working Papers* (May/June): 26–35.

————. 1982b. "Fighting Crime." *Working Papers* (July/August): 16–25.

————. 1985. *Confronting Crime.* New York: Pantheon Books.

Currie, E., R. Dunn, and D. Fogarty. 1980. "The New Immiserations: Stagflation, Inequality, and the Working Class." *Socialist Review* 10: 7–31.

Curtin, K. 1975. *Women in China.* New York: Pathfinder Press.

Curtis, L. 1975. *Violence, Race, and Culture.* Lexington, Mass.: D.C. Heath.

Dahl, T.S., and A. Snare. 1978. "The Coercion of Privacy: A Feminist Perspective." In *Women, Sexuality, and Social Control,* ed. C. Smart and B. Smart. Boston: Routledge & Kegan Paul.

Daly, M. 1978. *Gyn/Ecology.* Boston: Beacon Press.

Datesman, S., and F. Scarpitti, eds. 1980. *Women, Crime and Justice.* New York: Oxford University Press.

Davidson, T. 1978. *Conjugal Crime.* New York: Hawthorne Books.

Davis, A. 1983. *Women, Race, and Class.* New York: Vintage Books.

Davis, M. 1980. "The Impact of Workplace Health and Safety on Black Workers: Assessment and Prognosis." *Labor Law Journal* 31: 718–44.

DeFronzo, J. 1983. "Economic Assistance to Impoverished Americans: Relationship to Incidence of Crime." *Criminology* 21: 119–36.

Dinnerstein, D. 1976. *The Mermaid and the Minotaur.* New York: Harper & Row.

Dobash, R.E., and R. Dobash. 1979. *Violence Against Wives.* New York: The Free Press.

Douglass, J., and J. Johnson. 1978. *Crime at the Top.* Philadelphia: J.B. Lippincott.

Dowie, M. 1977. "Pinto Madness." *Mother Jones* (September-October): 18–34.

————. 1979. "The Corporate Crime of the Century." *Mother Jones* (November): 24–25.

Draper, P. 1975. "!Kung Women: Contrasts in Sexual Egalitarianism in Foraging and Sedentary Contexts." In *Toward and Anthropology of Women,* ed. R. Reiter. New York: Monthly Review Press.

Earley, P. 1982. "OSHA Shift Means Cutback in Its Inspections." *The Washington Post,* February 3, A21.

Edwards, R.C., M. Reich, and T.E. Weisskopt. 1978. *The Capitalist System.* Englewood Cliffs, N.J.: Prentice-Hall.

Edwards, S. 1981. *Female Sexuality and the Law.* Oxford: Martin Robertson.

Ehrenreich, B.,and D. English. 1978. *For Her Own Good.* Garden City, N.Y.: Anchor Press.

Ehrensaft, D. 1980. "When Women and Men Mother." *Socialist Review* 49: 37–73.

Eisenstein, Z. 1979. "Developing a Theory of Capitalist Patriarchy and Socialist Feminism." In *Capitalist Patriarchy and the Case for Socialist Feminism,* ed. Z. Eisenstein. New York: Monthly Review Press.

————. 1984. *Feminism and Sexual Equality.* New York: Monthly Review Press.

Eitzen, D.S., and D. Timmer. 1985. *Criminology: Crime and Criminal Justice.* New York: John Wiley.

Engels, F. 1958. *The Condition of the Working Class in England,* Stanford, Calif.: Stanford University Press. [1845]

————. 1972. *The Origin of the Family, Private Property, and the State.* Moscow: Progress Publishers. [1884]

Engler, R. 1986. "Political Power Aids Health and Safety." *In These Times,* January 15–21.

Enloe, C. 1983. *Does Khaki Become You?* Boston: South End Press.

Ermann, M.D., and R.C. Lundman. 1982. *Corporate Deviance.* New York: Holt, Rinehart & Winston.

Esselstyn, T.C. 1968. "Prostitution in the United States." *Annals* (March): 123–35.

Fagan, J., K.V. Hansen, M. Jang. 1983. "Profiles of Chronically Violent Juvenile Offenders: An Empirical Test of an Integrated Theory of Violent Delinquency." In *Evaluating Juvenile Justice,* ed. J.R. Kluegel. Beverly Hills, Calif.: Sage Publications.

Farley, L. 1978. *Sexual Shakedown.* New York: McGraw-Hill.

Federal Bureau of Investigation. 1985. *Uniform Crime Reports.* Washington, D.C.: U.S. Government Printing Office.

Fellmeth, R.C. 1970. "The Regulatory-Industrial Complex." In *With Justice for Some,* ed. B. Wasserstein and M.J. Green. Boston: Beacon Press.

Ferguson, A. 1979. "Women as a New Revolutionary Class." In *Between Labor and Capital,* ed. P. Walker. Boston: South End Press.

———. 1980. "The Che-Lumumba School: Creating a Revolutionary Family Community." *Quest* 5: 1–25.

Firestone, S. 1970. *The Dialectic of Sex.* New York: William Morrow.

Fisher, E. 1979. *Women's Creation.* Garden City, N.Y.: Anchor Press/Doubleday.

Flax, J. 1976. "Do Feminists Need Marxism?" *Quest* 3: 46–58.

Fleisher, B.M. 1966. *The Economics of Delinquency.* Chicago: Quadrangle Books.

Fleishman, J. 1984. "The Health Hazards of Office Work." In *Women's Health Hazards on the Job and at Home,* ed. W. Chavkin. New York: Monthly Review Press.

Friedan, B. 1963. *The Feminine Mystique.* New York: W.W. Norton.

Friedman, S., and J. Ladinsky. 1967. "Social Change and the Law of Industrial Accidents." *Columbia Law Review* 67: 50–82.

Frith, S. 1978. *The Sociology of Rock.* London: Constable Press.

Fuentes, A., and B. Ehrenreich. 1983. *Women in the Global Factory.* Boston: South End Press.

Fyfe, J.J. 1982. "Blind Justice: Police Shootings in Memphis." *Journal of Criminal Law and Criminology* 73: 707–22.

Gay, J. 1985. "The 'Patriotic' Prostitute." *The Progressive* (February): 34–36.

Geis, G. 1967. "White Collar Crime: The Heavy Electrical Equipment Antitrust Cases of 1961." In *Criminal Behavior Systems: A Typology,* ed. M. Clinard and R. Quinney. New York: Holt, Rinehart & Winston.

———. 1978. "Deterring Corporate Crime." In *Corporate and Government Deviance,* ed. M.D. Ermann and R.C. Lundman. New York: Oxford University Press.

Geis, G., and R.F. Meier, eds. 1977. *White Collar Crime.* New York: Free Press.

Gelles, R. 1977. "Power, Sex, and Violence: The Case of Marital Rape." *The Family Coordinator* 26: 339–47.

Glaser, D., and K. Rice. 1959. "Crime, Age, and Employment." *American Sociological Review* 24: 679–86.

Glasgow, D.G. 1980. *The Black Underclass.* San Francisco: Jossey-Bass Publishers.

Glick, P. 1981. "A Demographic Picture of Black Families." In *Black Families,* ed. H. McAdoo. Beverly Hills, Calif.: Sage.

Gordon, D. 1971a. "Class and the Economics of Crime." *Review of Radical Political Economics* 3: 51–75.

———. 1971b. *Problems in Political Economy.* Lexington, Mass.: D.C. Heath.

Gordon, D.R. 1984. "Doing Violence to the Crime Problem: A Response to the Attorney General's Task Force." *Annual Editions: Criminal Justice.* Guildford, Conn.: Dushkin Publishing.

Graham, J.M. 1972. "Amphetamine Politics on Capitol Hill." *Society* 9: 14–23.

Green, E. 1970. "Race, Social Status, and Criminal Arrest." *American Sociological Review* 35: 476–90.

Green, M., B.C. Moore, and B. Wasserstein. 1972. *The Closed Enterprise System.* New York: Bantam Books.

Greenberg, D. 1977a. "Delinquency and the Age Structure of Society." *Contemporary Crises* 1: 189–223.

———. 1977b. "The Dynamics of Oscillatory Punishment Processes." *The Journal of Criminal Law and Criminology* 68: 643–51.

———. 1983. *Crime and Capitalism: Readings in Marxist Criminology.* Palo Alto, Calif.: Mayfield.

Greenwald, H. 1970. *The Elegant Prostitute.* New York: Ballantine Books.

Greer, G. 1975. "Seduction Is a Four-Letter Word." In *Rape Victimology,* ed. L. G. Schultz. Chicago: C.C. Thomas.

Griffin, S. 1971. "Rape: The All American Crime." *Ramparts* 10: 26–35.

Gross, B. 1982. "Some Anticrime Proposals for Progressives." *The Nation* (February 6): 137–40.

Gross, E. 1978. "Organizational Sources of Crime: A Theoretical Perspective." In *Studies in Symbolic Interaction,* ed. N.K. Denzin. Greenwich, Conn.: JAI Press.

Grozuczak, J. 1982. *Poisons on the Job: The Reagan Administration and American Workers.* Report no. 4. San Francisco: Sierra Club.

Hagan, J., J.H. Simpson, and A.R. Gillis. 1979. "The Sexual Stratification of Social Control: A Gender-Based Perspective on Crime and Delinquency." *British Journal of Sociology* 30: 25–38.

Hall, S., C. Critcher, T. Jefferson, J. Clarke, and B. Roberts. 1978. *Policing the Crisis: Mugging, the State, and Law and Order.* London: Macmillan and Co.

Harding, S. 1981. "What Is the Real Material Base of Patriarchy and Capital?" In *Women and Revolution,* ed. L. Sargent. Boston: South End Press.

Harring, S., T. Platt, R. Speiglman, and P. Takagi. 1977. "The Management of Police Killings." *Crime and Social Justice* 8: 34–43.

Hartmann, H. 1979. "Capitalism, Patriarchy, and Job Segregation by Sex." In *Capitalist Patriarchy and the Case for Socialist Feminism,* ed. Z. Eisenstein. New York: Monthly Review Press.

———. 1981a. "The Unhappy Marriage of Marxism and Feminism: Towards a More Progressive Union." In *Women and Revolution,* ed. L. Sargent. Boston: South End Press.

———. 1981b. "The Family as the Locus of Gender, Class and Political Struggle: The Example of Housework." *Signs* 6: 336–94.

Hay, G., and D. Kelly. 1974. "An Empirical Survey of Price-Fixing Conspiracies." *Journal of Law and Economics* (April): 13–38.

Hayden, D. 1976. *Seven American Utopias: The Architecture of Communitarian Socialism, 1790–1975*. Cambridge: MIT Press.

———. 1980. "What Would a Non-Sexist City Be Like? Speculations on Housing, Urban Design, and Human Work." *Signs* 5 (supplement): 170–87.

Heitlinger, A. 1979. *Women and State Socialism*. Montreal: McGill-Queens University Press.

Henifin, M.S. 1984. "The Particular Problems of Video Display Terminals." In *Women's Health Hazards on the Job and at Home*, ed. W. Chavkin. New York: Monthly Review Press.

Henry, A.F., and J.F. Short. 1954. *Suicide and Homicide: Some Economic, Sociological, and Psychological Aspects of Aggression*. New York: The Free Press.

Hepburn, J. 1977. "Social Control and the Legal Order: Legitimated Repression in a Capitalist State." *Contemporary Crises* 1: 77–90.

Hill, J. 1975. *Class Analysis: United States in the 1970s*. San Francisco: Synthesis Publishing.

Hills, S.L. 1971. *Crime, Power and Morality*. Scanton, Penn.: Chandler Publishing.

Hindelang, M. 1979. "Sex Differences in Criminal Activity." *Social Problems* 27: 143–56.

Hite, S. 1977. *The Hite Report*. New York: Dell Publishing.

Hoffman-Bustamante, D. 1973. "The Nature of Female Delinquency." *Issues in Criminology* 8: 117–32.

Hooks, B. 1981. *Ain't I a Woman?* Boston: South End Press.

Howe, L.K. 1977. *Pink Collar Ghetto*. New York: G.P. Putnam.

Hughes, J.C., and L. May. 1980. "Sexual Harassment." *Social Theory and Practice* 6: 249–80.

Humphries, D. 1979. "Crime and the State." In *Sociology: Class, Consciousness, and Contradictions*, ed. A.J. Szymanski and T.G. Goertzel. New York: D. Van Nostrand.

Humphries, D., and D. Wallace. 1980. "Capitalist Accumulation and Urban Crime, 1950–1971." *Social Problems* 28: 179–93.

Hunt, M. 1979. "Legal Rape." *Family Circle*, January 9, 24, 37–38, 125.

Hunt, V.R. 1979. "A Brief History of Women Workers and Hazards in the Workplace." *Feminist Studies* 6: 276–85.

Institute for Labor Education and Research. 1982. *What's Wrong with the U.S. Economy?* Boston: South End Press.

Jacoby, N., P. Nehemkis, and R. Eells. 1977. *Bribery and Extortion in World Business*. New York: Macmillan.

Jaggar, A. 1983. *Feminist Politics and Human Nature*. Totowa, N.J.: Rowman & Allanheld.

James, J. 1976. "Motivations for Entrance into Prostitution." In *The Female Offender*, ed. L. Crites. Lexington, Mass.: D.C. Heath.

———. 1982. "The Prostitute as Victim." In *The Criminal Justice System and Women*, ed. B.R. Price and N.J. Sokoloff. New York: Clark Boardman.

Jankovic, I. 1977. "Labor Market and Imprisonment." *Crime and Social Justice* 8: 17–31.

Jasso, S., and M. Mazorra. 1984. "Following the Harvest: The Health Hazards of Migrant and Seasonal Farmworking Women." In *Women's Health*

Hazards on the Job and at Home, ed. W. Chavkin. New York: Monthly Review Press.

Johnson, A.G. 1980. "On the Prevalence of Rape in the United States." *Signs* 6: 136–46.

Jones, B. 1970. "The Dynamics of Marriage and Motherhood." In *Sisterhood Is Powerful,* ed. R. Morgan. New York: Vintage.

Kanter, R.M. 1977. *Men and Women in the Corporation.* New York: Basic Books.

Klein, D. 1979. "Can This Marriage Be Saved? Battery and Sheltering." *Crime and Social Justice* 12: 19–33.

————. 1982a. "The Etiology of Female Crime: A Review of the Literature." In *The Criminal Justice System and Women,* ed. B.R. Price and N.J. Sokoloff. New York: Clark Boardman.

————. 1982b. "Violence Against Women: Some Considerations Regarding Its Causes and Elimination." In *The Criminal Justice System and Women,* ed. B.R. Price and N.J. Sokoloff. New York: Clark Boardman.

Kobler, A.L. 1975. "Police Homicide in a Democracy" and "Figures (and Perhaps Some Facts) on Police Killing of Civilians in the United States, 1965–1969." *Journal of Social Issues* 31: 163–91.

Kolko, G. 1965. *Railroads and Regulation: 1877–1916.* New York: W.W. Norton.

Krisberg, B. 1975. *Crime and Privilege: Toward a New Criminology.* Englewood Cliffs, N.J.: Prentice-Hall.

Kristera, J. 1977. *About Chinese Women.* New York: Unizen.

Kuhn, A., and A. Wolpe. 1978. *Feminism and Materialism: Women and Modes of Production.* Boston: Routledge & Kegan Paul.

Leacock, E. 1981. *Myths of Male Dominance.* New York: Monthly Review Press.

Lebergott, S. 1964. *Manpower in Economic Growth: The American Record Since 1880.* New York: McGraw-Hill.

Lee, R. 1979. *The !Kung San.* Cambridge: Cambridge University Press.

Lenze, I. 1979. "Tourism Prostitution in Asia." *ISIS International Bulletin* 13: 4–21.

Leonard, E. 1982. *Women, Crime and Society.* New York: Longman.

Levi-Straus, C. 1971. "The Family." In *Man, Culture and Society,* ed. H. Shapiro. London: Oxford University Press.

Lewis, D.K. 1981. "Black Women Offenders and Criminal Justice." In *Comparing Female and Male Offenders,* ed. M.Q. Warren. Beverly Hills, Calif.: Sage.

Liazos, A. 1982. *People First.* Boston: Allyn & Bacon.

Lipset, S.M., and E. Raab. 1970. *The Politics of Unreason: Right Wing Extremism in America, 1790–1970.* New York: Harper & Row.

Loftin, C., and R.H. Hill. 1974. "Regional Subculture and Homicide: An Examination of the Gastil-Hackney Thesis." *American Sociological Review* 39: 714–24.

Lombroso, C. 1876. *Criminal Man.* New York: G.P. Putnam.

Lombroso, C., and W. Ferrero. 1894. *The Female Offender.* New York: Appleton.

MacKinnon, C.A. 1979. *Sexual Harassment of Working Women.* New Haven: Yale University Press.

Malcolm X. 1965. *The Autobiography of Malcolm X.* New York: Grove Press.

Mann, C.R. 1984. *Female Crime and Delinquency.* University: University of Alabama Press.

Manpower Report. 1976. *Manpower Report of the President, April 1975*. Washington, D.C.: U.S. Government Printing Office.

Marable, M. 1983. *How Capitalism Underdeveloped Black America*. Boston: South End Press.

Maris, R.W. 1969. *Social Forces in Urban Suicide*. Homewood, Ill.: Dorsey Press.

Marshall, L. 1976. *The !Kung of the Nyae Nyae*. Cambridge: Harvard University Press.

Marx, K. 1868. Letter to Dr. Kugelman.

———. 1967. *Capital, Vol. I*. New York: International Publishers. [1867]

Marx, K., and F. Engels. 1947. *The German Ideology*. New York: International Publishers. [1846]

———. 1970. *The Communist Manifesto*. New York: Pathfinder Press [1848]

Matsui, Y. 1984. "Why I Oppose Kisaeng Tours." In *International Feminism: Networking Against Female Sexual Slavery*, ed. K. Barry et al. New York: International Women's Tribune Center.

Mayer, C.E. 1981. "Easing of Hazardous Exports Studied." *The Washington Post*, September 9, B4.

McCaghy, C. 1976. *Deviant Behavior*. New York: Macmillan.

McCormick, A.E. 1977. "Rule Enforcement and Moral Indignation: Some Observations on the Effects of Criminal Anti-Trust Convictions Upon Societal Reaction Processes." *Social Problems* 25: 30–38.

———. 1979. "Dominant Class Interests and the Emergence of Anti-Trust Legislation." *Contemporary Crises* 3: 399–417.

McDermott, J. 1979. *Rape Victimization in 26 American Cities*. Washington, D.C.: U.S. Government Printing Office.

McIntosh, M. 1973. "The Growth of Racketeering." *Economy and Society* (February): 35–69.

Meyer, M.W. 1980. "Police Shootings at Minorities: The Case of Los Angeles." *Annals* 452: 98–110.

Michalowski, R. 1981. "The Politics of the Right." *Crime and Social Justice* 15: 29–35.

———. 1983. "Crime Control in the 1980's: A Progressive Agenda." *Crime and Social Justice* 19: 13–23.

———. 1985. *Order, Law, and Crime*. New York: Random House.

Miller, E.M. 1983. "International Trends in the Study of Female Criminality: An Essay Review." *Contemporary Crises* 7: 59–70.

———. 1986. *Street Woman: The Illegal Work of Underclass Women*. Philadelphia: Temple University Press.

Miller, W.B. 1975. *Violence by Youth Gangs and Youth as a Crime Problem in Major American Cities*. Washington, D.C.: U.S. Government Printing Office.

Millett, K. 1970. *Sexual Politics*. New York: Doubleday.

Milton, C. 1977. *Police Use of Deadly Force*. Washington D.C.: The Police Foundation.

Mintz, M. 1985. "At Any Cost: Corporate Greed, Women, and the Dalkon Shield." *The Progressive* (November): 20–25.

———. 1986. "A Crime Against Women: A.H. Robbins and the Dalkon Shield." *Multinational Monitor* 7 (January 15): 1–7.

Moberg, D. 1985. "Corporate Execs Guilty of Murder." *In These Times* (June 26): 2.

Muwakkil, S. 1984. "Slaying of 'Benjy' Wilson accents Violence Epidemic." *In These Times*, December 12.

National Commission on Product Safety. 1971. *Report.* Washington, D.C.: U.S. Government Printing Office.

Newton, J. 1973. "The Political Economy of Women's Oppression." In *Women on the Move: A Feminist Perspective,* ed. J.R. Lepalvoto. Eugene: University of Oregon Press.

Niemi, B., and C. Lloyd. 1975. "Sex Differentials in Earnings and Unemployment Rates." *Feminist Studies* 2: 195–200.

Oakley, A. 1972. *Sex, Gender, and Society.* New York: Harper & Row.

O'Connor, J. 1973. *The Fiscal Crisis of the State.* New York: St. Martins Press.

Olesen, V.L., and F. Katsuranis. 1978. "Urban Nomads: Women in Temporary Clerical Services." In *Women Working,* ed. A. Stromberg and S. Harkness. Palo Alto, Calif.: Mayfield.

Page, J.A., and M.W. O'Brien. 1973. *Bitter Wages.* New York: Grossman Publishers.

Parenti, M. 1983. *Democracy for the Few.* New York: St. Martins Press.

Pearce, F. 1976. *Crimes of the Powerful.* London: Pluto Press.

Perkins, R. 1969. *Criminal Law.* Mineola, N.Y.: The Foundation Press.

Petchesky, R. 1979. "Dissolving the Hyphen: A Report on Marxist Feminist Group 1–5." In *Capitalist Patriarchy and the Case for Socialist Feminism,* ed. Z. Eisenstein. New York: Monthly Review Press.

———. 1984. *Abortion and Woman's Choice: The State, Sexuality, and Reproductive Freedom.* New York: Longman.

Petersen, S.R. 1977. "Coercion and Rape: The State as a Male Protection Racket." In *Feminism and Philosophy,* ed. M. Vetterling-Braggin, F.A. Elliston, and J. English. Totowa, N.J.: Littlefield, Adams.

Phillips, L., H.L. Votey, and D. Maxwell. 1972. "Crime, Youth and the Labor Market." *Journal of Political Economy* 80: 491–504.

Piven, F.F., and R.A. Cloward. 1982. *The New Class War: Reagan's Attack on the Welfare State and Its Consequences.* New York: Pantheon.

Platt, T. 1978. " 'Street' Crime—A View from the Left." *Crime and Social Justice* (Spring/Summer): 26–34.

———. 1984. "Criminology in the 1980s: Progressive Alternatives to 'Law and Order.' " *Crime and Social Justice* 21–22: 191–99.

Pleck, J.H., and J. Sawyer, eds. 1974. *Men and Masculinity.* Englewood Cliffs, N.J.: Prentice-Hall.

Pollock J.C., and A.E. Rosenblat. 1984. "Fear of Crime: Sources and Responses." In *Criminal Justice,* ed. J.J. Sullivan and J.C. Victor. Guildford, Conn.: Dushkin Publishing.

Prescott, S., and C. Letko. 1977. "Battered Women: A Social Psychological Perspective." In *Battered Women,* ed. M. Roy. New York: Van Nostrand, Reinhold.

Procek, E. 1981. "Psychiatry and the Social Control of Women." In *Women and Crime,* ed. A. Morris and L. Gelsthorpe. Cambridge: Cambridge Institute of Criminology.

Quinney, R. 1973. *Critique of Legal Order.* Boston: Little, Brown.

———. 1980. *Class, State and Crime.* New York: Longman.

Rainwater, L. 1970. *Behind Ghetto Walls.* Chicago: Aldine.

Randall, M. 1974. *Cuban Women Now.* Toronto: Women's Press.

———. 1982. *Sandino's Daughter.* London: Crossing Press.

Ratner, R.S., and J.L. McMullen. 1983. "Social Control and the Rise of the

'Exceptional State' in Britain, the United States, and Canada." *Crime and Social Justice* 19: 31–43.

Regenstein, L. 1982. *America the Poisoned.* Washington, D.C.: Acropolis Books.

Reich, W. 1970. *Character Analysis.* New York: Longman.

Reiman, J. 1979. *The Rich Get Richer and the Poor Get Prison* New York: John Wiley & Sons. Second edition 1984.

Reiss, A.J., and A.L. Rhodes. 1961. "The Distribution of Juvenile Delinquency in the Social Class Structure." *American Sociological Review* 26: 720–32.

Reiter, R., ed. 1975. *Toward an Anthropology of Women.* New York: Monthly Review Press.

Rich, A. 1976. *Of Woman Born: Motherhood as Experience and Institution.* New York: W.W. Norton.

Robin, G.D. 1963. "Justifiable Homicide by Police Officers." *Journal of Criminal Law, Criminology, and Police Science* 54: 225–31.

———. 1982. "Forcible Rape: Institutionalized Sexism in the Criminal Justice System." In *The Criminal Justice System and Women,* ed. B.R. Price and N.J. Sokoloff. New York: Clark Boardman.

Rosaldo, M., and L. Lamphire, eds. 1974. *Women, Culture and Society.* Stanford, Calif.: Stanford University Press.

Rosenberg, H.G. 1984. "The Home Is the Workplace: Hazards, Stress, and Pollutants in the Household." In *Double Exposure: Women's Health Hazards on the Job and at Home,* ed. W. Chavkin. New York: Monthly Review Press.

Rosenblum, K. 1975. "Female Deviance and the Female Sex Role: A Preliminary Investigation." *British Journal of Sociology* 25: 169–85.

Rossi, P.H., E. Waite, C.E. Bose, and R.E. Berk. 1974. "The Seriousness of Crimes: Normative, Structural and Individual Differences." *American Sociological Review* 39: 224–37.

Rowbotham, S. 1973. *Women's Consciousness, Man's World.* London: Penguin Books.

Rubin, G. 1975. "The Traffic in Women." In *Toward an Anthropology of Women,* ed. R. Reiter. New York: Monthly Review Press.

———. 1984. "Thinking Sex: Notes for a Radical Theory of the Politics of Sexuality." In *Pleasure and Danger: Exploring Female Sexuality,* ed. C.S. Vance. Boston: Routledge & Kegan Paul.

Russell, D.E.H. 1975. *The Politics of Rape.* New York: Stein and Day.

———. 1982. *Rape in Marriage.* New York: Macmillan.

———. 1984. *Sexual Exploitation.* Beverly Hills, Calif.: Sage Publishing.

Salmans, S. 1981. "Resurgence of Sweatshops Reported in New York." *New York Times,* February 26, A1.

Sanday, P. 1981. "The Socio-Cultural Context of Rape: A Cross-Cultural Study." *Journal of Social Issues* 37: 5–27.

Sanders, W. 1981. *Juvenile Delinquency.* New York: Holt, Rinehart & Winston.

Sandmaier, M. 1980. *The Invisible Alcoholic: Women and Alcohol Abuse in America.* New York: McGraw-Hill.

Sargent, E.D. 1986. "The Curse of Blacks Killing Blacks." *Washington Post,* March 2, C1, C3.

Sarri, R. 1976. "Juvenile Law: How It Penalizes Females." In *The Female Offender,* ed. L. Crites. Lexington, Mass.: D.C. Heath.

Sartre, J. 1963. *Search for a Method.* New York: Alfred A. Knopf.

Schecter, S. 1982. *Women and Male Violence.* Boston: South End Press.

Schlossman, S., and S. Wallach. 1978. "The Crime of Precocious Sexuality: Female Juvenile Delinquency in the Progressive Era." *Harvard Educational Review* 48: 65–94.

Schlozman, K.L. 1979. "Women and Unemployment." In *Women: a Feminist Perspective,* ed. J. Freeman. Palo Alto, Calif.: Mayfield.

Schmid, C.F. 1960. "Urban Crime Areas." *American Sociological Review* 25: Part I, 527–42; Part II, 655–78.

Schur, E. 1984. *Labeling Women Deviant: Gender, Stigma, and Social Control.* New York: Random House.

Schwendinger, H., and J. Schwendinger. 1970. "Defenders of Order or Guardians of Human Rights." *Issues in Criminology* (Summer): 123–57.

———. 1974. *Sociologists of the Chair: A Radical Analysis of the Formative Years of American Sociology.* New York: Basic Books.

———. 1985. *Adolescent Subcultures and Delinquency.* New York: Praeger Publishing.

Schwendinger, J.R., and H. Schwendinger. 1976. "Rape Victims and the False Sense of Guilt." *Crime and Social Justice* 6: 4–17.

———. 1981. "Rape, Sexual Inequality, and Levels of Violence." *Crime and Social Justice* 16: 3–31.

———. 1983. *Rape and Inequality.* Beverly Hills, Calif.: Sage.

Scott, H. 1976. *Women and Socialism.* London: Allison & Busby.

Scott, J. 1984. "Keeping Women in Their Place: Exclusionary Policies and Reproduction." In *Double Exposure: Women's Health Hazards on the Job and at Home,* ed. W. Chavkin. New York: Monthly Review Press.

Scully, D., and J. Marolla. 1985. " 'Riding the Bull at Gilley's': Convicted Rapists Describe the Rewards of Rape." *Social Problems* 32: 251–63.

Shaw, C., and H. Mckay. 1942. *Juvenile Delinquency and Urban Areas.* Chicago: University of Chicago Press.

Sheehy, G. 1973. *Hustling: Prostitution in Our Wide-Open Society.* New York: Delacorte.

Sheils, M., and J. Walcott. 1978. "Behind the Tower Tragedy." *Newsweek,* June 19, pp. 59–60.

Sheldon, R. 1982. *Criminal Justice in America: A Sociological Approach.* Boston: Little, Brown.

Sherman, L.W., and P.H. Langworthy. 1979. "Measuring Homicide by Police Officers." *Journal of Criminal Law and Criminology* 70: 546–60.

Shostak, M. 1983. *Nisa: The Life and Words of a !Kung Woman.* New York: Vintage Books.

Silberman, C. 1978. *Criminal Violence, Criminal Justice.* New York: Random House.

Silverman, D., and S.L. McCombie. 1980. "Counseling the Mates and Families of Rape Victims." In *Rape Crisis Intervention Handbook,* ed. S.L. McCombie. New York: Plenum Press.

Silverman, M., P.R. Lee, and M. Lydecker. 1982. *Prescriptions for Death: The Drugging of the Third World.* Berkeley: University of California Press.

Silverstein, M. 1977. "The History of a Short, Unsuccessful Academic Career." In *For Men Against Sexism,* ed. J. Snodgrass. Albion, Calif.: Times Change Press.

Simon, D. 1981. "The Political Economy of Crime." In *Political Economy: A Critique of American Society,* ed. S.D. McNall. Glenview, Ill.: Scott, Foresman.

Simon, D., and D.S. Eitzen. 1982. *Elite Deviance*. Boston: Allyn & Bacon.

Simon, R. 1975. *Women and Crime*. Lexington, D.C. Heath.

Slim, I. 1967. *Pimp: The Story of My Life*. Los Angeles: Holloway House.

Smart, C. 1976. *Women, Crime and Criminology: A Feminist Critique*. Boston: Routledge & Kegan Paul.

Smith, D. 1975. "Women, the Family, and Corporate Capitalism." *Berkeley Journal of Sociology* 20: 55–90.

Smith, R.J. 1982. "Gorsuch Strikes Back at EPA Critics." *Science*, July 16, p. 233.

Smithyman, S.C. 1979. "Characteristics of 'Undetected' Rapists." In *Perspectives on Victimology*, ed. W.H. Parsonage. Beverly Hills, Calif.: Sage.

Sokoloff, N.J. 1980. *Between Money and Love*. New York: Praeger.

Sokoloff, N.J., and B.R. Price. 1982. "The Criminal Law and Women." In *The Criminal Justice System and Women*, ed. B.R. Price and N.J. Sokoloff. New York: Clark Boardman.

Spitzer, S. 1975. "Toward a Marxian Theory of Deviance." *Social Problems* 22: 638–51.

Stallard, K., B. Ehrenreich, and H. Sklar. 1983. *Poverty in the American Dream*. Boston: South End Press.

Steffensmeier, D.J. 1981. "Crime and the Contemporary Woman: An Analysis of Changing Levels of Female Property Crimes, 1960–1975." In *Women and Crime in America*, ed. L. Bowker. New York: Macmillan.

Stellman, J.M. 1977. *Woman's Work, Woman's Health*. New York: Pantheon.

Stern, M. 1978. *Women in Soviet Society*. Berkeley: University of California Press.

Stoltenberg, J. 1977. "Toward Gender Justice." In *For Men Against Sexism*, ed. J. Snodgrass. Albion, Calif.: Times Change Press.

Takagi, P. 1974. "A Garrison State in 'Democratic' Society." *Crime and Social Justice* 1: 27–33.

———. 1982. "Delinquency in School and Society: The Quest for a Theory and Method." *Crime and Social Justice* 17: 37–49.

Takagi, P., and T. Platt. 1978. "Behind the Gilded Ghetto: An Analysis of Race, Class, and Crime in Chinatown." *Crime and Social Justice* (Spring/Summer): 2–25.

Taylor, I. 1981. *Law and Order: Arguments for Socialism*. London: Macmillan.

Tolson, A. 1977. *The Limits of Masculinity*. New York: Harper & Row.

Tong, R. 1984. *Women, Sex, and the Law*. Totowa, N.J.: Rowman & Allanheld.

Twopines, C. 1985. "My Life in Crime." *The Progressive* 49: 50.

U.S. Bureau of the Census. 1983. *Estimates of the Population of the U.S. by Age, Race, and Sex: 1980–1982*. Washington, D.C.: U.S. Government Printing Office.

U.S. Commission on Civil Rights. 1982. *Unemployed and Underemployed Among Blacks, Hispanics and Women*. Washington, D.C.: U.S. Commission on Civil Rights.

U.S. Department of Commerce. 1981. *Current Population Reports, Household and Family Characteristics: March 1980*. Washington, D.C.: U.S. Government Printing Office.

U.S. Department of Justice. 1981. *Attorney General's Violent Crime Task Force Report*. Washington, D.C.: U.S. Government Printing Office.

U.S. Department of Labor. 1982. *Employment and Earnings*. Washington, D.C.: U.S. Government Printing Office.

U.S. Department of Labor. 1984. *20 Facts on Women Workers*. Washington, D.C.: Women's Bureau, U.S. Department of Labor.

"U.S. Foreign Policy in the 1980's." *Monthly Review* (April): 1–12.

U.S. General Accounting Office. 1979. *Female Offenders: Who Are They and What Are the Problems Confronting Them*. Washington, D.C.: General Accounting Office.

U.S. House of Representatives, Subcommittee on Crime. 1981. *Increasing Violence Against Minorities*. Washington, D.C.: U.S. Government Printing Office.

Vanek, J.A. 1978. "Housewives as Workers." In *Women Working*, ed. A.H,. Stronberg and S. Harkness. Palo Alto, Calif.: Mayfield.

Walker, L. 1977–78. "Battered Women and Learned Helplessness." *Victimology* 2: 525–34.

———. 1978. *The Battered Woman*. New York: Harper & Row.

Warr, M. 1985. "Fear of Rape Among Urban Women." *Social Problems* 32: 238–50.

Weis, K.,and S.S. Borges. 1973. "Victimology and Rape: The Case of the Legitimate Victim." *Issues in Criminology* 8: 71–116.

Wilson, J.Q. 1975. *Thinking About Crime*. New York: Random House.

Wilson, J.Q., and R. Herrnstein. 1985. *Crime and Human Nature*. New York: Simon & Schuster.

Wood, P. 1973. "The Victim in a Forcible Rape Case: A Feminist View." *American Criminal Law Review* 11: 194–217.

Woolf, V. 1938. *Three Guineas*. New York: Harcourt, Brace & World.

Wright, E.O. 1973. *The Politics of Punishment*. New York: Harper & Row.

Wright, M.J. 1979. "Reproductive Hazards and 'Protective' Discrimination." *Feminist Studies* 5: 302–9.

Yayori, M. 1977. "Sexual Slavery in Korea.' *Frontiers: A Journal of Women's Studies* (Spring): 22–30.

Yeager, M.G. 1979. "Unemployment and Imprisonment." *Journal of Criminal Law and Criminology* (Winter): 586–88.

Zaretsky, E. 1978. "The Effects of the Economic Crisis on the Family." In *U.S. Capitalism in Crisis*, ed. Radical Political Economic Collective. New York: Union for Radical Political Economics.

Index